Defectors and the Liberal Party 1910–2010

Defectors and the Liberal Party 1910–2010

A study of inter-party relations

Alun Wyburn-Powell

Manchester University Press

Copyright © Alun Wyburn-Powell 2012

The right of Alun Wyburn-Powell to be identified as the author of this work has been asserted by him in accordance with the Copyright, Designs and Patents Act 1988.

Published by Manchester University Press
Altrincham Street, Manchester M1 7JA, UK
www.manchesteruniversitypress.co.uk

British Library Cataloguing-in-Publication Data is available

Library of Congress Cataloging-in-Publication Data is available

ISBN 978 1 7849 9397 9 *paperback*

First published by Manchester University Press in hardback 2012

This edition first published 2016

The publisher has no responsibility for the persistence or accuracy of URLs for any external or third-party internet websites referred to in this book, and does not guarantee that any content on such websites is, or will remain, accurate or appropriate.

Printed by Lightning Source

For Diana and Christopher

Contents

List of illustrations	*page* viii
Foreword	ix
Abbreviations	xi
Acknowledgements	xii
1 Introduction	1
2 Defectors and loyalists	6
3 Liberal defectors to Labour	27
4 Liberal defectors to the Conservatives	93
5 Liberal defectors to minor parties	149
6 Inward defectors	179
7 Conclusions	191
Bibliography	198
Index	203

List of illustrations

Figures

2.1	Scale and direction of defections from Liberal Party by year	page 7
2.2	Outward defectors in chronological order	8
2.3	Defectors by grouping	22

Tables

2.1	Parliamentary status of outward defectors at defection	6
2.2	Destination of defectors from the Liberals	11
2.3	Party leaders' records on defections	12
2.4	Geographical distribution of defections	14
2.5	Defections by type of constituency	14
2.6	Defectors and religion	15
2.7	Defectors by gender	15
2.8	Profession outside parliament	16
2.9	Military experience (including National Service)	16
2.10	Military rank achieved	16
2.11	'Toffs' defect	17
2.12	Divorce	17
2.13	Parliamentary careers of defectors and loyalists	18
2.14	Motivation for defection	20
3.1	Fate of the 35 Liberal MP War Policy Objectors	34
3.2	Future political careers of the 35 War Policy Objectors	35
3.3	Labour candidates unopposed by Liberals	51
3.4	Labour overtakes the combined Liberals' seats and votes	51
4.1	Electoral record of the 1924 Constitutionalists	112
4.2	Lloyd George Policy Objectors defecting to the Conservatives	121
4.3	Protection Convert Industrialist defectors	128
5.1	Paths of Liberal MPs elected in 1929 at the 1931 election	156
6.1	Fate of SDP defectors at 1983 general election and after	183
6.2	Returning former defectors	189

Foreword

Alun Wyburn-Powell's fascinating study of defections of MPs from the Liberals and Liberal Democrats highlights one remarkable fact: how few defections there have been in the past few decades. The party has been able to maintain a stable parliamentary position despite a hostile electoral system, which makes parliamentary survival tough and might therefore be conducive to defection. That this has not happened to any notable extent testifies to the strength and vitality of British liberalism.

The Westminster electoral system works heavily against the third party, a fact most clearly demonstrated by the 1983 general election, where the Liberal-SDP Alliance's 25.3% share of the popular vote was translated into a mere 23 MPs – just 3.5% of the total. Even in 1997, when electoral support for Tony Blair was at its peak, and New Labour appeared at its most unstoppable, the Lib Dems were still able to poll almost 17% of the popular vote. So there has always been the political space for a Liberal party, but the shift from major to minor party in the 1920s was traumatic and the cause of significant defections.

Being a broad church, the Liberals suffered losses to both the left and the right. Those who looked towards Labour in the immediate post-war years did so because, in the main, they saw Labour as the only credible progressive option, wanting to continue where Asquith's pre-war government had started. However, on the right, Labour's rise only intensified the fear of socialism, driving Winston Churchill and others into – or in his case, back into – the arms of the Tories.

While the party was able to come together in defence of free trade at the 1923 general election, the failure to capitalise on any sense of unity following the formation of the first Labour government proved its undoing. And once Baldwin had abandoned protection, the Tories had little difficulty picking off much of the Liberal right.

Nearly a century later, the Lib Dems are in coalition with the Conservatives. Going in with the Tories was the toughest political decision the party had taken since Asquith decided to put MacDonald and Labour in power in 1924. Strikingly, not a single MP has yet defected to Labour. Alun Wyburn-Powell's study helps to explain why.

Andrew Adonis

Abbreviations

BSP   British Socialist Party
DLB   *Dictionary of Liberal Biography*
ILP   Independent Labour Party
LCC   London County Council
LWC   Liberal War Committee
NDP   National Democratic Party
NPS   National Party of Scotland
ODNB   *Oxford Dictionary of National Biography*
RNVR   Royal Naval Volunteer Reserve
UDC   Union of Democratic Control

Acknowledgements

I would like to thank the staff of the following archives and libraries: the Bodleian Library, Oxford; University of Bristol Library Special Collections; the British Library Newspaper Collections, Colindale; Cambridge University Library; the Churchill Archives Centre, Cambridge; University of Glasgow Library Special Collections; University of Leicester Library; London Probate Registry; the National Archives, Kew; the National Archives of Scotland; the National Library of Scotland; the National Library of Wales; Nuffield College, Oxford; the Parliamentary Archives; the John Rylands University Library, Manchester; Southampton University Library Special Collections; the Scottish Probate Registry; University of Warwick Library and the National Trust, Whitwick Manor.

The following people very kindly gave me their views on aspects of my research: the late Lord Allen of Abbeydale, Lord Ashdown, David Alexander, Professor Vernon Bogdanor, the late Roderic Bowen QC, Duncan Brack, Dr Peter Catterall, the late Stanley Clement-Davies, Dr Matthew Cole, Professor Russell Deacon, Lord Hooson QC, Dr Glyn Tegai Hughes, Dr J. Graham Jones, Tony Little, the late Lord Livsey, Graham Lypiatt, Lembit Opik MP, Roger Pincham CBE, Peter Price, the late Lord Renton, Viscount Tenby, Lord Thomas of Gresford, Rt Hon. Jeremy Thorpe and Mark Williams MP. I would like especially to thank Dr Stuart Ball and Professor Robert Colls at the University of Leicester, Tony Mason at Manchester University Press, Lord Adonis and Professor David Dutton.

My late wife, Ann, then apparently in good health, encouraged me to start this research. But, in an uncanny parallel with the fortunes of the Liberal Party, unexpected disaster hit and Ann died. I and the project survived and eventually fortunes revived and I met my new wife, Diana. Diana and my son, Christopher, have not only been very supportive, but have made many of my research visits more enjoyable by coming with me to Glasgow, Edinburgh, Manchester, Oxford,

ACKNOWLEDGEMENTS

Bristol, London, Southampton, Cambridge and even to Colindale – although they chose to visit the RAF Museum instead of the Newspaper Library!

1
Introduction

The Liberal Party was the dominant party of British Government from its emergence in the 1850s until the Great War, but by the 1950s it was virtually wiped off the political map. Controversy still rages over the reasons and responsibility for the collapse. Defections played a significant part in the decline, but until now they have never received detailed attention from historians or political analysts. This book studies all the defections of serving and former Liberal MPs from 1910 to 2010. The sheer scale of the exodus is striking: one in every six people elected as a Liberal MP defected at some point from the party. Each defection is explored, providing new perspectives on the controversies surrounding party leadership, divisions over policy and the impact of the Great War. It sheds light on the long-term relationship between the Liberals/Liberal Democrats and the Conservatives and the Labour Party. In the light of these findings, the conclusion of the coalition negotiations with the Conservatives in 2010 and the failure of the discussions between Labour and the Liberal Democrats are not surprising. This research also finds that there are statistically significant personal differences between defectors as a group and their loyalist colleagues.

Defection is defined as a 'falling away from allegiance to a leader or party'. The defection of a person who has served as an MP is effectively the verdict on their party at a specific date of a well-informed person with vested interests. A political defection is a significant act, which usually involves a public explanation, a severing of old links, a forging of new relationships and, in some cases, significant financial and career implications. The reasons for a defection may have developed over a long period of time, but, if circumstances had changed, the proposed defection could have been abandoned at any stage. A defection to another party will normally have been intended as an irrevocable act. The starting point for this book is December 1910, when the Great War was unforeseen and the Liberal Party was cohesive and in government. Seats in Ireland, where the Liberals were unrepresented at Westminster after December 1910, are therefore not included in this study, but mainland university seats are included.

An outward defector is defined as someone who sat as a Liberal or Liberal Democrat MP at Westminster at any time between the December 1910 general election and the dissolution before the 2010 election, and who, at any time afterward, also sat as an MP, or stood as a candidate, for any other party or as an independent, or whose departure from the Liberal Party or joining of another party was reported or announced by them, or which can be deduced from the circumstances.

This research is focused on MPs and former MPs who made a deliberate individual decision to change party allegiance. These people should be distinguished from those who were involved in party splits and who would not have made a deliberate decision to change party. The following are therefore included in the definition of defectors in this study, as they made a deliberate personal decision to change their party status: candidates who stood as Constitutionalists in 1924; Liberal MPs who moved from the Liberals to the Liberal Nationals or vice versa from November 1933 onward, when the two factions were on opposite sides of the House of Commons; Liberal MPs who publicly renounced the Liberal whip; former Liberal MPs who were elevated to the House of Lords and became cross-benchers or who took another party's whip; former Liberal MPs who became candidates or MPs who were effectively Conservatives but styled themselves Liberal National and Conservative, Conservative and Liberal, Conservative and National Liberal, or (after 1948) National Liberal; and former Labour MPs who joined the SDP and who later became Liberal Democrat MPs (but SDP MPs but who did not later become Liberal or Liberal Democrat MPs are not included).

The following are not classed as defectors in this study, as they did not make a deliberate decision to leave one party for another: MPs who changed labels between Liberal and Lib-Lab; Coalition Liberals up to 1922; and National Liberals in 1922 (who are all counted as members of the Liberal Party for this study). Liberal MPs who joined the Liberal Nationals or vice versa before November 1933, when both wings of the party were on the same side in the Commons and the divisions between the factions were unclear, are also not counted as defectors in this research.

In addition to the MPs and former MPs covered in this study, there have, of course, been defections among MEPs, peers, party members, constituency activists, benefactors, councillors and voters. This study focuses on the MPs, as they are a clearly defined category who have the highest profile and are generally the most committed group within any party.

For contrast and completeness, this research also investigated the smaller number of inward defectors and the part they played in the party's revival. The definition of an inward defector has been taken as one who served as an MP for another party or as an independent before becoming a Liberal or Liberal Democrat MP. In the cases of both outward and inward defectors the person must have served as an MP before the defection and in both cases must have served at some stage as a Liberal or Liberal Democrat MP. However, this inevitably means that the criterion for qualifying as an inward defector is more stringent. A person who was simply a member of another party, who then became a Liberal or Liberal Democrat MP would not be included, as a person's allegiance before they enter parliament is of less significance than it is after they have been elected. The above definitions enable an unequivocal decision to be made in virtually all cases about whether a person was a defector.

This book adds new evidence to an under-researched field. No previous work has taken a long-term view of political defections. Existing writing about the history of the Liberal Party has concentrated heavily on Gladstone, Lloyd George, Asquith and the party's decline. Attention has been given to the major party splits, such as the Liberal Unionists and the Liberal Nationals.[1] A few overall histories of the party covering longer spans of time have been written, but all of them take a chronological rather than thematic approach. Long-term thematic and analytical study of the party has been very limited, and essentially confined to election performance.

In addition to the areas of the party's history which remain unexplored, there are also other areas where there is no settled view. Aspects of the party's history which are still the subject of controversy include the health of the party on the eve of the Great War and the extent and impact of the Lloyd George Fund. Since the Asquith–Lloyd George split of 1916, controversy has raged over the respective responsibility of the two leaders and their followers in the damage done to the party. In fact, the impact of a majority of the party's leaders is still subject to debate, re-evaluation and disagreement – Clement Davies and Jo Grimond for their respective roles in the party's revival since the 1950s; Jeremy Thorpe due to his achievements being eclipsed by his controversial departure and his subsequently being charged with incitement and conspiracy to murder;[2] David Steel for his role in the merger with the SDP; Paddy Ashdown for his attempt to forge an alliance with the Labour Party under Tony Blair's leadership; Charles Kennedy due to his departure after revealing a long-term alcohol problem and Nick Clegg for leading the party into coalition with the Conservatives.

Dangerfield's *Strange Death of Liberal England,* published in 1935, was one of the first attempts to trace the start of the decline of the Liberal Party and placed the origins earlier than that proposed by most subsequent writers.[3] He argued that the decline started in the period 1910 to 1914. McKibbin followed this theme, as did Pelling, who argued that the decline was the 'the result of long-term social and economic changes'.[4] Cline put emphasis on the Pre-War Single Tax proposals as being of importance in linking those who defected from the Liberals to Labour.[5]

In 1966 Trevor Wilson's *The Downfall of the Liberal Party, 1914–35* challenged Dangerfield's assertion of a pre-war decline and placed the responsibility for the collapse firmly on the party's leadership during the war.[6] Later, Tanner also subscribed to this view.[7] Agreeing with the timescale, Bentley asserted that 'Liberalism tore its heart out between 1914 and 1918 in a private agony about true and false Liberals'.[8] Dutton argued that 'the more evidence that has been accumulated to show that the Liberal Party was in no imminent danger of collapse in 1914, the more significance must be attached to the war as the key explanation of what subsequently occurred'.[9] A few commentators agreed with Asquith's claim that the 'disintegration of the Liberal Party began with the Coupon election'.[10] Hart follows this view and made the case that the mechanics of the 1918 election were primarily responsible for the near-collapse of the party, as objectors to the Great War were rejected by the party.[11] Successive revisions of the causes of the Liberal Party's decline have tended to place the problems in a later era than did the older analyses. This research provides new evidence on the causes, responsibility and timing of the decline of the party, challenging the conclusions of previous studies.

Notes

1 See Cawood, Ian, *The Liberal Unionist Party: A History* (Tauris, 2012); Dutton, David, *Liberals in Schism* (Tauris, 2008); Goodlad, Graham, 'The Liberal Nationals, 1931–1940: The Problems of a Party in "Partnership Government"', *Historical Journal*, 38(1) (1995): 133–144; David, Edward, 'The Liberal Party Divided 1916–1918', *Historical Journal,* 13(2) (1970): 509–32.
2 Thorpe was acquitted.
3 Dangerfield, George, *The Strange Death of Liberal England* (Serif, 1935).
4 McKibbin, Ross, *The Evolution of the Labour Party, 1910–1924* (Oxford, 1994); Pelling, H., 'Labour and the Downfall of Liberalism', in Pelling, *Popular Politics and Society in Late Victorian Britain* (London, 1968).
5 Cline, Catherine Ann, *Recruits to Labour* (Syracuse, 1963).

6 Wilson, Trevor, *The Downfall of the Liberal Party 1914–35* (Collins, 1966).
7 Tanner, D.M., 'Political Realignment in England and Wales c.1906–1922', London, Ph.D. (1985).
8 Bentley, Michael, *The Climax of Liberal Politics: British Liberalism in Theory and Practice, 1868–1918* (Arnold, 1987).
9 Dutton, David, *A History of the Liberal Party* (Palgrave Macmillan, 2004), p. 55.
10 Oxford and Asquith, *Memories and Reflections, 1852–1927*, Vol. 2 (Cassell, 1928), p. 172.
11 Hart, Michael, 'The Decline of the Liberal Party in Parliament and in the Constituencies, 1914–1931', Oxford, D.Phil. (1982).

2

Defectors and loyalists

From the December 1910 election to the dissolution of May 2010, a total of 707 individuals served as a Liberal or Liberal Democrat MP.[1] Of these, 116, about one in six (16%), defected from the party, representing a serious loss of talent and, in many cases, money. Conversely, despite the party's manifest and serious problems, the majority of MPs did remain loyal to the party. This chapter identifies the scale and pattern of defections and some of the attributes which distinguished those who defected from those who stayed loyal.

The vast majority of the defectors were still actively seeking a political role, aiming to apply their skills in opposition to the Liberals. Of the 116 defectors, 83 (72%) sat in the House of Commons or in the House of Lords after their defection. An additional 21 (18%) were involved in further unsuccessful parliamentary contests. Only 12 (10%) played no further role in elections or in parliament, although most of them too continued to exert some influence on others. Table 2.1 shows the parliamentary status of all the defectors.

The timings of the defections reveal that most defectors left individually with few departing in concert with others. Defections peaked at times of rapidly fluctuating party fortunes; after the end of coalitions; and in election years (see Figure 2.1).[2] There were virtually no defections in the period 1910 to 1917. The year 1918 saw the first

Table 2.1 *Parliamentary status of outward defectors at defection*

In the House of Commons	49
In the House of Lords	6
Out of the Commons, but later returned	22
Out of the Commons, but later in the Lords	6
Out of the Commons and tried unsuccessfully to return	21
Out of Parliament and never tried to return	12
Total	**116**

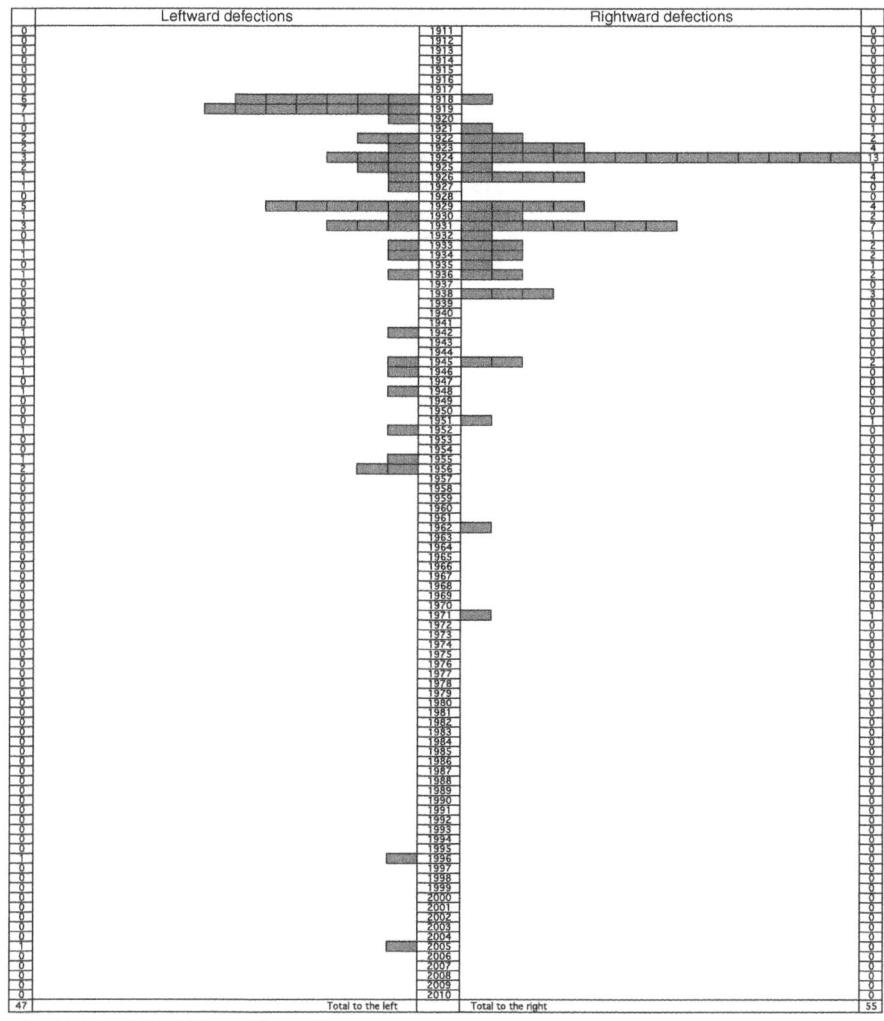

Leftward defections include to Labour and Communist
Rightward defections include to Conservative, Constitutionalist, New Party, National Party, Bottomley Party and Liberal Nationals
Independents not shown

Figure 2.1 Scale and direction of defections from Liberal Party

serious outflow of defectors. The vast majority of the defectors, 85 of the 116 (73%), departed in the thirteen years from November 1918 to November 1931. The year 1924 saw the highest number of defectors, with 16; followed by 1931, with 10. One of the striking features overall is the range of destinations, encompassing eight different parties, excluding those who left to be independents (see Figure 2.2).

7

DEFECTORS AND THE LIBERAL PARTY

	Defector	First defection			Subsequent defections			
1	Bottomley, Horatio	Jun	1911	Ind Lib	1918	Bott		
2	Mason, David	Jan	1914	Ind Lib	1919	Lib	1938	Lib Nat
3	Outhwaite, Robert	Dec	1914	Ind Lib	1919	Lab		
4	John, Edward	Nov	1918	Lab				
5	Trevelyan, Charles	Nov	1918	Lab	1931	Ind Lab		
6	Money, Leo Chiozza	Nov	1918	Lab	1924	Ind		
7	Ponsonby, Arthur	Dec	1918	Lab	1940	Ind		
8	Whitehouse, John Howard	Dec	1918	Ind Lib	1919	Lib		
9	Lambert, Richard	Dec	1918	Lab				
10	Wedgwood, Josiah	Apr	1919	Lab	1931	Ind Lab	1935	Lab
11	Haldane, Richard	Apr	1919	Ind	1922	Lab		
12	Lees-Smith, Hastings	Jun	1919	Lab				
13	White, James Dundas	Aug	1919	Lab	1924	Ind		
14	Malone, Cecil	Nov	1919	Ind	1920	Comm	1924	Lab
15	Buxton, Noel		1919	Lab				
16	Alden, Percy	Apr	1919	Lab	1927	Lib		
17	King, Joseph	Dec	1919	Lab				
18	Hemmerde, Edward		1920	Lab				
19	Beck, (Arthur) Cecil	Aug	1921	Bott				
20	Hopkinson, Austin	Feb	1922	Ind				
21	Munro, Robert	Sep	1922	Ind	1934	Lib Nat	1945	Con
22	Munro-Ferguson, Ronald	Oct	1922	Con				
23	McKenna, Reginald	Oct	1922	Con				
24	Hope, John	Nov	1922	Ind Lib				
25	Arnold, Sydney		1922	Lab	1938	Ind		
26	Philipson, Hilton	May	1923	Con				
27	Evans, Arthur	Jul	1923	Con				
28	Cowan, (William) Henry	Oct	1923	Con				
29	Addison, Christopher	Nov	1923	Lab				
30	Waring, Walter	Dec	1923	Con				
31	Edwards, John		1923	Ind Lib				
32	Churchill, Winston	Jan	1924	Const	1924	Con		
33	Moreing, Algernon	Jan	1924	Const	1924	Con		
34	Jarrett, George	Jan	1924	Con				
35	Allen, William	Oct	1924	Const				
36	Greenwood, Hamar	Oct	1924	Const	1924	Con		
37	Ward, John	Oct	1924	Const	1924	Lib		
38	Edwards, (John) Hugh	Oct	1924	Const	1924	Lib		
39	Robinson, Thomas	Oct	1924	Const	1924	Lib	1929	Ind
40	Sturrock, John Leng	Oct	1924	Const	1924	Con		
41	England, Abraham	Oct	1924	Const	1924	Lib		
42	Hogbin, Henry Cairn	Oct	1924	Const	1924	Con		
43	Denman, Richard	Oct	1924	Lab	1931	Nat Lab		
44	Scott, Alexander McCallum	Nov	1924	Lab				
45	Spears, Edward	Dec	1924	Con				
46	Lamb, Ernest		1924	Lab	1931	Nat Lab		
47	Bennett, Albert		1924	Con				
48	Spero, George	Apr	1925	Lab				

Figure 2.2 Outward defectors in chronological order

	Defector	First defection			Subsequent defections			
49	Thornton, Maxwell	Dec	1925	Ind				
50	Rendall, Athelstan		1925	Lab				
51	Mond, Alfred	Jan	1926	Con				
52	Mond, Henry	Jan	1926	Con				
53	Young, Edward Hilton	Feb	1926	Ind	1926	Con		
54	Entwistle, Cyril	Feb	1926	Con				
55	Mansel, Courtenay	Mar	1926	Con				
56	Kenworthy, Joseph	Oct	1926	Lab				
57	Davies, David	Nov	1926	Ind Lib				
58	Benn, William Wedgwood	Jan	1927	Lab				
59	Royle, Charles	Apr	1929	Ind Lib				
60	Pattinson, Samuel	May	1929	Con				
61	Livingstone, Mackenzie	May	1929	Ind Lib	1930	Lab	1931	Nat Lab
62	Guest, Frederick	May	1929	Con				
63	Guest, (Christian) Henry	May	1929	Con				
64	Guest, Oscar Montague	May	1929	Con				
65	Marks, George Croydon	Jun	1929	Lab	1931	Nat Lab		
66	Jowitt, William	Jun	1929	Lab	1931	Nat Lab	1936	Lab
67	Martin, Frederick	Sep	1929	Lab				
68	Garro-Jones, George	Nov	1929	Lab	1958	Lib		
69	Fletcher, Reginald		1929	Lab				
70	Illingworth, Albert	Apr	1930	Con				
71	Forrest, Walter	Sep	1930	Con	1935	Lib Nat		
72	Dickinson, Willoughby		1930	Lab	1931	Nat Lab		
73	Grigg, Edward	Feb	1931	Con				
74	Williams, Rhys	Mar	1931	Con				
75	Simon, John	Jun	1931	Ind Lib				
76	Hutchison, Robert	Jun	1931	Ind Lib				
77	Brown, Ernest	Jun	1931	Ind Lib				
78	Lloyd George, David	Oct	1931	Ind Lib	1935	Lib		
79	Lloyd-George, Gwilym	Oct	1931	Ind Lib	1935	Lib	1945	Con
80	Owen, Goronwy	Oct	1931	Ind Lib	1935	Lib		
81	Lloyd George, Megan	Oct	1931	Ind Lib	1935	Lib	1955	Lab
82	Owen, Frank	Oct	1931	Ind Lib	1935	Lib		
83	Barnes, Harry		1931	Lab				
84	Alexander, Maurice		1931	Lab	1937	Lib Nat		
85	Pratt, John	Oct	1931	New				
86	Dudgeon, Cecil	Oct	1931	New				
87	Thorne, George	Nov	1931	Ind				
88	Simon, Ernest	Nov	1931	Ind	1946	Lab		
89	Dalziel, (James) Henry	Sep	1932	NPS				
90	Nathan, Harry	Feb	1933	Ind	1934	Lab		
91	Hunter, Joseph	Nov	1933	Lib Nat				
92	Maclay, Joseph	Nov	1933	Ind Lib Nat				
93	McKeag, William	Jun	1934	Lib Nat	1936	Lib	1955	Con
94	Davies, Ellis	Oct	1934	Lab	1939	Lib Nat		
95	Morrison, George	Jul	1935	Lib Nat				
96	Murray, Arthur	Apr	1936	Lib Nat	1938	Lib		

Figure 2.2 (continued)

	Defector	First defection		Subsequent defections				
97	Bernays, Robert	Sep	1936	Lib Nat				
98	Janner, Barnett	Sep	1936	Lab				
99	Harvey, (Thomas) Edmund	Feb	1937	Ind Lib				
100	Holdsworth, Herbert	Oct	1938	Lib Nat				
101	Roberts, Aled		1938	Lib Nat	1945	Con		
102	Acland, Richard	Sep	1942	C Wealth	1947	Lab	1955	Ind
103	Mallalieu, (Edward) Lance	May	1945	Lab				
104	Hore-Belisha, Leslie	Aug	1945	Con				
105	Horabin, Thomas	Oct	1946	Ind Lib	1947	Lab		
106	Mander, Geoffrey	Jun	1948	Lab				
107	Wadsworth, George	Feb	1951	Con				
108	Granville, Edgar	Jan	1952	Lab	1974	Ind		
109	Foot, Dingle	Jul	1956	Lab				
110	Roberts, Wilfrid	Jul	1956	Lab				
111	Bennett, Donald		1962	Ind				
112	Macdonald, Archibald	Mar	1971	Con				
113	Meadowcroft, Michael	Feb	1989	Ind Lib	2007	Lib		
114	Pitt, Bill		1996	Lab				
115	Alton, David	Apr	1997	Ind				
116	Marsden, Paul	Apr	2005	Lab				

Key
Lab   Defection to Labour   Lib Nat   Defection to Liberal Nationals 1933-
Con   Defection to Conservatives   New   Defection to New Party
NPS   Defection to National Party of Scotland   Bott   Defection to Bottomley Party
Comm Defection to Communist Party   C Wealth   Defection to Common Wealth
Const Constitutionalist   Nat Lab   National Labour
Lib   Return to Liberals   Ind   Independent

Figure 2.2 (continued)

The initial destination for many defectors was not their final political home, as many of the defectors made further party moves and eighteen returned to the Liberals.

There was a preponderance of departures to Labour among the early defectors, followed by clusters of defections to the Conservatives and then to the Liberal Nationals. The outward defections to the Conservatives were almost entirely a phenomenon of the period 1922 to 1931. Rightward defectors continued to the Liberal Nationals until 1938, but this was virtually the end of the rightward losses. From 1956 to 2010 there were extremely few outward defections.[3] Overall, similar numbers defected to the right as to the left. Table 2.2 below shows the destinations of the defectors. The highest total for any individual party was 47 defectors who went to the Labour Party, but 34 went to the Conservatives and another 21 went to other right-of-centre parties, making a total of 55.

Table 2.2 *Destination of defectors from the Liberals*

	Number Defecting
To the Conservatives, Liberal Nationals, Constitutionalists and radical populist parties	55
To Labour*	47
To be independent	14
Total	**116**

* Includes defectors to Labour who also joined another party at some stage.

There were 83 defectors (72% of the total) who left during the leaderships of Asquith and Lloyd George: 50 under Asquith and 33 under Lloyd George. However, Asquith was leader from the start of this study in 1910 until 1926, while Lloyd George was only party leader from 1926 to 1931. The annual attrition rate gives a measure of how extensive was the loss of defectors under each party leader, allowing for the varying lengths of leadership and allowing for the fact that there was a vastly varying pool of potential defectors (current MPs and living former MPs) at different stages, ranging from a high point of 443 in 1923 to a low point of 40 between 1980 and 1982. The worst annual attrition of defectors was during Lloyd George's leadership of the party. During his tenure the annual attrition rate was 1.6% per year, followed by Asquith's leadership, when the rate was 0.9%. Davies at 0.6% annual attrition and Samuel at 0.5% were the leaders suffering the next highest rates.

Table 2.3 shows the attrition by defection figures for each leader from 1910 to 2010.[4] These figures can reasonably be taken as a reflection of the opinions of the defectors on the individual leaders: despite the fact that each defection may have resulted from years of dissatisfaction, the planned defection could have been aborted at any stage. A defector would have known that his or her departure would be seen at the time as a judgement on the current leadership of the party. Two of the more recent leaders, Steel and Campbell, suffered no outward defections during their time as leader. During Asquith's leadership the level of defections varied widely from year to year. From 1911 (the first full year included in this study) to 1917 the attrition rate was very low, but from 1918 to 1926 the rate increased significantly. Despite the greater difficulty of entering parliament as a Liberal by then, those MPs who entered in the 1931 parliament were the most prone to defect: nine of the fifteen (60%) of the Liberal MPs elected in that parliament defected.

Table 2.3 *Party leaders' records on defections*

Leader	Number of outward defections during leadership	Average outward defections per year	Average number of MPs and living former MPs	Attrition during leadership	Annual attrition rate+
Asquith* (Dec 1910–Oct 1926)	50	3.1	346	14.5%	0.9%
Lloyd George (Oct 1926–Nov 1931)	33	6.6	409	8.1%	1.6%
Samuel (Nov 1931–Nov 1935)	7	1.8	365	1.9%	0.5%
Sinclair (Nov 1935–Jul 1945)	8	0.8	276	2.9%	0.3%
Davies (Aug 1945–Nov 1956)	10	0.9	164	6.1%	0.6%
Grimond (Nov 1956–Jan 1967)	1	0.1	76	1.3%	0.1%
Thorpe (Jan 1967–Jul 1976)	1	0.1	48	2.1%	0.2%
Steel (Jul 1976–Jul 1988)	0	0.0	46	0.0%	0.0%
Ashdown (Jul 1988–Aug 1999)	3	0.3	58	5.2%	0.5%
Kennedy (Aug 1999–Mar 2006)	1	0.2	91	1.1%	0.2%

Table 2.3 (continued)

Leader	Number of outward defections during leadership	Average outward defections per year	Average number of MPs and living former MPs	Attrition during leadership	Annual attrition rate+
Campbell (Mar 2006– Oct 2007)	0	0.0	110	0.0%	0.0%
Clegg (Dec 2007– May 2010)	0	0.0	108	0.0%	0.0%

* Asquith assumed the party leadership in April 1908, before the starting date of this study.
^ Total number of defectors during the leadership as a percentage of the average number of Liberal MPs and living former Liberal MPs elected since 1910.
\+ Average percentage of the total MPs and living former MPs defecting each year.

Defections were not a peculiarly English, Scottish or Welsh phenomenon: they were distributed evenly across Great Britain according to the level of Liberal representation in each country. Table 2.4 below shows the geographical distribution of defections.[5]

During the span of the study, as there were well over 100 defectors and nearly 600 who remained loyal, there is a large enough population to investigate, statistically, some of the apparent differences between the defectors and the loyalists. Where appropriate, a statistical test (chi-squared test), has been applied to establish if some apparent differences between the loyalists and the defectors are statistically significant – i.e., not just the result of chance.[6]

MPs representing an urban constituency were slightly more likely to defect than those representing a rural constituency, as shown in Table 2.5.

However, applying the chi-squared test shows that the nature of the constituency represented was not a statistically significant determinant of likelihood to defect. So, overall, there was no overriding geographical pattern to defections.

Since Victorian times, Liberal support was strongest in constituencies with high levels of religious nonconformism and the Liberal Party had a majority of MPs who were from a nonconformist background. Representatives of the minority religions within the Liberal Party – Unitarian, Anglican, Quaker and Jewish MPs and former MPs – were

Table 2.4 *Geographical distribution of defections**

	Defectors		Loyalists	
England	73	71%	427	74%
Wales	11	11%	51	9%
Scotland	19	19%	99	17%

* 103 defectors and 577 non-defectors sat for seats in one country only. Those who represented seats in more than one country are excluded.

Table 2.5 *Defections by type of constituency**

	Defectors		Loyalists	
Rural	50	50%	341	60%
Urban	49	49%	223	40%
University	1	1%	2	0%

* Excludes MPs who sat for more than one type of seat.

more likely to defect than were the majority Nonconformists (see Table 2.6).[7]

Men were more likely to defect than women, as Table 2.7 demonstrates. However, the Parliamentary Liberal Party was male-dominated and therefore there were very few female potential defectors. The only female defector was Megan Lloyd George.[8]

The Liberal Party was dominated by lawyers and business people. These groups tended to be fairly equally represented among the defectors and the non-defectors. The profession where there is the most noticeable difference in the proportion of defectors and loyalists are politicians whose career outside parliament was in the armed forces: they are over-represented among the defectors. Possible reasons for this can be speculated. People with a military background typically tend to be self-confident, to be willing to take decisive actions and not be prepared to tolerate a lack of clarity or weak leadership. Conversely, educationalists and ministers of religion, who were perhaps more likely to have been conciliatory and tolerant by professional training and personality, were under-represented among the defectors. Table 2.8 illustrates the spread of professions among defectors and loyalists.

In addition to the MPs whose main profession outside parliament had been in the armed forces, many other MPs had military service, as the study includes the periods of the two world wars. Table 2.9 shows that outward defectors were more than twice as likely to have been in the armed forces than were non-defectors.

Table 2.6 *Defectors and religion*

	Defectors		Loyalists	
Religion known*	57		242	
of these:				
Nonconformist	38	69%	186	77%
Jewish	7	12%	10	4%
Unitarian	4	7%	11	5%
Anglican	3	5%	4	2%
Presbyterian	2	4%	15	6%
Quaker	2	4%	5	2%
Catholic	1	2%	4	2%
Other	0	0%	7	3%

* A major source for MPs' religions is Catterall, Peter, 'The Free Churches and the Labour Party in England and Wales 1918–1939', London, Ph.D. (1989).

Table 2.7 *Defectors by gender*

	Defectors		Loyalists	
Male	115	99%	564	97%
Female	1	1%	20	3%

The difference between the rates of military service of the defectors and the loyalists is statistically significant.[9] Those with military service were more likely to defect. Furthermore, of those with military service, the highest ranks were disproportionately represented among the defectors: with proportionately three times as many of the rank of lieutenant-colonel or above compared to the non-defectors (see Table 2.10).[10]

Among those with military experience, the difference between the ranks achieved by the defectors and non-defectors is also statistically significant.[11] Defectors were significantly more likely to have been of high military rank than were the non-defectors. This may have reflected that those having achieved a high military rank were more willing to trust their own judgement and more willing to accept responsibility in an adverse situation, such as a political defection.

While serving as leader of the Liberal Democrat Party, Paddy (later Lord) Ashdown proposed a theory that 'toffs defect'. His views originated in his earlier military and diplomatic career, where he observed the type of people who had defected to the Soviet Union (including, ironically, Donald Maclean, son of the eponymous Liberal MP and

Table 2.8 *Profession outside parliament*

	Defectors		Loyalists	
Legal	35	33%	145	31%
Business/finance	29	27%	157	34%
Journalism/writing	15	14%	48	10%
Military (regular)	14	13%	30	6%
Education	5	5%	36	8%
Engineer	4	3%	10	2%
Medical	2	2%	14	3%
Architect	2	2%	5	1%
Accountant	1	1%	6	1%
Farmer	1	1%	9	2%
Minister of Religion	0	0%	6	1%

Table 2.9 *Military experience (including National Service)*

	Defectors		Loyalists	
No military experience	74	64%	488	84%
Military experience	42	36%	96	16%

Table 2.10 *Military rank achieved*

	Defectors		Loyalists	
Lieutenant	7	6%	12	2%
Captain	7	6%	28	5%
Major	8	7%	27	5%
Lt-Colonel or Colonel	15	13%	25	4%
Major-Gen. or Lt-General	3	3%	3	1%

cabinet minister).[12] Ashdown considered that his theory also applied to politics. If 'toffs' are defined as being aristocratic, wealthy, Eton-educated and of high military rank, 'toffs' were indeed more likely to have defected (see Table 2.11). Defectors were more likely to be Eton-educated, to have had a hereditary peerage and to have been wealthier than non-defectors.[13]

Defectors appear to have been much more likely to have divorced than were the non-defectors. Of the defectors, 9.5% divorced, compared to only 2.7% of the loyalists (see Table 2.12). Some divorces preceded the defection and some succeeded it. However, a tendency

Table 2.11 *'Toffs' defect*

	Defectors	Loyalists
Hereditary Peerage	2.6%	1.5%
Median wealth at death	£42,457	£28,919
Eton-educated	5.2%	4.4%

Table 2.12 *Divorce*

	Defectors	Loyalists
Divorced	9.5%	2.7%

to be divorced could be considered to be an indicator of a person who will take radical action if not satisfied with his or her circumstances, and hence make that person more likely, if dissatisfied, to defect from a political party. Defectors were more than three times as likely to divorce as were loyalists. However, the numbers of divorcés is slightly too small to apply the chi-squared test to demonstrate the statistical significance of this finding.

There was virtually no difference between the ages at which the two groups died: defectors on average lived for seventy-four years – just one year longer than did the loyalists, suggesting that the defectors were no more physically robust than the non-defectors. The average age at defection was fifty years. The youngest defector was Arthur Evans, aged twenty-five, and the oldest George Thorne, at seventy-eight.

On average, defectors started their political careers at a younger age than did the loyalists. In many cases this was possible because the defectors came from wealthier backgrounds. Many defectors also had greater ambition and a focus on the achievement of ministerial office.

There was no significant difference between the electoral success rates of the defectors and the non-defectors. Defectors' success rate per election, either standing as a Liberal or for another party, was virtually the same as that of the loyalists – averaging between 61% and 65%. The defectors on average had a longer parliamentary career, primarily because they fought more elections: defectors on average fought 6.4 contests compared to 4.8 for the non-defectors (Table 2.13).

Defectors were no more successful as candidates and no more highly educated than loyalists – 60% of both groups received a university education. However, despite this, defectors were significantly more likely to have achieved ministerial office.

Table 2.13 *Parliamentary careers of defectors and loyalists*

	Defectors	Loyalists
Age at first parliamentary contest	35.3	41.2
Age on entering Commons	37.2	44.2
Time between first contest and election	1.9	3.1
Overall election success rate	61%	65%
Electoral success standing as a Liberal	64%	65%
Total number of contests fought*	6.4	4.8
Average total years in Commons+	14.4	10.4
Percentage achieving ministerial office	33%	14%
Age at highest ministerial appointment	54.8	50.6
Percentage receiving a peerage	31%	13%

* Includes by-elections.
+ Excludes MPs still serving at May 2010.

Defectors overall were more than twice as likely to have achieved ministerial office as non-defectors, with 33% of defectors achieving ministerial office compared to only 14% of the loyalists. This difference is statistically significant.[14] The peak of the defectors' careers was more commonly reached after their defection than before: of the 38 defectors who achieved ministerial office at some stage in their careers, 15 achieved their highest position prior to their defection and 23 reached a higher post after defecting.

The defectors were also more than twice as likely as the loyalists to have received a peerage – 31% compared to 13%.[15] This difference is also statistically significant.[16] Thirty-three defectors were created new hereditary peers or life peers. Of these, only five had received their peerage before their defection, while twenty-eight were honoured after defection. In overall terms, defection was, therefore, a career-enhancing move. The defectors' careers were more successful in terms of peerages and ministerial office, despite the fact that their electoral success and education were only equivalent to those of the loyalists.

Overall, comparing all the defectors and the non-defectors demonstrates that there was no significant difference between the two groups in terms of their education, electoral appeal or longevity, and the incidences of defections were equally spread around the country. On the other hand, the defectors were on average wealthier and more determined on a political career, which they had started at an earlier age. They were more likely to have been educated at Eton, to have had military experience and, if so, to have achieved higher rank than the non-defectors. The defectors were also more likely to have been divorced and to belong to a religion which was in a minority within the Liberal Party. Thus, faced with similar sets of circumstances, some people were more predisposed to defect than others, depending on a range of factors, some of which have been identified and analysed here.

Each defection resulted from a politician's decision based on, among other factors, the individual's view of his or her personal circumstances and future prospects, as well as national and local electoral conditions. Where a single or predominant reason for a defection can be identified (which is the case in all but 17 of the 116 defections) the breakdown of motivations is shown in Table 2.14.

In the majority of cases, a 'policy' motivation was a reaction against an undesired Liberal policy, rather than the attraction of another party's policies. 'Prospects' as a motivation were related to the perceived better electoral or ministerial prospects offered by another party. In only three cases was the defection almost totally ascribed to 'personality' issues: in each case the catalyst for defection was Lloyd George's personality.

Although very few defectors left at the same time as others, or in any concerted manner, common directions of, and reasons for, the defections link most, but not all, into one of several virtually mutually exclusive groupings. The only overlaps between membership of the groupings are two defectors who joined Labour and then defected to the Liberal Nationals and some who sat as independents, and at a different time, for another party. No defector went to the Conservatives and then to Labour or vice versa.

Defectors to Labour are studied in Chapter 3. The 'War Policy Objectors' were individuals who objected to the First World War governments' war policies from a principled and instinctive point of view, and in some cases because of their religious beliefs. They objected initially to secret diplomacy and later became opponents of conscription. They were not necessarily pacifists and in some cases were willing to go to war themselves, but were not willing to force others to do so. Many were drawn into contact with Ramsay MacDonald through membership of the Union of Democratic Control. Faced with vilification from their local press, rifts opened up between them and their local Liberal associations. In effect the Liberal Party left them at a local level: they were reluctant to leave the Liberal Party. All ended up in the Labour Party, but most had not formally joined by the time of the 1918 election. There were some personal links between them, but they did not act as a group. Most were caught unprepared at the time of the 1918 election, some in mid-transfer; and many stood under halfway house labels. The 1918 election interrupted their journey, but did not cause, hasten,

Table 2.14 *Motivation for defection*

Policy	43
Prospects	53
Personality	3
Mixed	17

delay or prevent their change of allegiance. The 'Idealists' were individualistic, idealistic loners, often unrealistic and impractical, unsettled in any party. Many sabotaged their own careers, due to their beliefs and actions. The 'Disillusioned Progressives' comprised the largest grouping of defectors. They left the Liberals for Labour over a period of twenty-seven years after the end of the Great War. Their decisions were based more on the decline of the Liberal Party and their eagerness for continued social progress, rather than on the attractions of the Labour Party. They did not tend to take sides between Asquith and Lloyd George, but were seriously discouraged by the fall-out from the party split. No one issue or personality determined their stance. They were sentimentally attached to the Liberal Party and agonised over leaving. They would have stayed if they had felt that the Liberals could form another effective government. Independent-minded, they tended to make similar decisions independently from each other. They were politically career-minded, but motivated by achievement, rather than position. The 'Lloyd George Objectors' were Asquithians who were motivated to leave by their personal dislike of Lloyd George. The 'MacDonald Supporter Careerists' had successful careers outside politics. They were not very party-minded or politically principled. They were influenced by their friendship with Ramsay MacDonald and the attractions of office and titles. With one exception, they followed MacDonald into the National Government. The 'Rightward Drift Objectors' objected to Clement Davies' leadership of the Liberal Party in an apparent rightward direction after the Second World War. They joined the Labour Party in the decade after 1946. There were personal links between the individuals, but theirs was not a concerted defection.

Defectors to the Conservatives are studied in Chapter 4. The 'Bonar Law Supporter-Third Coalitionists' were strongly opposed to the Lloyd George Coalition. They were on good terms with Bonar Law and were willing to take office in a Conservative Government. They were the nucleus of what might have become a Third Coalition – between Asquithians and the Conservatives opposed to Lloyd George. The 'Fusionists' were followers of Lloyd George, who wished to see a merger of Coalition Liberals and Conservatives. They were career-, but not party-, minded. The 'Constitutionalists' briefly gained prominence at the 1924 election. They centred on Churchill, but were never an organised party. Many of them had military backgrounds. Their objective was to avoid a Liberal-Conservative contest in their own constituencies. The 'Lloyd George Policy Objectors' were right-leaning defectors who objected to Lloyd George's policies – especially the land policies. They were not necessarily personally hostile to Lloyd George, and in some cases retained a good personal relationship with him after their parting of the ways. The 'Protection Convert Industrialists' were industrialists, for whom politics was a secondary career. They saw political policies in terms of their shareholders' interests and were willing to sacrifice political principles for economic expediency. They defected from the Liberal Party between 1923 and 1930. The 'Faux Fusionists' were former Liberals who stood under labels such as Conservative and Liberal or Liberal-Conservative, who claimed to be nominees of the local Liberal and Conservative parties, but were, to all intents and purposes, purely Conservatives. They exploited a lack of clarity, or in some cases, even misled voters over their party status.

Defectors to minor parties are considered in Chapter 5. The 'Proto-Liberal Nationals' comprised Simon, Hutchison and Brown, who left the Liberals before the formation of the National Government in 1931. They were motivated by their objection to the Liberals' support for the Labour Government and by the potential electoral consequences. Those who changed labels between Liberal and Liberal National between the formation of the National Government and November 1933 are not considered as defectors in this study as the boundaries between the two groups were fluid while both groups sat on the same side of the House of Commons. However, the 'Post-November 1933 Liberal National Defectors' were those who made the clear decision to change allegiance between the Liberals and Liberal Nationals after November 1933, when Samuel's group had crossed the floor of the House of Commons. The earlier among these defectors were generally motivated by electoral advantage or ministerial career prospects, while the later converts were mainly motivated by foreign affairs. Some former Liberals became 'Radical Populists'. Two Liberals became members of the Bottomley Group in the House of Commons. Two Liberals joined the New Party and stood unsuccessfully as candidates for that party at the 1931 election. The National Party of Scotland claimed a former Liberal convert and the right-wing National Party also inherited a former Liberal MP. Those who became Independent Liberals are also included in Chapter 5. The 'Lloyd George Family Group' comprised David, Gwilym and Megan Lloyd George, together with Goronwy Owen and Frank Owen, who all

Defector	Year	Grouping	Chapter
Trevelyan, Charles	1918	War Policy Objector	3
Ponsonby, Arthur	1918	War Policy Objector	3
Outhwaite, Robert	1918	War Policy Objector	3
Lambert, Richard	1918	War Policy Objector	3
King, Joseph	1919	War Policy Objector	3
Whitehouse, John Howard	1918	War Policy Objector	3
Lees-Smith, Hastings	1919	War Policy Objector/Disillusioned Progressive	3
John, Edward	1918	Idealist/War Policy Objector	3
Money, Leo Chiozza	1918	Idealist	3
Wedgwood, Josiah	1919	Idealist	3
White, James Dundas	1919	Idealist	3
Hemmerde, Edward	1920	Idealist	3
Malone, Cecil	1919	Idealist	3
Alexander, Maurice	1931	Idealist	3
Davies, Ellis	1934	Idealist	3
Acland, Richard	1942	Idealist	3
Buxton, Noel	1919	Disillusioned Progressive	3
Alden, Percy	1919	Disillusioned Progressive	3
Haldane, Richard	1922	Disillusioned Progressive	3
Addison, Christopher	1923	Disillusioned Progressive	3
Scott, Alexander MacCallum	1924	Disillusioned Progressive	3
Spero, George	1925	Disillusioned Progressive	3
Rendall, Athelstan	1925	Disillusioned Progressive	3
Kenworthy, Joseph	1926	Disillusioned Progressive	3
Martin, Frederick	1929	Disillusioned Progressive	3
Garro-Jones, George	1929	Disillusioned Progressive	3
Fletcher, Reginald	1929	Disillusioned Progressive	3
Barnes, Harry	1931	Disillusioned Progressive	3
Simon, Ernest	1931	Disillusioned Progressive	3
Nathan, Harry	1933	Disillusioned Progressive	3
Janner, Barnett	1936	Disillusioned Progressive	3
Mallalieu, (Edward) Lance	1945	Disillusioned Progressive	3
Morris, Rhys Hopkin	1924	Lloyd George Objector	3
Benn, William Wedgwood	1927	Lloyd George Objector	3
Livingstone, Mackenzie	1929	Lloyd George Objector	3
Arnold, Sydney	1922	MacDonald Supporter Careerist	3
Denman, Richard	1924	MacDonald Supporter Careerist	3
Lamb, Ernest	1924	MacDonald Supporter Careerist	3
Jowitt, William	1929	MacDonald Supporter Careerist	3
Marks, George Croydon	1929	MacDonald Supporter Careerist	3
Dickinson, Willoughby	1930	MacDonald Supporter Careerist	3
Horabin, Thomas	1946	Rightward Drift Objector	3
Mander, Geoffrey	1948	Rightward Drift Objector	3
Granville, Edgar	1945	Rightward Drift Objector	3
Lloyd George, Megan	1931	Lloyd George Family Group/Rightward Drift Objector	3
Foot, Dingle	1956	Rightward Drift Objector	3
Roberts, Wilfrid	1956	Rightward Drift Objector	3
Pitt, Bill	1996	Individual Defector	3

Figure 2.3 Defectors by grouping

Defector	Date	Grouping	Chapter
McKenna, Reginald	1922	Bonar Law Supporter - Third Coalitionist	4
Munro-Ferguson, Ronald	1922	Bonar Law Supporter - Third Coalitionist	4
Guest, Frederick	1929	Fusionist	4
Guest, (Christian) Henry	1929	Fusionist	4
Guest, Oscar (Montague)	1929	Fusionist	4
Philipson, Hilton	1923	Fusionist	4
Evans, Arthur	1923	Fusionist	4
Waring, Walter	1923	Fusionist	4
Jarrett, George	1924	Constitutionalist	4
Moreing, Algernon	1924	Constitutionalist	4
Churchill, Winston	1924	Constitutionalist	4
Greenwood, Hamar	1924	Constitutionalist	4
Sturrock, John Leng	1924	Constitutionalist	4
Hogbin, Henry Cairn	1924	Constitutionalist	4
Ward, John	1924	Constitutionalist	4
Allen, William	1924	Constitutionalist	4
Edwards, (John) Hugh	1924	Constitutionalist	4
Robinson, Thomas	1924	Constitutionalist	4
England, Abraham	1924	Constitutionalist	4
Thornton, Maxwell	1925	Lloyd George Policy Objector	4
Davies, David	1926	Lloyd George Policy Objector	4
Mond, Alfred	1926	Lloyd George Policy Objector	4
Mond, Henry	1926	Lloyd George Policy Objector	4
Young, Edward Hilton	1926	Lloyd George Policy Objector	4
Mansel, Courtenay	1926	Lloyd George Policy Objector	4
Entwistle, Cyril	1926	Lloyd George Policy Objector	4
Pattinson, Samuel	1929	Lloyd George Policy Objector	4
Illingworth, Albert	1930	Lloyd George Policy Objector	4
Grigg, Edward	1931	Lloyd George Policy Objector	4
Cowan, (William) Henry	1923	Protection Convert Industrialist	4
Bennett, Albert	1924	Protection Convert Industrialist	4
Forrest, Walter	1930	Protection Convert Industrialist	4
Spears, (Edward) Louis	1924	Faux Fusionist	4
Williams, Rhys	1931	Faux Fusionist	4
Munro, Robert	1922	Faux Fusionist	4
Lloyd-George, Gwilym	1931	Lloyd George Family Group/Faux Fusionist	4
Hore-Belisha, Leslie	1945	Faux Fusionist	4
Wadsworth, George	1951	Faux Fusionist	4
Macdonald, Archibald	1971	Individual defector	4
Defector	Date	Grouping	Chapter
Simon, John	1931	Proto Liberal National	5
Hutchison, Robert	1931	Proto Liberal National	5
Brown, Ernest	1931	Proto Liberal National	5
Hunter, Joseph	1933	Post-November 1933 Liberal National Defector	5
Maclay, Joseph	1933	Post-November 1933 Liberal National Defector	5
McKeag, William	1934	Post-November 1933 Liberal National Defector	5
Morrison, George	1935	Post-November 1933 Liberal National Defector	5

Figure 2.3 (continued)

Defector	Date	Grouping	Chapter
Bernays, Robert	1936	Post-November 1933 Liberal National Defector	5
Murray, Arthur	1936	Post-November 1933 Liberal National Defector	5
Holdsworth, Herbert	1938	Post-November 1933 Liberal National Defector	5
Roberts, Aled	1938	Post-November 1933 Liberal National Defector	5
Mason, David	1938	Post-November 1933 Liberal National Defector	5
Bottomley, Horatio	1911	Bottomley Party	5
Beck, (Arthur) Cecil	1921	Bottomley Party	5
Hopkinson, Austin	1922	Independent Liberal	5
Dudgeon, Cecil	1931	New Party	5
Pratt, John	1931	New Party	5
Dalziel, (James) Henry	1932	National Party of Scotland	5
Bennett, Donald	1962	National Party	5
Lloyd George, David	1931	Lloyd George Family Group	5
Owen, Goronwy	1931	Lloyd George Family Group	5
Owen, Frank	1931	Lloyd George Family Group	5
Thorne, George Rennie	1931	Independent National Government Objector	5
Hope, John	1922	Deselected Liberal	5
Royle, Charles	1929	Deselected Liberal	5
Edwards, John	1923	University MP	5
Harvey, (Thomas) Edmund	1937	University MP	5
Meadowcroft, Michael	1989	Liberal Democrat Policy Objector	5
Alton, David	1997	Liberal Democrat Policy Objector	5
Mayhew, Christopher	1974	Proto SDP Inward Defector	6
Maclennan, Robert	1988	SDP Inward Defector	6
Nicholson, Emma	1995	Conservative Inward Defector	6
Thurnham, Peter	1996	Conservative Inward Defector	6
Marsden, Paul	2001	Labour Inward Defector	6
Sedgemore, Brian	2005	Labour Inward Defector	6

Figure 2.3 (continued)

objected to Samuel's acquiescence to the 1931 election. They sat on the opposition benches in the House of Commons and remained aloof from the remainder of their party. The 'Deselected Liberals' decided to fight elections as independent Liberals after losing the party's official backing. The 'University MPs and Candidates' include several politicians who contested elections as Independent Liberals: adherence to party labels in the university contests was less rigid than in the geographical constituencies. The 'Liberal Democrat Policy Objectors' were Michael Meadowcroft and David Alton, who both left the party over their strong objections to a particular policy.

Inward Defectors are studied in Chapter 6. The 'SDP and its Antecedents' include the first inward defection of a sitting MP for over sixty years – Christopher Mayhew – and the one MP, Robert Maclennan, who defected from Labour via the SDP and who eventually sat as a Liberal Democrat MP. The 'Defectors from the Conservatives' arrived during the Major Government in the 1990s, while Ashdown was leader of the Liberal Democrats. The 'Defectors from Labour' arrived during Kennedy's leadership of the Liberal Democrats during the 2001 parliament, angered by the policies and attitudes of Blair's Labour Government. Eighteen 'Returning Defectors' came back between 1922 and 2007 after an earlier defection from the Liberal/Liberal Democrat Party, although some defected away from the party again.

Figure 2.3 lists the defectors by their grouping and shows where they appear in the study.

Notes

1 Includes MPs who were elected as Liberals, Lib-Lab MPs, Coalition Liberals and National Liberals in 1922 and those whose elections were later declared void.
2 Of the 116 defections, 59 (51%) occurred in election years. Elections occurred in 24 of the 100 years in the study (24%).
3 Six in total, of whom one returned. Another was a defector into the party who left again. Two of the others did not join another major party.
4 Excludes Constitutionalists who re-took the Liberal whip after 1924 election, but includes Thomas Robinson, a Constitutionalist who took Liberal whip but who defected again in 1929. Excludes Leslie Hore-Belisha, who defected to the Conservatives, having previously joined the Liberal Nationals in 1931. Paul Marsden was the only defector from the party under Kennedy's leadership. Marsden had defected into the party in 2001, also under Kennedy's leadership.
5 Wales and Scotland are over-represented in the survey of Liberal defections, compared to the proportion of constituencies in each country (Scotland had 11% of the constituencies, Wales 6% and England 83%), but this is due to the higher density of Liberal-held seats in Wales and Scotland than in England.
6 The chi-squared test is appropriate for large enough samples in discrete groups. The results are claimed to be statistically significant above the 0.05 level – i.e., where there is a 95% or greater probability that the differences between defectors and loyalists are not simply the result of chance.
7 The numbers in some of the categories are too small to enable the chi-squared analysis of statistical significance to be applied to religious affiliation.
8 The number of women involved was too small to apply the chi-squared test.
9 Applying the chi-squared test.
10 Air force and navy ranks have been grouped with the equivalent army rank. Virtually all the MPs were commissioned officers. One former lieutenant, Austin Hopkinson, rejoined the army as a private; he is included as a lieutenant.

11 Applying a chi-squared test.
12 Interview, Lord Ashdown, 10 September 2009.
13 Figures from Central Registries, London and Edinburgh. Wealth has been calculated as the median of the wealth at death of all the eighty-nine defectors where wealth is known (the earliest date of death being 1928) and a sample of non-defecting MPs drawn to match the population of defectors as far as possible in terms of year of death and age at death. Comparisons between the defectors and the non-defectors should be meaningful, as the distorting effects of tax avoidance and trusts should have applied equally to the defectors and the non-defectors.
14 Applying the chi-squared test.
15 Achievement of ministerial office is likely to have increased the opportunity for a peerage, as a peerage was normally bestowed on all former cabinet ministers.
16 Applying the chi-squared test.

3

Liberal defectors to Labour

Kenworthy having thus forced his fat body through the hedge you may be sure that a large number of sheep will go dribbling through the gap.[1]

This chapter considers all the defectors who left the Liberal/Liberal Democrat Party to join the Labour Party during the hundred years covered by this study. The defectors are studied by grouping, according to their reasons for defection, as described at the end of Chapter 2. Figure 2.3 gives an overview of the membership of each grouping.

For nearly a quarter of a century after recovering from the Liberal Unionist split of 1886, the Liberal Party remained relatively cohesive, despite the fact that it was in opposition for all except three of the first twenty of these years. In fact, during this period it was the beneficiary of a net inward migration of defectors – the most prominent among them being Churchill, Seely and the Guest brothers in 1904. In December 1910 the Liberal Government was re-elected, albeit still without an overall majority, but its share of the vote increased from 43.2% in January to 43.8% in the December election. The Liberal Party appears therefore to have been in a reasonably healthy state and it had no reason to expect defections to the Labour Party, as the two parties were allied under the Gladstone-MacDonald Pact of 1903. However, the Liberal and Labour Parties were not everywhere working in harmony in the pre-war years. At the December 1910 election, eleven of the fifty-nine Labour candidates were opposed by Liberals.[2] In 1912, after an altercation over the Hanley by-election, Ramsay MacDonald wrote: 'Hanley is a Labour seat and the Liberals are the aggressors.' Snowden thought 'it would be war to the knife'.[3] The Hanley by-election and that at Crewe in the same month (where Labour stood in a former Liberal seat in retaliation), were fought with 'extraordinary virulence'. *The Times* believed it was the 'beginning of the end of the coalition'. Labour was defeated at both these by-elections and was also humiliated by the volte-face of the Chesterfield MP, Barnett Kenyon, who took the Labour whip after his by-election victory in 1913, only to reject it just nine days later.

Any decision about the future of the Gladstone-MacDonald Pact was overtaken by events on a much larger scale. The outbreak of war on 3 August 1914 caused instinctive unity among the Conservatives, a split from top to bottom in the Labour Party and a divergence of views among Liberals – soon to be demonstrated by the gulf between the anti-war Union of Democratic Control (UDC) and the fervently pro-war Liberal War Committee (LWC). However, war also heralded an electoral truce and a delay in the next general election, removing the normal contests for support among the parties. When the Liberal Foreign Secretary Sir Edward Grey made his speech to the House of Commons, justifying Britain's involvement in the European conflict, the overwhelming majority of MPs accepted his arguments. However, a significant minority dissented and spoke out in the House, rejecting Grey's analysis of the situation and the inevitability of war. They included the Liberals Arthur Ponsonby, Robert Outhwaite, Richard Denman and Joseph King. Burns, Morley and Trevelyan resigned their ministerial posts. These dissenting Liberals were opposed to the diplomatic policy of their own party and remained so. Many of the same MPs later became implacable opponents of conscription, but their objection to government policy was well established and public, long before the debate on conscription. During the adjournment after Grey's speech a group of twenty radical Liberal MPs signed a resolution stating that 'no sufficient reason exists ... for Great Britain intervening in the war and [we] most strongly urge [the] Government to continue negotiations with Germany'.[4]

On 5 August 1914 the Labour Party voted in favour of War Credits and MacDonald resigned the leadership, lamenting that 'it was no use remaining as the Party was divided and nothing but futility could result ... the Chairmanship was impossible ... The Party was no party in reality. It was sad, but [I was] glad to get out of harness'. MacDonald's political ambitions were temporarily almost extinguished by his frustration at his party's lack of cohesion, also by his continuing grief over his wife's death and by the absence of financial pressures.[5] With knowledge of MacDonald's earlier ambition and his later premierships, it is tempting to picture MacDonald during the war as a leader-in-waiting, suffering a period in the wilderness. He did not see himself like this at the time and was not seen by dissenting Liberals as a likely future leader for them, or for the country. Those who adhered to MacDonald up to 1918, and even beyond, could not have been doing so for career reasons, as during the war MacDonald was 'as remote from power as it is possible for a politician of his stature to be'. His support came from 'rebels and outcasts'. He had no conceivable hope of putting his policies into effect.[6] Beatrice Webb even commented that MacDonald 'would welcome a really conclusive reason for joining the Liberal Party'.[7] MacDonald's motivation appears to have been primarily the preservation of the integrity of his political views, in contrast to that of Henderson who generally put the interests of the Labour Party above his own personal interests and was prepared to adjust his policies according to his perception of the longer-term benefits to his party. Hence Henderson was willing to resign and then withdraw his resignation from the cabinet, in accordance to the wishes of his party. MacDonald, in a masochistic and melancholic frame of mind, determined to promote his policies, irrespective of the impact on himself or on his former colleagues. He kept his silence in the Commons for a year and a half, until January 1916, when he confided to his diary: 'I am back in the Parliamentary harness. God alone knows how unwilling I have been to put it on. Now I must keep it on.'

MacDonald was brought into close contact with dissenting Liberals through the Union of Democratic Control. Charles Trevelyan was the prime mover behind the UDC, although MacDonald saw himself as the centre, commenting: 'Trevelyan, Morrell ... Ponsonby, Angel + myself ... decided to form a committee to voice our views. The few who stuck to me cheered me much; their devotion humiliated me'. The UDC members believed that secret diplomacy had led to war, but that foreign policy should be as amenable to parliamentary debate as was any other aspect of politics. The UDC coexisted with, and in some cases overlapped and cooperated with, the No-Conscription Fellowship, founded in November 1914 by Fenner Brockway of the Independent Labour Party (ILP). Two other groups, the Bryce Group and the League of Nations Society, both focused on post-war international cooperation. Later in the War, another predominantly social Liberal-Labour organisation was formed – the 1917 Club – of which MacDonald, Trevelyan, Morel, John and Ponsonby became members. In the very early days of the UDC, its founders believed that they were representative of a large body of Liberal opinion and that they were seeking Labour support merely to strengthen their argument. By collaborating with MacDonald, the dissenting Liberals were certainly not motivated by any future career prospects within the Labour Party. Until mid-September 1914, the founders of the UDC had reason to believe that Lloyd George might have joined them and carried with him a substantial number of left-wing Liberals. Lloyd George claimed that he and Beauchamp had resigned from the cabinet on 1 August over Grey's pledges to France, but that Asquith had persuaded them to remain. Lloyd George had described his position as that of 'an unattached member of the Cabinet' who sat 'very lightly'.[8] In the event, the Conservative Party, the majority of Liberals and most of the Labour movement, apart from the ILP, backed the war effort and supported the voluntary recruiting drive. The dissenters who continued to oppose the war, and who did not support the voluntary recruitment drive, were a small proportion of the House of Commons. They became labelled as 'pacifists', even though they represented a wide range of views, all opposed to the war, but from many different standpoints. Membership of the UDC did not necessarily imply pacifism. Quakers such as Arnold Rowntree and Edmund Harvey objected to war on religious grounds, and were genuinely pacifist. Many others, including MacDonald and Denman, were opposed on political, economic or diplomatic grounds, but were not pacifists. However, their isolation from mainstream political opinion and, increasingly, their shared vilification in the press and in the street, brought them together for mutual support. The existence of the ILP attracted potential anti-war recruits to the Labour Party, while at the same time acting as a divisive influence: it was more attractive to the middle class than to the workers to whom it was directed. In fact about 10,000 working-class members (about one-third of its membership) left the ILP in the first months of the war.[9]

Trevelyan was not a pacifist and had supported the expansion of naval capacity. However, like many Liberals, he despised Grey's support of the Russian Government and detested autocratic rule. Until the outbreak of war, Trevelyan felt that he had been 'accepted by and accepted the Liberal tradition. I was definitely a Radical, but never outside the limit of party . . . Then I was thrown on my own resources ... lonely as ever could be in opposition to the . . . war'.[10] Arthur Ponsonby had been a founder of the Liberal Foreign Affairs Group and its last chairman, when the war put a stop to its activities. In 1912 Ponsonby had been offered the post of Junior Lord of the Treasury, but had refused in order to remain free to speak out on foreign policy. He had tried to mobilise opposition to British involvement in war and had organised five meetings of the Liberal Foreign Affairs Group between 29 July and 3 August 1914.

A majority of Liberal MPs supported all the moves towards military recruitment – the key legislation being the Registration Bill of July 1915, the Bachelors' Bill of January 1916 and full conscription in May 1916. Within this supportive majority, there was a group wholeheartedly advocating conscription, including Freddie Guest, Henry Cowan and Alfred Mond, all of whom later defected to the Conservatives. Other prominent pro-conscriptionists included Cathcart Wason, Ivor Herbert, Frederick Cawley and Edwin Cornwall, who all remained within the

Liberal Party. But also included among the pro-conscriptionists were Josiah Wedgwood, Chiozza Money and MacCallum Scott, who all eventually defected to Labour. It was hard to imagine a group of Liberals more diverse in their wider political opinions than those who came to embrace conscription. The Liberal conscriptionists included a number of very wealthy industrialists, but their ranks also contained a significant number of MPs who had been enthusiastic social reformers before the war.

The existence of a group of Liberal MPs strongly supporting conscription added to the tensions within the party and further alienated some of the most ardent anti-conscriptionists. Freddie Guest, founder of the Liberal War Committee in 1916, was among the most outspoken of the pro-conscriptionists. The *Nation* reported that Guest's 'extreme' stance on the question of compulsion had 'the advantage of dividing the conscriptionists, the more moderate openly dissociating themselves' from him.[11] This was an early example of Guest's ability to cause controversy and to alienate like-minded colleagues. At the outbreak of war, Guest had enthusiastically re-joined the army, setting an example which he encouraged others to follow. Many other Liberal MPs did join the forces and six were killed in action.[12]

While the UDC members always opposed conscription, they were not alone in the Commons in the first month of the war. At this stage, the Liberal Cabinet on balance was opposed to conscription, as was the Conservative Leader, Bonar Law. However, by November 1914 Bonar Law began to accept that conscription would become necessary if sufficient volunteers were not forthcoming. Lloyd George was also coming to the conclusion that compulsion could become necessary, but the lack of munitions delayed his demand for its introduction, as the shortage of shells was more acute than the lack of troops. Twenty-five Liberal MPs voted against the Registration Bill, six weeks after the formation of the Asquith Coalition. When compulsion became inevitable after the failure of the Derby Scheme, Asquith introduced the Bachelors' Bill on 5 January 1916. It was presented not as conscription, but as redemption of his pledge to married men, that single men would be called up ahead of them. Over thirty Liberals this time voted against the Bill. Simon resigned as Home Secretary. McKenna was opposed on practical and financial grounds, believing that the economy could not support a larger army, but he was persuaded to stay. The mounting military losses meant that on 3 May 1916 Asquith had to introduce the Military Services Bill. It provided for all men, regardless of marital status, between 18 and 41 to be conscripted. Twenty-eight Liberals voted against this measure.

The formation of the Lloyd George Coalition in December 1916 heralded a period of turmoil for party politics. Most European socialist parties split over the war, and in Britain, adherence to the existing party system was challenged on several fronts. MacDonald's dogged adherence to his anti-war stance meant that the Labour Party was split. Henderson told MacDonald that some Labour Ministers 'do not mean to return to the Party', believing that Lloyd George wanted to form a new party and that 'some Labour men will join him'.[13] Some within the UDC entertained hopes of setting up a new radical party to fight the next general election. However, by the end of March 1918, Ponsonby thought that the opinion that the Union attracted was 'too diffused . . . to justify the formation of a new party'.[14] MacDonald commented forlornly on the 'further combined meeting of Liberals + ourselves. [I] have not much hope of them doing anything effective'. MacDonald also doubted the wisdom of Liberals who joined the ILP: 'It would have been better had they managed to create a marginal group in touch with Radicalism on the Right + ourselves on the Left.'[15] However, Henderson's final resignation from the government in August 1917 gave the Labour Party the freedom to develop an independent war policy. The Labour Party's Memorandum on War Aims, adopted in December 1917, was in fact closely aligned to the UDC's policies. Labour was then in a position to coalesce around an agreed set of policies, while the Liberal Party was pulling itself further apart.

There is a continuing controversy surrounding the importance of the war in the decline of the Liberal Party. Dangerfield argued that the Liberal Party was in serious decline before the war and Pelling that the decline of Liberalism was not the result of wartime quarrels but 'the result of long-term social and economic changes'.[16] Evidence of the cohesion of the Liberal Party, even when in opposition for lengthy periods after 1886, the net inward migration of defectors and the election results of 1906 and 1910 suggest that the party *was* still in a healthy state up to the outbreak of war. There is no doubt that during the war, the Liberal Party was divided over policy; but Labour was more so. Bentley claimed that 'Liberalism tore its heart out between 1914 and 1918 in a private agony about true and false Liberals'.[17] Wilson imagined that the Liberal Party was struck down by an omnibus, representing the war. Dutton, surveying a wide range of historians' research, concluded that 'the more evidence that has been accumulated to show that the Liberal Party was in no imminent danger of collapse in 1914, the more significance must be attached to the war as the key explanation of what subsequently occurred'.[18] A minority of historians put a later date on the decline, including Asquith, who, from a clearly partial point of view, claimed that the 'disintegration of the Liberal Party began with the Coupon election'. Hart also attached importance to the circumstances of the 1918 election in explaining the decline and asserted that 'Constituencies not only disagreed with dissentient [Liberal] MPs, they would not tolerate their continuance in parliament'.[19]

By studying the Liberal MPs and former MPs who defected, it is possible to chart their attitudes and behaviour and to identify when they believed that a point of no return for the Liberal Party had been reached. These people embodied the fragmentation: they were the crumbling edge of the glacier. Table 3.1 shows the individual political fate of all the Liberal War Policy Objectors, defined as those who voted against at least two of the three conscription measures, or abstained on two and voted against on the third – a total of thirty-five MPs.

Table 3.2 then analyses whether war policy objection spelt the end of a career in the Liberal Party for these thirty-five MPs. For twenty-eight of the thirty-five Liberal MPs (80%) who were War Policy Objectors, their wartime stance was not a barrier to their future careers in the Liberal Party. In many cases their careers suffered setbacks, but this was the case with virtually all Liberals, due to the overall state of the party. This evidence directly contradicts Hart's assertion that constituencies would not tolerate the continuation of objectors in parliament.

In some cases the War Policy Objectors defected from the Liberal Party later, but for reasons other than the war. This suggests that Wilson's omnibus at worst struck the Liberal Party a glancing blow, temporarily leaving it reeling.

As can be seen from Table 3.2, in the case of just five MPs (Trevelyan, Ponsonby, Outhwaite, Lambert and King), their wartime objections resulted in their leaving the Liberal Party. Two other Liberal MPs (Lees-Smith and Edward John) also defected from the Liberals, but only partly due to their wartime objections. The cases of these seven Liberal MPs illuminate the local events which led to their defections.

War Policy Objectors

Trevelyan and Ponsonby, together with Robert Outhwaite, Richard Lambert and Joseph King, became isolated from the Liberal Party, not through their wish to leave, but because of a developing rift with their local Liberal constituency associations. They were forced out by pressure from within their constituencies, not by the party centrally, and in some cases they made strenuous attempts to remain within the party. By the time of the 1918 election all were estranged from the Liberal Party, but none stood as a Labour candidate at the 1918 election.

Table 3.1 *Fate of the 35 Liberal MP War Policy Objectors*

MP	Registration Bill vote 5/7/15	Bachelors' Bill vote 6/1/16	Conscription Bill vote 4/5/16	Fate at 1918 election	Date of defection (if any)
Arnold	no vote	opposed	opposed	won – Lib	1922
Glanville	supported	opposed	opposed	won – Lib	none
Hogge	opposed	opposed	opposed	won – Lib	none
Wilson, JW	no vote	no vote	opposed	won – Lib	none
Alden	no vote	opposed	no vote	lost – Lib	1919
Barlow	no vote	opposed	opposed	lost – Lib	none
Chancellor	opposed	opposed	opposed	lost – Lib	none
Holt	opposed	opposed	opposed	lost – Lib	none
Jones L	no vote	opposed	opposed	lost – Lib	none
Lees-Smith*	no vote	opposed	opposed	lost – Lib+	1919
Lough	opposed	opposed	no vote	lost – Lib	none
Molteno	no vote	opposed	opposed	lost – Lib	none
Pringle	opposed	opposed	opposed	lost – Lib	none
Rowntree	no vote	opposed	opposed	lost – Lib	none
Simon J	no vote	opposed	opposed	lost – Lib	1931
Outhwaite	opposed	opposed	opposed	lost – Ind Lib	1918
Mason D	supported	opposed	opposed	lost – Ind Lib	1938
Whitehouse	opposed	opposed	no vote	lost – Ind Lib	1914
Ponsonby	opposed	opposed	opposed	lost – Ind Dem	1918
Trevelyan	opposed	opposed	opposed	lost – Ind Lab	1918
John ET	opposed	opposed	no vote	lost – Lab	1918
Burns	no vote	opposed	opposed	not candidate	none
Clough	opposed	opposed	no vote	not candidate	none
Denman	opposed	opposed	no vote	not candidate	1924
Harvey A	no vote	opposed	opposed	not candidate	none
Harvey T	no vote	opposed	opposed	not candidate	1937
King	opposed	opposed	opposed	not candidate	1919
Lamb	no vote	no vote	opposed	not candidate	1924
Lambert	opposed	opposed	opposed	not candidate	1918
Runciman	opposed	opposed	opposed	not candidate	none
Sherwell	opposed	opposed	no vote	not candidate	none
Williams WL	no vote	opposed	opposed	not candidate	none
Morrell	supported	opposed	opposed	not candidate	none
Baker	opposed	opposed	opposed	dead	none
Byles	supported	opposed	opposed	dead	none

* Bold type indicates that the MP was a member of the UDC.
+ Counted here as a Liberal. Although he was described in some sources as an 'Independent Radical', Lees-Smith had the backing of his local Liberal association.

Table 3.2 *Future political careers of the 35 War Policy Objectors*

War Policy Objectors with continued Liberal careers:

4	Won seats as Liberals in 1918 (Hogge, Glanville, Wilson, Arnold*)
3	Lost as Liberals in 1918, but returned later as Liberal MPs (Pringle, Jones, Simon*)
4	Lost as Liberals in 1918, but fought later elections unsuccessfully as Liberals (Holt, Molteno)
4	Lost as Liberals, retired, but remained in the Liberal Party (Chancellor, Rowntree, Barlow, Lough)
1	Lost as Liberal in 1918, later defected to Labour, but returned to Liberals (Alden*)
1	Lost as Independent Liberal in 1918, but returned later as a Liberal MP (Mason*)
1	Lost as Independent Liberal in 1918, returned to the Liberals, stood but lost (Whitehouse)
1	Did not stand in 1918, but returned later as a Liberal MP (Harvey, TE*)
1	Rejected by constituency in 1918, did not stand, but later a Liberal candidate (Denman*)
2	Died, having remained in Liberal Party to their deaths (Baker, Byles)
7	Retired from Parliament in 1918, but remained in Liberal Party (Runciman, Sherwell, Harvey, A., Burns, Clough, Williams, Morrell)
1	Did not stand in 1918, but remained in Liberal Party until 1924 (Lamb*)
__	
28	**total**

Those who defected partly because of War Policy Objections:

1	stood as Labour in 1918 mainly due to his support for Welsh Nationalism, lost (John)
1	stood unsuccessfully as a Liberal in 1918, joined Labour in June 1919 (Lees-Smith)
__	
2	**total**

Those who defected entirely due to War Policy Objections:

1	defected to Labour before the 1918 election, but did not stand, retired (Lambert)
1	left Liberals, did not stand in 1918, defected to Labour after the 1918 election (King)
3	rejected by their constituency Liberal associations and stood as Independents (Ponsonby, Trevelyan, Outhwaite)
__	
5	**total**

* Defected later for reasons unconnected with the war.

Before he resigned from the Government at the outbreak of war, **Charles Trevelyan** had enjoyed a 'particularly close' relationship with his constituency executive in Elland, but his resignation from the Board of Education, where he had been Parliamentary Secretary, received a 'very cool reception' locally. However, by the end of 1914 his Liberal association had taken no action, worried that if Trevelyan stood down, it would place the seat 'in the hands of the hereditary enemy'.[20] Trevelyan wrote optimistically in November 1914 to his like-minded colleague, Ponsonby, saying that his local party association had decided that he 'conceivably might still be the best Liberal candidate if circumstances changed ... This surely ought to be a lead to your people'.[21] Another letter, undated, but probably between November 1914 and April 1915, illustrated the hopes which Trevelyan still harboured of returning to favour: 'the Executive ... don't expect me to resign and don't really want it.' However, the relationship between Trevelyan and his association deteriorated and by April 1915 a resolution was passed unanimously declaring 'the futility of again adopting as their candidate their present member'. Trevelyan 'respectfully but decidedly' declined his executive's request for him to resign.[22] In November 1917, Trevelyan wrote to his brother, Robert: 'I am interested to hear you have joined the ILP. If I were in your [position] I probably should do the same'.[23] Trevelyan, clearly torn, hesitated publicly over his political future, then announced his intention of contesting Elland against all comers. He was urged formally to join the Labour Party, but, although he was 'prepared to go a long way, he could not bring himself to sign the constitution'. In November 1918 he eventually announced that he had joined Labour, but he had left his decision so late that there was an official Labour candidate, Hardaker, already adopted for the constituency. Trevelyan tried to have himself adopted to replace Hardaker, and declined a proposal that both names should be submitted to the divisional council. The Labour Party refused to withdraw Hardaker, who had already opened his campaign. The Labour Party argued that 'the graceful thing' would have been for Trevelyan to retire.[24] In the event, Elland was won by a Coalition Conservative. The Liberals had selected H. Dawson, who came a close second. Hardaker was third and Trevelyan a very poor last. Trevelyan was an intense and brooding character, who felt that the war had 'taken away our reputations as it has done our careers'.[25] Unlike many other War Policy Objectors, Trevelyan was still dwelling on the war, when, as the prospective Labour candidate for Newcastle Central, his work *From Liberalism to Labour* was published in 1921. He wrote: 'The Liberal leaders ... pretended that they left the vital decision of war with the House of Commons. They, in fact, arranged to come into the war before they told the House of Commons the real nature of their policy.'[26] Trevelyan was a man of principle, but the obverse was his inflexibility and brittle personal relationships – traits he shared with MacDonald. Trevelyan was elected as the Labour MP for Newcastle Central in 1922 and MacDonald appointed him President of the Board of Education in the first and second Labour Governments. In January 1924 Trevelyan wrote to MacDonald: 'you can rely on [Ponsonby] and myself in a different way from so many others. Nothing could shake our feeling which grew during the war . . . And you know that we have no personal axes to grind'. But by February 1931 their relationship had broken down and Trevelyan wrote: 'I have realized that I am very much out of sympathy with . . . Government policy . . . I therefore place my resignation in your hands. I have to thank you personally, especially during the dark years of the war when you made it easy for me to come into the Labour Party.' Four days later Trevelyan petulantly tried to hurry MacDonald into a response: 'I think that you are leaving a matter of this kind a very long time . . . I cannot now be responsible for decisions of policy and I do not propose to attend Cabinet meetings.'[27] Trevelyan therefore earned the dubious distinction of becoming the only person to resign from the same department in the governments of two different parties. MacDonald felt that Trevelyan had become 'a poor fussy figure + unpleasantly sophistical'.[28] His draft reply gave vent to his loss of confidence in Trevelyan, and by implication some of the other former Liberals: 'We gave you and others who were not at all acceptable to our friends . . . a generous welcome . . . they will laugh at me . . . all I did . . . was to give you a chance of walking out and giving the Govt. a nasty stab in the back'.[29] At a meeting of the Parliamentary Labour Party to explain his resignation, Trevelyan made a blunt personal attack upon MacDonald, which received little support and much objection. He was heavily defeated at the 1931 election, standing as an Independent Labour candidate. For a few years after leaving the Commons, Trevelyan continued to attend Labour Party conferences. He felt vindicated and 'rather enjoyed the atmosphere', after what he called MacDonald's 'greatest treachery on record in British politics'.[30]

Arthur Ponsonby arguably had more at stake over his political career than did Trevelyan, in that he was much less wealthy. Trevelyan offered (slightly) to subsidise him, offering: 'whenever the election comes you may reckon on my paying . . . £400 over to you as a loan at 5% interest'. Trevelyan also offered Ponsonby moral support: 'I and others now know that you are good to go tiger hunting with . . . you have not taken some excellent excuse to slip off the howdah.'[31] But Ponsonby suffered for his views. He was physically attacked at Kingston in the summer of 1915 and he and Joseph King had their premises raided by the police. Ponsonby's relationship with his constituency Liberal association followed a similar trajectory to that of Trevelyan. In March 1915 Ponsonby's constituency chairman, Robertson, wrote sadly and respectfully to him, saying that he was 'satisfied that you are honestly following what you believe to be the right line ... any breach between us personally, will be very painful to me. I have all along respected you, and admired your courage'.[32] Ponsonby tried to enlist the party whips to intervene on his behalf with his constituency. Gulland's reply was sympathetic, but of little practical value:

> I am very sorry that this difference should have occurred between you and your constituents, and I fear it is more serious than you imagine. We whips have given no encouragement in any way to the protesting constituents of members of the U.D.C., though we have been very strongly urged to take action.[33]

The urging was not from Asquith, but from vocal pro-conscriptionist members of the party. Ponsonby resisted what he saw as attempts by his constituency chairman, Robertson, to 'insert' his own preferred candidate and he refused to resign his seat.[34] The local situation continued to deteriorate and Ponsonby's agent resigned in October 1916. Ponsonby became defiant in the face of an ultimatum issued by his constituency in January 1917. He rejected what he saw as a 'notice to quit' and the assertion that he could not hold the seat for the Liberal party at an election, asking Robertson the very pertinent questions: 'what [is] the Liberal Party ... and who are its leaders? Which is the orthodox wing, the Asquithites or the Georgites? Which do you belong to?'[35] MacDonald went to Dunfermline in March 1918 and tried, unsuccessfully, to persuade the miners not to put up a candidate against Ponsonby. 'Ponsonby for Labour itself is worth twenty of the average candidate.'[36] MacDonald was censured by his party's executive for supporting Ponsonby, when he was not even a Labour candidate. At this point, MacDonald was more committed personally to Ponsonby than he was to the local Labour Party and he wrote to Ponsonby: 'I am ashamed of my friends'.[37] When the election arrived Ponsonby stood in the renamed Dunfermline Burghs seat as an 'Independent Democrat'. He came last, with 3,491 votes, to his Independent Labour opposition's 5,076 and the winning Coaltion Liberal's 6,886. Immediately after the election Ponsonby joined the Labour Party.

Ponsonby was elected as Labour MP for Sheffield Brightside in 1922 and served as parliamentary under-secretary at the Foreign Office in the first Labour Government. However, after Labour's defeat 'his invidious position as an aristocratic socialist who was in the party but not of it' was further emphasised by his failure to be elected to the shadow cabinet.[38] He was created Lord Ponsonby in January 1930 and the following year appointed Chancellor of the Duchy of Lancaster. On the creation of the National Government, Ponsonby did not follow MacDonald, instead becoming Labour leader in the Lords. He wrote sadly to MacDonald: 'I deeply regret breaking so long an association with you'.[39] Ponsonby supported disarmament, in opposition to Labour's official policy, and this led him in September 1935 to resign the leadership. After the start of the Second World War he virtually withdrew from active politics, resigning from the Labour Party on 15 May 1940.

Robert Outhwaite fell out with the Hanley Liberal association over his war policy objections early in the conflict. He had won the seat in the fiercely contested by-election in 1912, when MacDonald had accused the Liberals of being the 'aggressors' in a 'Labour seat'. In December 1914 Outhwaite explained his views to his local constituency association who decided to 'hold themselves free not to nominate ... Outhwaite at the next election or to give him support', but the opinion was general that Outhwaite's attitude was dictated by 'the highest motives' and the opinion of his 'character and principles had been enhanced rather than otherwise'.[40] At the 1918 election, Outhwaite stood as an Independent Liberal. He faced a Liberal, as well as a Labour, and the winning Coaltion NDP, candidate. He joined the Labour Party in 1919, but did not contest any further elections, due to poor health. In 1917 Outhwaite had published *The Land or Revolution*, in it asking: 'Will the constitutional systems of the West be sundered by the forces generated by war? That depends upon the decision ... between revolution by force and an economic reform. [The] alternative to revolution was ... the Single Tax.'[41] Outhwaite was driven to the Labour Party over his alienation from the Liberals due to his war policy objections, rather than by his expectation that Labour would adopt the single tax – which was never the Labour Party's policy.

Richard Lambert, a vicar's son, sat as a Liberal in parliament for eight years, but in December 1918 he joined the ILP. He explained his conversion in the *Labour Reader* in which he declared that as the result of 'four years' experience of broken faith and broken pledges ... the Liberal Party of to-day has neither policy nor leaders nor even principles'.[42] Lambert had spoken out in the Commons against the Registration Bill in 1915, reminding his audience that he had willingly helped at recruitment rallies, but condemning the bill as 'Prussianism', declaring: 'We shall never defeat Prussianism ... by adopting Prussianism ourselves. We shall never be able to Prussianise half as well as the Germans'.[43] He then went on to oppose the Bachelors' Bill and the Conscription Bill. Lambert's constituency of Cricklade was abolished in the 1918 boundary changes, and he never sought re-election under any party label. He abandoned politics after the War and instead became the Librarian at the Athenaeum Club; an occupation which he found more congenial than politics or his earlier career as a barrister.

Joseph King, another former barrister, served as Liberal MP for North Somerset from January 1910. He had been outspoken in the Commons debate on 3 August 1914, riling many of the government's supporters by asking if they were 'afraid' or 'ashamed' to speak out in defence of the government's policy. King remained an opponent of government war policy, also voting against the Bachelors' and Conscription Bills. He did not stand in the 1918 election, but he supported the Labour candidature of Ben Riley in Dewsbury, against Walter Runciman for the Liberals and the winning Coalition Conservative candidate. King claimed that the reason that he left the Liberal Party was that 'it had proved disappointing, without courage, and false to its principles'. He said that he still admired Lloyd George and entertained hopes that he (Lloyd George) would join the Labour Party.[44] King made the move to Labour himself and later fought two unsuccessful election campaigns on the party's behalf in 1920 and 1923.

These five cases of War Policy Objectors, whose Liberal careers were ended – Trevelyan, Ponsonby, Outhwaite, Lambert and King – can be contrasted with others, such as those of Richard Holt, John Howard Whitehouse, David Mason and Philip Morrell, who were among the twenty-eight War Policy Objectors who continued their careers in the Liberal Party. Richard Holt, a War Policy Objector, resigned from his seat in Hexham in July 1918 after falling out with his local association, but he was found another seat by the whips, at Eccles, in time to fight the 1918 election.[45] **John Whitehouse**, another War Policy Objector, was elected Liberal MP for Mid-Lanarkshire in January 1910 and served as PPS to Lloyd George from 1913 to 1915. He resigned his post in September 1915, writing: 'I wish to do all in my power, as a member of Parliament, to resist [conscription] . . . I think it is my duty to place my resignation in your hands. But I cannot do so without saying how deeply I have valued the association of the past two years.'[46] Whitehouse was secretary of the deputation to Asquith on conscription on 17 December 1915. In 1918, his constituency of Mid-Lanarkshire was abolished. He unsuccessfully contested the 1918 election as an Independent Liberal candidate for Hamilton, but he was accepted back into the Liberal fold and contested Hanley in 1922, Hereford in 1923 and 1924, Southampton in 1929, Thornbury in 1931 and Stoke

Newington in 1935 as a Liberal candidate. **David Mason**, elected as Liberal MP for Coventry in December 1910, was at odds with the Coventry Liberal Party from 1913 onward for proposing a reduction in the naval estimates and for opposing other government policies. Mason had resigned the Liberal Whip well before the war was even foreseen, in January 1914. His policy positions were extreme and individualistic. He sat as an Independent Liberal during the war and was defeated under that label in 1918. However, he also later stood again as a Liberal candidate, although he eventually defected to the Liberal Nationals in 1938 (see Chapter 5). Philip Morrell, was also a Liberal MP and War Policy Objector, but who did not leave the Liberal Party. He should not be confused with his near-namesake, Edmund Morel, who was the first of the UDC's founders to leave the Liberal Party.[47] He was a Liberal prospective candidate, but he was never a Liberal MP. He suffered physical attacks and police raids, and was imprisoned for six months for a technical violation of the Defence of the Realm Act. He went on to be elected for Labour at Dundee in 1922, ousting Churchill.

In addition to the five War Policy Objectors whose departure from the Liberals was entirely the consequence of their objections, there were two others for whom it was a contributing factor – Bertie Lees-Smith and Edward John. **Hastings (Bertie) Lees-Smith** was one of two Liberal MPs for Northampton, elected along with Charles McCurdy in January 1910. Lees-Smith was a War Policy Objector and UDC member, described as 'a pacifist' and 'a radical of the most pronounced type'. However, he volunteered for service in the ranks and, in May 1916, addressed parliament in his corporal's uniform. He was described in the press as the only Member of Parliament enlisted in the ranks. In 1918 the Northampton constituency was reduced to a single-member seat, which was fought and won by McCurdy as a Coalition Liberal. Lees-Smith moved to the Don Valley constituency in Yorkshire. The local press and Craig described him as the 'Liberal' candidate, although other sources labelled him as an 'Independent Radical'. He did have the backing of the local Liberal association and did not face any form of Liberal opposition, although he refused party funds for his election campaign. During the election campaign a miner asked him why he was not a Labour candidate. He replied that he had 'seen nothing better than Radicalism yet, and was rather disappointed with Labour leadership'.[48] He was not elected, coming a distant second. In June 1919, seven months after the end of hostilities, and without making reference to the war, Lees-Smith announced: 'I am about to join the Labour Party . . . My principles have in no way changed but . . . I cannot look to any section of the Liberal Party to carry them into effect . . . practically all the men who share these views . . . are in the ranks of labour.'[49] Lees-Smith's war policy objections had brought him into contact with other eventual Liberal defectors and with MacDonald, but the timing and the reasons given for his defection suggest that the war was certainly not the overriding reason.

Edward John was the only one of the Liberals' thirty-five War Policy Objectors to stand as a Labour candidate in the 1918 election. However, he was not the leader, or even an outrider, of any group, nor was he typical of the War Policy Objectors, and his defection was not primarily motivated by the war. His main concern was Welsh nationalism, and his standing for Labour in 1918 was not actually his preferred platform. John's attitude to conscription was coloured by his experience as an industrialist. He explained that: 'apart from the objections to conscription in principle . . . the transfer of one million men from industrial pursuits to military service would be most disastrous'.[50] In January 1916, John confided to Simon, whose attitude to conscription he shared: 'Nothing is more disappointing than the attitude of the Labour Party'. In June 1918, John was aware of plots to undermine his position in his constituency, but he was still undecided over which party to adhere to and over which constituency to fight. The indecision continued for six months. He felt that accepting the nomination for East Denbighshire as a Liberal would place him in a 'false position' and that he was 'much more likely to secure a substantial measure of both Liberal and Labour support by standing as a Welsh Nationalist. I may, of course, be driven to definitely declare myself as Labour, but I scarcely think so'.[51] By November 1918, under pressure to make a decision, John wrote to the neighbouring constituency of West Denbighshire: 'We are rapidly reaching the point where I shall have to declare whether I desire to stand as Labour, Liberal or as a Welsh Nationalist. My own preference is to stand in the latter capacity . . . though . . . if they care formally to adopt me, I would be prepared to associate myself definitely with the Labour Party.'[52] It the event, it was the Western Division (renamed Denbigh) where John fought and lost as a Labour candidate in 1918: his margin of defeat was massive. He secured 2,958 votes to 14,773 for his only opponent, a Coalition Liberal. After 1918 John's hopes that the Labour Party would strongly advocate Welsh nationalism were to be disappointed, as were his further attempts to re-enter parliament. He stood unsuccessfully for Labour in three more elections in other Welsh constituencies, but never gave the party his full confidence.

Only two former Liberal MPs, of whom Edward John was one, stood as Labour candidates in the 1918 election. The other was the highly individualistic case of **Leo Chiozza Money**, who was not a War Policy

Objector, and there is little to link the two cases. Money's views and behaviour marked him out as an even more untypical Liberal than Edward John. Money had been parliamentary private secretary to Lloyd George, for whom he always retained respect, at the Ministry of Munitions in 1915.[53] He then served as parliamentary secretary to the Ministry of Shipping, becoming so convinced of the merits of public ownership that he eventually wrote a book, *The Triumph of Nationalization*, claiming that 'National organization triumphed in a land where it had been denied'.[54] At the end of the war Money resigned from the ministry, having tried unsuccessfully to persuade Lloyd George not to return shipping to private ownership.[55] Money decided not to re-contest East Northamptonshire in 1918, but Lloyd George and the coalition whips offered to find him another seat, even accommodating his wish not have to compete against Labour. On 6 November 1918 Money was still undecided about contesting the election as a Liberal. Under pressure to make a decision, in mid-November Money joined the Labour Party and received forty-two invitations to contest seats for the party. He chose to stand as the Labour candidate at South Tottenham and came just 853 votes behind the winning Coalition Unionist. However, he never re-entered parliament, although he stood in one more contest at Stockport (a two-member constituency) for Labour in 1920, coming third. Never on good terms with MacDonald, whom he considered 'spiteful', Money informed the press in 1924 that he had 'refused to become a Labour Candidate', and would not be supporting Labour at the election as 'its defeat is as certain as it is deserved'. Money reflected ruefully that the Labour Party had 'failed lamentably ... and I had to admit to myself that my resignation was a futility'.[56] Money's personal life and increasingly extreme political views undermined his political credibility. He was twice charged with indecent behaviour. He was acquitted the first time. On the second occasion, in 1933, he was found guilty and fined for indecency with a woman in a railway carriage. His unusual, and unsuccessful, defence was that he was wearing a distinctive hat that day and that, had he done anything wrong, a signalman in one of the signal boxes would have noticed.[57] In later years he became an increasingly convinced supporter of the Fascist dictatorships.[58]

The detailed examination of the War Policy Objectors' careers does bring into question the extent to which the Great War was the political catastrophe for the Liberal Party, which it has often been portrayed to be. Five War Policy Objectors defected from the Liberals because of their objections, but they were vastly out-numbered by the twenty-eight who remained, at least for the time being, in the Liberal Party. The significance of the 1918 election in the Liberal decline is also questioned, as only two former Liberal MPs stood in that election as Labour candidates – Money and John. With a gap of ten years since the previous election, an attrition of two MPs standing for other parties at the 1918 election was actually low compared to the figures for the century as a whole. However, by the time of the following general election in 1922, it was clear for all to see that the Liberal Party was in dire straits. A closer examination of the defections between the elections of 1918 and 1922, especially the earlier part of that period, reveals much about the turmoil which afflicted the party during those crucial years.

Idealists

Between 1919 and 1920 a small group of idealistic former Liberals left for the Labour Party. They were not War Policy Objectors. Three of them were linked to each other and to Outhwaite by their former association in the pre-war campaign for a single land tax, but this was not their motivation for defecting. Their reasons were all highly individualistic.

Josiah Wedgwood was a rebel with many – sometimes incompatible – causes. He was a pacifist who was prepared to risk his own life on the battlefield. He condemned the UDC for their defeatism early in the war, only to encourage their persistence six months later.[59] He divorced his first wife and took custody of their children, only to decide that his temperament was 'better fitted to be a dashing bandit than the responsible parent of seven'. His second wife was a pacifist from a background 'Puritan to the point of austerity'. Wedgwood was motivated by freedom, but in escaping from the constraints of the Liberal Party he volunteered for the straitjacket of Labour discipline, only to find it suffocating. He had started his career as a naval architect, gave that up to become a resident magistrate in South Africa, then came back to England with no career plans. Politics suited his temperament, but political parties did not. He found friends and admirers in all parties, but a philosophical home in none. His mother, uncle, cousin and eldest brother were stalwart Conservatives, but Wedgwood was a keen proponent of a single land tax. Wedgwood became Liberal MP for Newcastle-under-Lyme in 1906 and held the seat, despite several changes of party allegiance, until 1942. On the outbreak of the Great War Wedgwood's opinions swayed: 'Though a pacifist . . . I would rather fight than leave the Kaiser triumphant . . . I do not think it right to *compel* people to go and face it by Act of Parliament unless I go myself.' He became a lieutenant-commander in the RNVR, and was wounded in the groin at Gallipoli. In 1918 Wedgwood was issued with the coalition coupon but repudiated it. Although adopted by the local Liberal association, he considered himself to be an independent Liberal. He was unopposed and claimed: 'I come before you, the same impenitent Independent Radical that you first elected in 1906; older and wiser perhaps . . . but with the same ideals.' In April 1919 he broke finally with the Liberals and joined the ILP. So determined an individualist found Labour Party discipline more irksome than the 'easier control' of the Liberals. He was soon protesting against the party's 'regimentation'. His discomfort was exacerbated by his poor relationship with MacDonald; and the dislike was mutual. Wedgwood was appointed Chancellor of the Duchy of Lancaster in 1924 – a more junior post than he had hoped for and 'a deflationary conclusion to the happiest years of his Parliamentary life'. When MacDonald did not offer him a seat in cabinet in the second Labour Government, Wedgwood commented: 'I cannot feel myself aggrieved as I have long been aware of the sentiments regarding myself held by the good MacDonald.' In 1931 Wedgwood refused to sign the pledge of obedience which the Labour Party imposed on its members, complaining to Lansbury: 'These standing orders turn a Member of Parliament into a voting dummy.'[60] He became an Independent Labour MP, until he returned to the party in 1935. In the lead-up to the Second World War he strongly condemned appeasement. He retained his seat in the Commons until he was created Lord Wedgwood in January 1942.

James Dundas White had been associated with Josiah Wedgwood, Robert Outhwaite and Edward Hemmerde in the pre-war campaign for a single land tax. He was not a War Policy Objector. He joined the ILP in August 1919, but was not at home in the party. In common with most of the other former Liberal defectors to Labour, he made no protestation of conversion to socialism. So when he joined the party, he was greeted with a less-than-effusive welcome by the journal *Forward*, which thundered: 'great disillusionment will be his if he imagines that the I.L.P. is only a haven of rest for Liberals who seek preservation of Peace and Free Trade and who favour taxation of land values'.[61] White contested two unsuccessful election campaigns for Labour, in 1922 and 1923, but left the party in 1924.

By the time **Edward Hemmerde** joined the Labour Party in 1920, four of the six most energetic land tax supporters were by then within Labour's ranks. The differences between their own policies and outlook and those of their new party were, however, 'abundantly clear' to them. Their change of party was motivated by despair of the Liberals, rather than any positive agreement with the Labour Party. In his personal affairs Hemmerde was always his own worst enemy: 'impulsive, tactless, unobjective'.[62] His personal life was a catalogue of embarrassing incidents. Hemmerde borrowed £1,000 in 1910 when he was in financial difficulties, and was later taken to court for repayment. The case went all the way to the Lords, where Hemmerde lost.[63] He was divorced from his wife on the grounds of her adultery and in this case the grounds were genuine, rather than the typical contrivance of the times, such as the 'legal fiction' employed by Josiah Wedgwood. Later, as Recorder of Liverpool, Hemmerde complained that he had been 'subjected for 13 years to a rigid ceremonial and professional boycott . . . as part of a deliberate attempt to belittle his office and humiliate him'.[64] Hemmerde did not contest the 1918 election. Having failed to get the ideals nearest to his heart realised by the Liberal Party, he joined the Labour Party, 'perfectly satisfied that none of the things he desired would be done by any other party'.[65] Hemmerde won Crewe for Labour in 1922 by 555 votes, but did not see his ideals realised. He held the seat until he was defeated in 1924, when he retired from politics.

Of all the convoluted career paths of former Liberals, that of **Cecil L'Estrange Malone** is probably the most unorthodox. Malone went from being elected in 1918 as a Coalition Liberal and member of the anti-communist Reconstruction Society to being the UK's first Communist MP. Although he later denied ever having been a Liberal, his 1918 election address described him as the 'Liberal, Radical and Coalition Candidate'. By July 1919 he declared that 'my inherent personal bias leads me more and more to the Left'.[66] His changing political allegiance gave rise to what must have been one of the strangest exchanges of correspondence between a constituency chairman and an MP. Malone was asked to explain a statement he had made at the Labour Party Conference that he 'never officially belonged to the Free Liberals, and was sent to the Labour Conference as a representative of the British Socialist Party'. His chairman went on that he 'found it very difficult to form any opinion as to what your political views really were and as to what party you, in fact, belong'.[67] Malone officially joined the Communist Party in July 1920, when the BSP merged with other groups to form the Communist Party of Great Britain. After a speech at the Albert Hall on 7 November 1920, Malone was charged with sedition. He had argued that during a revolution, it would be legitimate to execute leading members of the bourgeoisie. He was convicted and sentenced to six months' imprisonment and he had his OBE withdrawn. On his release, Malone returned to the House of Commons, but seemed to have 'lost his mental equilibrium'.[68] However, during his time in prison, he had changed his views on revolutionary politics and decided to join the ILP. The Communist Party concluded that his temporary allegiance had been genuine, despite allegations that he had been an infiltrator. However, they believed that 'the suddenness of his conversion' meant that his 'intellectual understanding of Communism was certainly questionable'.[69] Malone did not contest the 1922 election, but was elected as Labour MP for Northampton at a by-election in 1928, holding the seat until his defeat in 1931 standing for Labour, having dissociated himself from MacDonald.

Maurice Alexander was a political chameleon. He was a Canadian-trained Jewish lawyer and army officer. Never married, he lived in Park Lane in central London and on an estate on the Surrey-Hampshire borders, where he eventually gave refuge to a hundred Basque children fleeing the Spanish Civil War. He was elected as a National Liberal for Southwark South East in 1922, having received official Conservative backing after he had 'given specific pledges of support to a Bonar Law Ministry'.[70] In 1923 he was rumoured to be about to join the Conservatives.[71] However, in the event, he fought and lost the 1923 and 1924 elections as a Liberal. By 1931, Alexander's political orientation had completely reversed, and he stood as a full-blooded Labour candidate for Newcastle East. He could not escape his political past and a letter to the local press remarked that seven years earlier Alexander had described Labour policies as 'disastrous'. Alexander's 1931 election address gave a clue to his level of attachment to his adopted Labour Party when he wrote:

> I have accepted the unanimous invitation of the East Newcastle Labour Party to stand as their candidate . . . The Labour Party . . . will demand the ownership of the nation's land by the people . . . I shall demand a reversal of the cut in unemployment insurance . . . The Liberal Party has been shattered into fragments. The handful of Labour supporters who have deserted their principles are the prisoners of Mr. Baldwin and his friends.

To add to the controversy surrounding Alexander's 1931 candidature, he managed to embroil himself in a public row with MacDonald, claiming that he refused the premier's offer of the post of Under Secretary for War. MacDonald repudiated the claim that he had made the offer, but Alexander stood by his version of events.[72] Alexander lost the 1931 contest to his National Liberal opponent. Although never a MacDonald supporter, Alexander changed his attitude to the National Government when Chamberlain was Prime Minister. On 17 February 1938 Alexander was reported in *The Times* to be likely to be chosen as the National Government candidate for West Bermondsey, in opposition to Labour's Dr Salter. Alexander died in 1945 and was never able to put this, his fourth political label, to the test.

Ellis Davies was elected unopposed as Liberal MP for Eifion, at a by-election in June 1906. Davies represented the neighbouring seat to that of Lloyd George and, although the pair were in agreement on questions such as land reform, Davies did not support Lloyd George's bellicose attitude in the Great War. As a result, Davies lost the seat (renamed Caernarvonshire) in 1918, after a bitter campaign, to a Coalition Liberal. An Independent Labour candidate was also ahead of him. However, in 1923 Davies was re-elected to parliament, as Liberal MP for Denbigh – a seat which he held until 1929, when he resigned on health grounds. In 1934, despite pressure from his friend the Liberal MP for Merionethshire, Henry Haydn Jones, Davies defected to the Labour Party. Jones tried to persuade Davies to change his mind, writing: 'Think what *you* have missed by leaving the true fold ... there are heaps of the working classes who will never trust a Labour Govt.'[73] 'Don't you think you have made a huge mistake in joining those humbugs ... Return, you prodigal at once. It is not too late.'[74] Jones failed to persuade Davies to return from the Labour Party in 1934, but in 1939, convinced of the need to avoid war, Davies switched his alliance to the Liberal National Party (see Chapter 5).

Richard Acland was elected for Barnstaple in 1935 – one of only two new Liberal MPs at that general election. An Oxford-educated barrister, he had the archetypical background for a Liberal MP and impeccable party antecedents – his father, grandfather and great-grandfather had all sat as Liberal MPs. However, soon after his election, Acland began a religious, philosophical and political journey, which was to take him far beyond the bounds of Liberalism. Acland wrote a series of publications calling for the abolition of profit-seeking and its urgent replacement with a brand of socialism, founded on Christian principles.[75] Acland's views led to (unheeded) calls for the Liberal whip to be withdrawn from him. In 1941 he formed the 'Forward March' movement, which he merged the following year with J.B. Priestley's '1941 Committee', to form 'Common Wealth'. Common Wealth espoused world unity and the common ownership of all property not essential for personal use. Acland practised what he preached and donated his wealthy family's estates to the National Trust. In September 1942 Acland resigned the Liberal whip. Free from the wartime electoral truce which bound the main parties, Common Wealth put up candidates in some by-elections where no progressive (either Labour or independent) candidate was standing. In other seats, the party gave support to independent left-wing candidates. Acland even tried, unsuccessfully, to enlist Lloyd George's support for his new party.[76] By exploiting the absence of other left-of-centre contestants in wartime by-elections in formerly Conservative- or Liberal National-held seats, Common Wealth managed to win Eddisbury in 1943, Skipton in 1944 and Chelmsford in 1945. Although

Labour officially proscribed membership of Common Wealth in 1943, the latter's activities undoubtedly helped Labour – by taking seats from the Conservatives (Chelmsford and Skipton) and the National Liberals (Eddisbury) and by attracting into politics new young professional middle-class supporters. In other seats, such as West Derbyshire in 1944, Common Wealth's support helped independent candidates to victory. The activities of Common Wealth, or 'Acland's Circus' as it was widely known, worried Churchill, as it eroded Conservative support in particular and kept some of his close allies, such as the Marquess of Hartington at West Derbyshire, out of parliament. The successes of Common Wealth and other independent left-wing candidates in the wartime by-elections weighed into the Labour Party's decision to refuse Churchill's offer to continue the coalition government at the end of the war.[77] At the 1945 general election, Common Wealth received a total of 110, 634 votes between its twenty-three candidates and only Ernest Millington survived, at Chelmsford. He and Acland joined the Labour Party immediately after the election. Acland's wartime defection had deprived the Liberal Party of one of its dwindling band of MPs, and a talented propagandist at that. It also ended a wealthy Liberal dynasty and provided a source of new support for the Labour Party. However, Acland did not find a permanent political home within Labour. He was elected as Labour MP for Gravesend at a by-election in 1947, but in 1955 he resigned his seat to precipitate a by-election over Labour's support for the hydrogen bomb. He was expelled from the Labour Party for putting himself forward as an independent, in opposition to the official Labour candidate. In the event, no by-election was held, as parliament was dissolved for the general election, called by Eden after his assumption of the premiership. Acland contested the seat, but came third, with 6,514 votes – enough to save his deposit and to deprive the Labour candidate of the seat, which went to the Conservatives by 2,909 votes – an ironic reversal of the consequences of Common Wealth's wartime interventions. Although in scale and consequences his actions were less critical, Acland's career had echoes of that of Joseph Chamberlain – a wealthy and talented policy-maker who deserted the Liberals before spending a period as an independent power-broker, then being adopted by, but ultimately sabotaging, another major party. Acland was the last of the Idealists to defect from the Liberals to Labour.

The Disillusioned Progressives

The Disillusioned Progressives were the most numerous of the defectors to Labour and were highly significant as they included many individuals of prestige, wealth and ability. Their numbers included Haldane, Addison and Buxton. They tended to agonise over leaving the Liberal Party, and based their decisions to leave more on the problems of the Liberal Party and on their eagerness to make social progress than on the attractions of the Labour Party. They did not tend to take sides between Asquith and Lloyd George, but were seriously discouraged by the fall-out from the party split. No single issue determined their stance. Most were strongly sentimentally attached to the Liberal Party. Crucially, they probably would have stayed with the Liberals if they had felt that the party were able to form another effective government. They were part of a vicious circle in which their lack of faith in the party's prospects encouraged them to defect, while in turn their defections reduced the prospects of a Liberal revival.

Table 3.3 illustrates the progress that the Labour Party had made in putting up candidates across the country between 1910 and 1918, and the extent of the failure of the Liberals to oppose them.

While in 1918 the Liberal Party was split, Labour was also in serious difficulty. In fact the backlash against anti-war MPs in the Labour Party was in some ways more severe than in the Liberal Party. After the 1918 election MacDonald was aged fifty-two and, after twelve years in the House of Commons, his political career appeared to be in ruins. The party he had helped to create appeared to be firmly under the control of those who had rejected his leadership. The anti-war section had all lost their seats; and even Henderson had been defeated. The major difference between the Liberals' and Labour's performance between 1918 and 1922 was the result of Labour's success in putting up increased numbers of candidates and the Liberals' failure to contest seats, especially those where they failed to oppose Labour candidates. The Liberals' failure was essentially a mechanical breakdown. The split party, even adding the two wings together, was not matching the Labour Party's challenge. The number of Labour candidates unopposed by a Liberal more than doubled between December 1910 and 1918, despite the ending of the Gladstone-MacDonald Pact. Table 3.4 shows that between 1918 and 1922 Labour comprehensively overtook the combined forces of the two wings of the Liberal Party.

These figures suggest that, had the Liberal Party reunited soon after 1918, it might have been able to hold back the Labour tide, but by 1922 a tipping point had been passed, and Labour had overtaken the Liberals in terms of seats and votes. This was confirmed by the 1923 election result, when, under favourable conditions, with a (more or less) united party, the Liberal recovery was only patchy and unsustainable. The 159-seat Liberal high watermark of 1923 was not even equal

Table 3.3 *Labour candidates unopposed by Liberals*

	December 1910	1918
Labour candidates	59	388
Labour candidates without Liberal opposition*	48	108
Labour MPs elected	42	63

* Includes Lib-Lab and Coalition Liberal as Liberal, excludes Independent Labour.

Table 3.4 *Labour overtakes the combined Liberals' seats and votes*

	1918		1922	
	% votes*	seats	% votes	seats
Conservative and Coalition Con	36.0	358	38.2	345
Liberal and Nat/Coalition Liberal	25.6	161	29.1	116
Labour and Coalition Labour	23.7	73	29.5	142

* Includes Ireland.

to the combined total of 161 Asquithian and Lloyd George Liberal victories in 1918. After the 1923 election Labour went on to form its first administration and to win the mantle of responsibility.

A striking feature of all the defections from the Liberals to Labour is that there was almost no coordinated exodus, although a total of forty-five MPs and former MPs made the move between 1918 and 1956.[78] The staggered timing of the defections, as shown in Figure 2.2, illustrates that the pattern of defections was more of a dribble than a rush. Some of the War Policy Objectors, discussed earlier, did liaise with each other, but failed to coordinate their actions. The only other significant attempt at coordination was by the Rightward Drift Objectors in the 1950s, and this fell apart. Cline points out that once the Liberal converts to Labour had made the transition, 'they ceased to be a group almost immediately, and were frequently to be found on opposite sides of issues under discussion' within the Labour Party. Her conclusion on the former Liberals' behaviour once in the Labour Party is an accurate observation, but in reality they had never been a group. Cline also put emphasis on the single tax as being of importance in linking those who defected from the Liberals to Labour, but while this was a connection, it was not a reason for the defections. The main damage to the Liberals was done by the steady drift of Disillusioned Progressives which started after the 1918 election. They tended to make similar decisions independently from each other and were not overly influenced by the actions of any one individual. Most were politically career-minded, but motivated by achievement, rather than position.

Noel Buxton had strongly held, individualistic convictions about the war, which to some extent coincided with those of the UDC, but he was never one of its members, even though he was a close friend and travelling companion of Ramsay MacDonald and uncle to Arthur Ponsonby. However, Buxton voted for conscription in 1916. Before the war, he had launched initiatives to defuse Anglo-German hostility, but his main focus was on conditions in Bulgaria, where he had been involved in pre-war relief work. He had returned to the country with his brother Charles after the outbreak of war, to try to secure Bulgaria's support for the allies. The mission failed and the two brothers nearly lost their lives when they were shot by a Turkish gunman. Noel Buxton was shot in the jaw, and his brother in the lung, but both survived. Buxton felt that the entry of the United States into the war spelt an end to hopes of a negotiated peace and he was also 'increasingly disenchanted with the Liberal Party and its leadership.'[79] However, he contested his North Norfolk seat as a Liberal in 1918, but lost by the narrow margin of 213 votes. Buxton joined the Labour Party in 1919, believing that the radical point of view was better represented by the Labour Party than by the Liberals. He wrote that 'to join the Labour Party was an alarming plunge, being regarded by one's relations and friends as a betrayal, and I hesitated long'. 'Without Charlie's example I doubt if I should have brought myself to such extreme action, being by nature a compromiser rather than a whole-hogger!'[80] Buxton returned to the Commons for his old seat of North Norfolk under Labour colours in 1922, and sat until elevated to the peerage in 1930, when his wife was elected, briefly, to succeed him. He was a rare member of the Parliamentary Labour Party in that he represented a rural seat. Buxton served as Minister of Agriculture in the first and early part of the second Labour Governments, until his elevation. He then drifted away from MacDonald and later became an advocate of appeasement. Buxton's son joined the Liberal Party in the House of Lords on succeeding to the title after his father's death.

Well before the war, **Percy Alden** had edited the Liberal daily paper the *Echo*, whose writers included Ramsay MacDonald. He was a social worker, member of the Fabian Society and secretary of the National Unemployed Committee. Alden was one of the progressive politicians with an appeal to Labour voters for whom Herbert Gladstone found a constituency and provided finance following the electoral pact with MacDonald in 1903.[81] He was elected to the Commons in 1906 for

Tottenham, as a Radical Liberal. In the war Alden did not vote on the Registration Bill or on Conscription in May 1916, but he voted against the Bachelors' Bill, stating in the Commons: 'I believe this Bill is wrong on principle, because it is contrary to everything I have ever believed.' But Alden did not leave the Liberal Party over his objections to the war and he contributed a chapter on housing to the Asquithian Liberals' manifesto at the 1918 election. However, he failed to retain his seat at Tottenham North in the coupon election, being beaten by a Coalition Conservative. His election address proposed the abolition of the House of Lords, nationalisation of the railways and the mines, drastic land reform, together with the taxation of land values, equality of women with men and self-government for Ireland. After losing his seat, and driven by his long-standing concerns for social issues, rather than his war policy objections, Alden joined the Labour Party in 1919. He set out his views on ethical socialism and public ownership in an article in *Contemporary Review* in April 1919. Between 1923 and 1924 Alden served as Labour MP for the neighbouring constituency of Tottenham South, but disappointed with the performance of Ramsay MacDonald's first Labour Government, and attracted by the innovative proposals for tackling unemployment developed by the Liberal industrial inquiry, he rejoined the Liberal Party in late 1927. However, in 1933 he was knighted on the recommendation of MacDonald. Alden was killed in an air raid in 1944.

Richard Haldane was a prestigious catch for the Labour Party, even though he was too individualistic to bring a Liberal following with him and the Labour leadership made little attempt to lure him. In the early stages of Haldane's migration, MacDonald was not over-enthusiastic about Haldane's approaches, writing in his diary: 'Disappointed when I had to go home to lunch as Haldane was coming to discuss the Party which he appears to think of joining (!)', and a week later: 'Haldane . . . thinks the Liberal Party is dead.' In April 1919 MacDonald recorded that Haldane had told him that he had ceased to belong to the Liberal Party.[82] Haldane was a semi-detached member of many groups throughout his life. He studied law, philosophy, geology and German – all with flashes of brilliance tempered by failure – in part due to a lack of commitment to any one field. When his doctoral thesis was rejected for weaknesses in botany, Haldane moved into law. Here he had success, but also stuck with the mundane work of conveyancing as part of his portfolio, for most of his legal career. He abandoned his Christianity as a teenager. His one recorded romance, an engagement to the sister of Munro-Ferguson, was ended by his fiancée. Beatrice Webb, who knew Haldane very well, noted that despite 'the beaming kindliness of his nature ... there is pathos ... he is a restless, lonely man'.[83] Haldane's detachment is reflected positively in his own assessment that he was 'never depressed by even the most violent abuse'.[84] Haldane was a key member of the Liberal Imperialists and had been one of the co-conspirators in the Relugas Compact with Grey and Asquith. He went on to serve successfully as Secretary of State for War from 1905 to 1912, when he was appointed Lord Chancellor. Haldane saw himself as a man of action and he gravitated to where the action was. His relationship with Asquith cooled after he was not included in the coalition cabinet in 1915. Haldane began to be more attracted to Lloyd George, even though he considered him to be 'an illiterate with an unbalanced mind'.[85] Then, as the Labour Party began to look like a potential party of power, Haldane began to integrate himself with the Labour leadership. Between 1917 and 1922 Haldane managed to maintain an ambiguous political stance, which could have allowed him to attach himself to whichever party promised the greater opportunities. In 1922, Haldane declined Asquith's invitation to a meeting, replying:

> I have the fullest desire to be by your side [but] three years ago I decided ... to work with whatever party was most in earnest with Education ... I observed then, as I observe now, the almost complete lack of harmony between my strong conviction on this subject and the programme of official Liberalism ... That is why I am driven to seek it where I see a chance of finding it.[86]

Haldane later admitted that his motives for changing party allegiance were not really that Labour offered a superior programme or party, but that its prospects appeared brighter than the Liberals'. Labour was gaining seats rapidly. Its programme fitted in with the educational work on which he had been engaged. Haldane considered that it was 'at least no more deficient' than the Liberals and for the four years before 1924 he found himself 'more and more driven by conviction' in the direction of the Labour Party. However, he reported that 'with the exception of the Sidney Webbs ... I was not intimate with their prominent men [sic], nor had I joined any organisation'. At the end of 1923, when it was evident that MacDonald was likely to form a government, Haldane told MacDonald that he wished to resume the Lord Chancellorship and to lead the party in the House of Lords. His wish was granted and he became a valuable member of the first Labour Government for his extensive knowledge of cabinet protocol and his experience of dealing with civil servants. His confidence, resilience and detachment had stood Haldane in good stead when he had served successfully as a reforming Liberal Secretary of State for War and Lord

Chancellor. The same attributes enabled him to make the transition to Labour without the debilitating self-doubt suffered by Jowitt, who later followed Haldane's path from the Liberals to Labour, also serving as Lord Chancellor. Haldane died in 1928, before the second Labour administration was formed.

Christopher Addison was from a farming family, but trained as a doctor. He was one of six Coalition supporters who, contrary to the general flow of defectors, went over to Labour. However, he had parted company with the coalition before its demise and the reasons for, and manner of, his departure partly explained his change of allegiance. Addison had been a loyal supporter of Lloyd George and was the member of the Coalition Government responsible for the 1919 Housing and Town Planning Act. As the economy worsened during the Lloyd George Coalition's term of office, Addison's department faced severe financial restrictions, which threatened to undermine his housing programme. Addison's policies were among the most expensive and the most socialist of the government's programmes. This made him particularly vulnerable to demands for budget cuts, the clamour for which increased significantly with the popular support for the Anti-Waste League. The League was sponsored by Lord Rothermere and supported in parliament by Horatio Bottomley. Anti-Waste candidates won three by-elections in early 1921 and the movement attracted the adherence of the Coalition Liberal, Cecil Beck (see Chapter 5). In April 1921, Addison was moved to become Minister Without Portfolio, but he resigned in July – estranged from Lloyd George. Addison's resignation letter revealed his frustrations over the curtailment of public expenditure and the consequences for his reputation. It ended: 'I am compelled, bitterly as I feel this ending of our long and intimate work together, to resign my position in your Government in order to be able freely to devote myself to the promotion of those things which I believe are essential.' Lloyd George drafted a less than conciliatory reply: 'I cannot accept your description of the Government decision as an abandonment of our housing policy.'[87] Addison was criticised for having been an ineffective minister and as a line of defence he argued vehemently for an expanded role for public sector housing. His estrangement from Lloyd George and from his Unionist former colleagues left him without a political home. In 1919 and early 1920 Addison had been one of the chief protagonists of Fusion between the Coalition Liberals and Unionists, but he left the Coalition and crossed the floor; although he was hardly welcomed or comfortable among the Asquithians, after his interventions against Asquith in the Paisley by-election and his pugnacious behaviour at the Leamington Conference (see Chapter 4). In

1922 the National Liberal association in Shoreditch worked to unseat Addison, who had to pay to revive the defunct local Independent Liberal Association for it to act on his behalf. He was third in a three-cornered contest and was called upon to pay over a thousand pounds in election expenses. Addison was driven almost to insolvency by these claims and applied to the London Liberal Federation for a contribution. The federation secretary rejected his request: 'our help has been given to men who stood by the Liberal Party in its darkest days, men who did not desert the faith and work with our political enemies in the great betrayal of 1918 for mere personal position and profit'.[88] After this financial and personal rebuff and the loss of his seat, Addison was in limbo between political parties. His policy positions, and his lack of an alternative political base, steered him towards the Labour Party. Henderson, more pro-active and conscientious about contacting potential recruits than MacDonald, asked about Addison's future plans, eliciting the reply that he could not afford to contest the 1923 election, but that he believed:

> [T]he Labour Party is more resolutely intent than any other political party on bettering the housing, health and education of the people . . . I know that there are differences in every Party, and it would not be honourable of me to conceal the serious misgivings I have. [In] this Division where no Labour Candidate is standing I think it would be my duty openly to do what I can to assist . . . the [Liberal] Candidate.[89]

In November 1923 the press reported that, although Addison felt that 'no man leaves a political party . . . without grave reasons',[90] he had decided to 'throw in his lot with the Labour Party.'[91] While Addison was another prestigious catch for the Labour Party, MacDonald was less than quick or effusive in welcoming his conversion, much as had been the case with Haldane: 'I am very much ashamed indeed that your letter has been unanswered for so long. The fact is that I am simply covered up with correspondence . . . perhaps we will meet soon after all this trouble is over.'[92] Addison stood unsuccessfully for Labour in 1924, returning to parliament as Labour MP for Swindon in 1929. He was appointed Minister of Agriculture in June 1930, in succession to Buxton. In 1931 Addison opposed MacDonald over the National Government and lost his seat at the general election. In the meantime he had been reconciled with Lloyd George, who had intervened on Addison's behalf at the Swindon by-election, where no Liberal had been standing. The rekindled friendship endured.[93] According to Frank Owen, former Liberal MP and later Lloyd George biographer, this rapprochement led to Lloyd George's suggestion in December 1937 that Addison, although by then a Labour peer, be appointed a trustee of the Lloyd George Political Fund. However, the chairman of the Fund's trustees blocked the proposal, avoiding the potential for serious conflicts of interest. Owen's accounts of events are not always to be relied upon, however. For instance Owen also claimed that General Seely left the Liberal Party in the mid-1920s,[94] when in fact Seely did not leave the party.[95] Addison became Labour leader in the Lords in 1940 (being advanced to a viscount in 1945) and served until his death in 1951.

Alexander MacCallum Scott was another one of the six Coalition Liberals who defected to the Labour Party. Scott received the coupon in 1918, but was ambivalent: 'As regards L.G. and Asquith . . . Personally, I am very little swayed by the respective personalities on either side.'[96] He criticised Lloyd George for neglecting his followers, complaining: 'We have all been left in the lurch. We are simply dropped like a sucked orange' and Asquith for lack of leadership: 'A leader is expected to lead, not merely to wait and see.'[97] Scott agonised about defecting after the 1924 election:

> I have been reluctant to break with the Liberal Party because I felt I had some small share of responsibility to the members + it was not fair to run away . . . The action of the leaders, however, in the recent election . . . finally determines me. I was asked to stand for Partick at this election, with Conservative support, but refused + gave my support to the ex-Labour member. I am not yet sure what course I shall take [and] I would like to get a number to act together.[98]

In the event, Scott acted alone and wrote to Asquith in December 1924 to explain his decision:

> I have decided to join the Labour Party . . . I have been uneasy as to the direction in which the Liberal Party was tending, whether under the direction of yourself or of Mr. Lloyd George . . . [T]he work of reform . . . has passed to the Labour Party . . . I have had to remain an onlooker while the party was more and more committed to a definitely anti-labour attitude . . . at the last election, a pact was made with the Conservative Party which reduced the Liberal Party to the position of a spare wheel in the Conservative car . . . I regard you as one of the most honourable and magnanimous men in public life . . . But I do not think you can restore the party to its former position.[99]

To his new leader Scott wrote: 'I have decided to offer myself as a recruit in the Labour Party . . . There are many Liberals who, like myself, have found themselves in agreement with the programme put forward by the Labour Party in recent elections . . . many of them still waver on the brink.'[100] Scott did not find it easy to sever his sentimental links with the Liberal Party, writing the month after his defection: 'I joined the ILP, the Fabian Society + the Labour Party . . . I felt the loss of the National Liberal Club most of all.' 'I say not a word in disparagement of my old leaders + colleagues. I respect them. I am sorry to part from them . . . I have no quarrel with them except that I do not agree with their policy + I agree with the policy of the Labour Party.' He was sorry that Lloyd George had 'cut me completely off'. Scott began to regret his move, realising that he had alienated potential key allies across the political spectrum: 'I have made no progress in the Labour Party + indeed I have made little effort. I have received over a dozen invitations to fight seats but they have mostly been duds . . . I have been heavy + clumsy handed + I have had little finesse . . . I made enemies of . . . Ponsonby . . . Noel Buxton . . . and I fear also of Lloyd George + Ramsay MacDonald . . . I failed with Churchill.' One year after his defection he complained 'I am left stranded . . . without a party – without a group – without even a circle of political friends . . . I have joined the Labour Party – but I have found few friends there + am looked upon with suspicious eyes. It is a poor result . . . I stopped too long in the Coalition . . . If Lloyd George, or Churchill, or even the Asquith crowd had shown any disposition to consult me . . . I would have recognised the obligation to play the team game . . . But they held out no hand . . . I am tempted to approach [LG] with a view to talking over [the Land League], for I could co-operate if he came out of the Liberal Party'.[101] Scott accepted his own part in his alienation from his former colleagues, but he also identified that the Liberal leadership had been too distracted by factional infighting to attend adequately to the management of the party. Scott, along with others, could have been persuaded to stay in the Liberal Party. Despite his misgivings about his new party, Scott was adopted as the prospective Labour candidate for East Aberdeenshire in 1926. However, he was denied the chance to fight an election under Labour colours, as he and his wife were killed in an air crash in August 1928. His untimely demise, paralleled by that of Robert Bernays (see Chapter 5), meant that Scott left an unvarnished, unadjusted account of his feelings about his defection.

Less than six months after Scott's defection, his exodus was followed by that of **George Spero**, who had served a single term in parliament as a Liberal MP for Stoke Newington between 1923 and 1924. In his letter to Asquith in April 1925, resigning from the Liberal Party, Spero wrote: 'I see a Liberalism so changed . . . There are no issues . . . that can arouse in me a semblance of my old-time enthusiasm. It cannot be sufficient . . . to rest . . . upon the laurels of the past . . . I now look to the Labour Party.'[102] Unlike Scott, Spero did stand and was elected, as Labour MP for Fulham West, in 1929. However, like Scott his parliamentary career was cut short by external events. Spero was declared bankrupt the following year and, when he was threatened with a court case over his business dealings, he fled the country for the United States. He took the Chiltern Hundreds in April 1930.

Athelstan Rendall was one of the four Liberal MPs to have voted for the Maurice Motion, but still to have received the Coupon in 1918. He was then to be one of the six Coalition Liberals to defect to Labour. His attachment to the coalition had been tenuous and he crossed the floor in July 1920 to sit with the Wee Frees. He lost his seat in 1922, but was re-elected in 1923. By the time of the 1924 election his frustration with the Liberal Party, and the political system generally, was clear from his election address:

> My first vote [was] to vote the Unionist Government out. This enabled the Labour Party . . . to form a Government. To the Labour Government, Liberals have given regular support . . . now everywhere Labour is seeking to destroy the Liberal Party . . . my party is now attacked as if it was an enemy of Labour.

Rendall lost his seat at the 1924 election and defected to Labour in 1925. He took part in no further elections. While Rendall was a modest, self-effacing lawyer, who had occupied himself with such interests as his 'Deceased Husband's Brother Bill', the next Liberal defector to Labour was a totally contrasting character.

Joseph Kenworthy was a would-be polar explorer turned naval officer, and heir to the Barony of Strabolgi, created in 1318. His parents were Conservatives. Kenworthy failed at his first attempt to enter parliament, as a Liberal, in 1918, when he refused the Coupon because he 'was disgusted with the Lloyd George Coalition [and] the vulgarizing of the war'. The following year he won a by-election in Hull Central, against only a Coalition Conservative opponent, overturning a 10,000 majority. He held the seat, despite a change of party allegiance, until 1931. Kenworthy was brash and confident and developed a hectoring style in parliament, which alienated many of his colleagues. He made a point of demonstrating his objection to the Versailles Treaty, being one of a small group who refused to rise and cheer Lloyd George on his return from Paris. After the 1923 election Kenworthy supported the Labour Government on every matter of policy except the warship programme.[103] A loyal Asquithian, Kenworthy did not accepted Lloyd George's leadership and associated himself with a Radical group, including Walter Runciman, Wedgwood Benn, McKenzie Livingstone and Percy Harris. Kenworthy saw that Asquith's resignation in 1926 affected the position of all members of the Liberal Party. 'We have to ask ourselves seriously whether our continued existence as a separate Party is in the best interests of the State and of Constitutional Government.' 'Very reluctantly therefore I have decided to transfer my energies' to the Labour Party.[104] Ironically, the timing of Kenworthy's defection meant that he was to leave the Liberal Party immediately after the only significant event which had drawn him and Lloyd George together – the General Strike. 'Lloyd George and myself were the only two Liberals left to preach Liberalism . . . The collapse of the General Strike left the Labour Party . . . in an extremely weak position . . . their moment of defeat, was, I felt, the time to join them.'[105] Kenworthy wrote to Lloyd George: 'I feel it my duty to leave the official Liberal Party . . . If this means the severance of our recently re-established political friendship, I am sorry.'[106] Kenworthy visited Churt to ask Lloyd George what he would have done in his situation; afterward claiming that Lloyd George had said: 'If I were your age I would do the same.' According to Kenworthy, they parted 'the best of friends'. Kenworthy initially held to the line that he would not resign his seat and trigger a by-election: 'I was returned as much by Labour as by Liberals, I had the official support of two seamen's unions . . . I have in no way changed my political opinions'.[107] However, the local Labour leaders, believing that the seat was winnable, persuaded Kenworthy to resign and re-contest the seat under Labour colours. Kenworthy had never faced a Labour opponent in his four contests at Hull and no other prospective Labour candidate had been adopted for a future contest, so he did not have to deal with the complication of displacing an incumbent prospective Labour candidate. Kenworthy had seen off a Conservative challenger at each election and, as long as the Liberals could not mount a strong challenge, he had a good prospect of success. In the event Kenworthy won the by-election, held on 29 November 1926, by a margin of 4,679 votes over his Conservative challenger, increasing his majority compared to that of his last contest. The Liberal lost his deposit. Kenworthy became close to MacDonald and was a frequent visitor to MacDonald's home. After the May 1929 election, Kenworthy claimed that he was instrumental in persuading William Jowitt to join the Labour Party and that he attempted unsuccessfully to persuade other Liberals to follow suit. As was the case with many of the Liberal defectors to Labour, Kenworthy eventually fell out with MacDonald, and even before the formation of the National Government. Kenworthy, perhaps self-flatteringly, believed that MacDonald looked upon him 'as a possible rival'.[108] He refused to join MacDonald in National Labour and was defeated as a Labour candidate in 1931. Kenworthy inherited his father's peerage in 1934. His son, on succeeding him in the Lords in 1953, joined the Liberal peers.

After Kenworthy's defection, Simon had commented wryly that 'Kenworthy having thus forced his fat body through the hedge you may be sure that a large number of sheep will go dribbling through the gap'. As it turned out, Simon's unflattering analysis did have a ring of truth to it. Kenworthy was bulky – he had been a heavy-weight boxer; others did follow his path and their exit from the Liberal field did resemble the behaviour of sheep, inasmuch as they tended to move in a common direction, but without an obvious leader or any meaningful communication between them. After Kenworthy, there dribbled another eight Liberals who defected to Labour for similar reasons.

Frederick Martin was elected, at his first attempt, as Liberal MP for Aberdeenshire and Kincardineshire East in 1922. This seat illustrated the self-imposed difficulties with which the Liberal Party was afflicted. Martin's only opponent was the incumbent National Liberal MP, Henry Cowan, who in turn had won in 1918 against only an Independent Liberal. Martin held the seat in 1923, before losing it in a three-cornered contest in 1924 to the Conservative Robert Boothby. As well as the unusual nature of the political contests in the constituency, Martin was an unusual candidate in that he was blind; his eyesight having seriously deteriorated while he was in training for the armed forces during the Great War. However, this did not prevent his working as a journalist or as an MP. In the 1929 election, Martin transferred his candidature to the neighbouring seat of Aberdeenshire and Kincardineshire Central, where he again stood unsuccessfully as a Liberal. Martin supported Lloyd George's policies to tackle unemployment and 'believed that the Liberal Party had the means and measures to mitigate it, and that they could find the finance'. However, four months after the 1929 election, Martin resigned from the Liberal Party to join Labour, saying that he wanted to pursue the same objectives, but by different means. He wrote cordially to Lloyd George that he hoped that 'personal friendships will survive this rupture of political alliance'. Martin was strongly against the National Government.[109] For the 1931 and 1935 general elections, he returned to his old seat as a Labour candidate and was defeated again by Boothby.

Only five weeks after Martin's defection, another Disillusioned Progressive joined the dribble to Labour. **George Garro-Jones** was one of only five new Liberal MPs to be elected in the 1924 general election, and the only one to have fought as a Lloyd George-supporting National Liberal candidate in 1922. Garro-Jones served a single term as the Liberal MP for Hackney South from 1924 to 1929, during which time he displayed a confident and combative approach, speaking on a wide range of issues and being willing to challenge the Speaker's authority.

Despite his earlier loyalty to Lloyd George, Garro-Jones decided to abandon the Parliamentary Liberal Party, even though it was now under the sole control of his former mentor. He did not stand again in 1929; he would almost certainly have lost, had he done so, as Herbert Morrison won the seat for Labour with a majority of over 7,000 against Conservative, Communist and Liberal candidates; the latter coming third. In early November 1929, Garro-Jones left the Liberal Party to join Labour, writing to MacDonald that in his opinion 'all virile progressive opinion . . . must identify itself with the Labour movement'. However, his political association with MacDonald was to be brief. Garro-Jones remained within the Labour Party after the 1931 split, but he did not contest that year's election. He did stand again for parliament in 1935, and was successful as the Labour candidate in Aberdeen North – the seat which William Wedgwood Benn had held for Labour from 1928 until his defeat in 1931. Garro-Jones' election in 1935 gave him a ten-year lease on his parliamentary seat, during which time he was appointed to the newly-created war-time post of parliamentary secretary to the Ministry of Production. He stood down from the Commons at the 1945 election and was created Lord Trefgarne in 1947. However, his allegiance to the Labour Party eroded and in 1952 he decided to become a cross-bencher, explaining that he had been concerned to see the tendency to swing 'from one extreme to another, which is bound to be very damaging to certain industries . . . I have always been a believer in compromise as being the essence of politics'. In 1958, disillusioned with his isolated position in the Lords, he re-joined the Liberal Party, by then under the leadership of Jo Grimond.[110] Garro-Jones was a bold and talented individual, with a successful track record in the armed forces, a qualified barrister, a combative politician and later chairman of the Television Advisory Committee. He was driven more by achievement than by party considerations and was never firmly attached to any political grouping. He was a Disillusioned Progressive at many stages of his career, and not just when he decided to defect from the Liberal Party.

Reginald Fletcher's career displayed striking similarities to that of Garro-Jones, although their career paths evolved from coincidence and individual decisions when faced with similar situations, rather than from any coordination or cooperation. Like Garro-Jones, Fletcher served a single term as a Liberal MP in the 1920s, defected to Labour in 1929, did not stand in 1929 or 1931, was elected at his first, and only, contest for Labour in 1935, held junior office during the war and ended up in the Lords, where he also drifted away from the Labour Party. Fletcher's family background was Conservative. He served as

Liberal MP for Basingstoke from 1923 to 1924 – the only Liberal tenure of that seat in over a century of Conservative domination. He then nursed Tavistock assiduously for three years, but lost at a by-election in 1928 by 173 votes, after the intervention of a Labour candidate. After this set-back, Fletcher began to wonder whether Labour was not 'destined to take the place of the Liberal Party'. He joined the Labour Party in 1929, but although 'in it, he was never really of it'. Having parted company with Ramsay MacDonald over support for the National Government, Fletcher was elected as Labour MP for Nuneaton in 1935, but in the House of Commons he spoke almost with the 'detachment of an independent'. In 1940 Fletcher became parliamentary private secretary to the First Lord of the Admiralty and in 1941, together with three other Labour members, he went to the Lords, taking the title Baron Winster. In 1945 Attlee invited Winster to be minister of civil aviation, which made him a minister of cabinet rank, but without a seat in the cabinet. In 1946 Winster was appointed Governor of Cyprus. Back in London, after February 1949, Winster took an even more independent line than ever before, and his 'strictures on left-wing members of his party were biting'.[111]

Like Fletcher, **Harry Barnes** remained a Liberal, fighting for the cause until a 1928 by-election defeat, before also defecting, disillusioned, to Labour. Barnes was an architect and town planner with a strong social conscience and a desire to see results for his efforts. He served a single term in the Commons, being elected as Coalition Liberal member for East Newcastle in 1918, but within a year of the election he crossed the floor of the House to sit as an Independent Liberal because he 'felt that the Unionists were dominating coalition policy'. He wrote to Guest saying that:

> I have for some time ceased to be in fact, a supporter of the Coalition . . . The Prime Minister is a great Liberal in an impasse . . . his real supporters are his nominal opponents, while his real opponents are his nominal supporters . . . I must go where my heart is. There could be no place for me in a Conservative Party, and if the only choice was between it and Labour I would not hesitate, but it is not yet that. Liberalism still survives.[112]

While Barnes wrote in respectful terms to Lloyd George, blaming the situation on the political circumstances of the times, chief whip Guest drafted a reply which was sure to engender animosity:

> When you offered yourself for election . . . you gained the active support of . . . the Coalition Unionists in the constituency . . . you actually appealed for this support. [T]he most elementary considerations of propriety and honesty make it necessary for you to give an opportunity [for

your constituents] to decide whether they prefer to be represented by yourself, or by a Member with greater claims to constancy and stability.[113]

Unsurprisingly, the executive committee of the Newcastle East Unionist Association added their voice to the chorus of disapproval, expressing their dissatisfaction and calling for his resignation.[114] Even after his change of allegiance between the Liberal factions, Barnes determined to retain his freedom of action. He wrote to the Independent Liberal Whip, Hogge, to warn him that: 'If I have shown some measure of independence you will, I am sure, not expect it to diminish in the society of Independent Liberalism.'[115] When the 1922 election arrived, Barnes faced a National Liberal as well as a Labour opponent, who won the seat after the Liberal vote was split into two roughly equal parts. Barnes abandoned national politics after his failure to win the by-election in Halifax in July 1928 for the Liberals. Halifax had been a Liberal-held seat, and it was at a time when the Liberals were having some by-election successes. Instead, Barnes concentrated on his work as a town planner. From 1923 to 1925 Barnes served as an alderman on the London County Council. This period saw a collapse in Liberal/Progressive representation on the LCC from a combined total of 31 councillors and aldermen to only six, while Labour representation increased from 19 to 41. At the LCC Barnes came into contact with Herbert Morrison, Labour leader on the council from 1925, whose housing improvement schemes inspired him.[116] In 1931 Barnes published *The Slum: its Story and Solution*, a major work which argued for high-quality publicly funded housing.[117] That year Barnes transferred his political allegiance to the Labour Party. However, he never stood for elected office under Labour colours and died in 1935.

Ernest Simon was elected to Manchester City Council in 1911 as a Liberal. Like Barnes, his primary concern was housing, but after the end of the war he began to consider whether he would be more at home in the Labour Party. However, seeing himself as an 'autocratic' employer with a gross income of £20,000 per year, he felt that he might be 'rather a fish out of water' in the Labour Party, even though 'four fifths of the people whose political views he admired' were in it. Simon was elected as Liberal MP for Manchester Withington at his second attempt in 1923, but after being defeated in 1924, he drew up a list of the pros and cons of remaining a Liberal: the Labour Party was clearly destined to be '*the* alternative party of the future', but the party's commitment to 'wholesale' nationalisation bothered him. He was concerned that his commitment to a party which advocated socialism might complicate his business relations. Simon Carves Ltd, of which he was a Director, had dealings with colliery companies to whom the idea of nationalisation was anathema. Simon's involvement with the Liberal Summer Schools reconfirmed his Liberal views and gave him an opportunity to contribute to party policy, including the industry 'Yellow Book'. He was re-elected in his old constituency in 1929 and served briefly as parliamentary secretary to the Ministry of Health in the National Government, before being defeated at the 1931 election, standing as a Liberal in Penryn and Falmouth. Simon distanced himself from the Liberals and counted himself as an independent after his 'final disillusionment' with party politics in 1931. He had already lost his council seat in 1925. Although his wife Shena joined the Labour Party in 1935, Simon remained unattached to any party until after the Second World War. He stood unsuccessfully as an independent for the Combined English Universities seat on the death of the independent (but Liberal-minded) Eleanor Rathbone in 1946. Simon then reassessed his political stance, using one of his lists of the pros and cons of joining the Labour Party, of which he had been on the brink twenty years earlier. This time the issue of nationalisation did not deter him, as the colliery owners had already accepted public ownership, so his business would not be affected. He joined his wife in the Labour Party in July 1946 and was elevated to the peerage the following year.[118] He served as Chairman of the BBC, but played little role in the Lords.

Harry Nathan was one of eighteen new Liberal MPs elected at the 1929 election, of whom only two (James de Rothschild and James Scott) remained members of the Liberal Party for the rest of their careers. Frank Owen left temporarily with the Lloyd George Family Group in 1931, eleven others went on to join the Liberal Nationals and four, including Nathan, defected to Labour. Barely more than a year after being elected, Nathan complained at a party meeting that the Liberal Party was 'done for'.[119] When the National Government was formed, Nathan remained in Samuel's group, but soon became dissatisfied with his leader's stance, feeling that Samuel should have withdrawn from the government side of the House. In February 1933 Nathan moved a resolution at a party meeting that the Samuelite Liberals should join the opposition. He received no support for it and ceremoniously crossed the floor of the Commons, when the House was packed for Question Time, to sit on the opposition benches with the Lloyd George Family Group. Nathan wrote to Samuel on 7 February 1933, 'I realize that this step involves, to my unfeigned regret, dissociating myself for the time from the Liberal Parliamentary Party ... By remaining on the Ministerial side of the House and thus giving the semblance of support to the government, the Liberal Party is in my opinion denying the beliefs and policies of Liberalism'. He was cold-shouldered by many of his old Liberal colleagues, but his constituency association in Bethnal Green endorsed his action. He met Labour opposition leader George Lansbury to discuss his immediate acceptance of the Labour whip. Although they found themselves in general agreement, Nathan decided to wait to see how far he was able to cooperate with Labour. On the eve of the summer recess in 1934 Nathan consulted Lloyd George. Nathan explained that he was thinking of joining Labour, but that he would not do so if Lloyd George felt that it would be 'desertion'. Lloyd George told him that if he took this step, Nathan would still retain his confidence.

Nathan had shown courage at various stages in his career. He had served as a major in the Great War, surviving a bullet through the back of his head. He withstood, better than most of the defectors, the opprobrium of his former Liberal colleagues on deserting the party and he risked much of his income by his transfer of political allegiance. In the 1930s a Labour solicitor in the City was unlikely to be consulted by leading bankers and industrialists.[120] Nathan unsuccessfully fought Cardiff South in the Labour interest in the 1935 general election, but was elected as Labour MP for Central Wandsworth at a by-election in 1937. In 1940 he was elevated to the Lords. He served in the Attlee Government, his political career culminating in the post of Minister of Civil Aviation from 1946 to 1948.

The next of the Disillusioned Progressives to defect to Labour was another Jewish solicitor, **Barnett Janner**. Janner was a member of the 1931 intake of Liberal MPs, which had almost as high a propensity to defect as had their preceding cohort. Of the twelve new Liberal MPs elected in 1931, only three remained loyal to the party for the remainder of their careers. Two joined the Conservatives, three (including Janner) defected to Labour and the others associated themselves with the Liberal Nationals. Janner sat as Liberal MP for Whitechapel. In the early 1930s he profoundly believed in Liberal philosophies but found the party 'impractical, disorganised and unlikely to achieve the results it sought'. After losing his seat at the 1935 general election, he found that he had lost the support of many of his Jewish constituents, who had switched to Labour. Largely under the influence of Morgan Phillips, Janner followed the voters and joined the Labour Party in 1936.[121] *The Times* commented that it was 'a matter of no surprise to his friends' that he changed his party allegiance. Janner was elected as a Labour MP in 1945 and served continuously until 1970, when he was given a life peerage. His son, Greville, succeeded him as Labour MP for Leicester North West. Janner's change of party allegiance is a rare example of a Liberal defector to Labour who was almost entirely content with his new party. Janner's most uncomfortable time was during the Suez Crisis, which brought a conflict of loyalties between his allegiance to his Jewish colleagues and to his party leader Gaitskell who had condemned Israel's part in the action.

Edward (Lance) Mallalieu was another of the 1931 cohort who defected from the Liberals to Labour. He represented Colne Valley, the seat which for which his father had sat as a Coalition Liberal from 1916 until his defeat in 1922. Lance Mallalieu was a 'strong radical' in his views, and found it difficult to support the National Government. When the Liberal Ministers resigned over the Ottawa agreements, Mallalieu reconsidered his position, and decided that he could no longer support the National Government. He crossed the floor of the House, and, though remaining a Liberal in name, felt that his political sympathies really lay with Labour. At the 1935 general election Mallalieu lost his seat to the Labour candidate, Ernest Marklew, by 3,779 votes. However, Marklew died in 1939 and Mallalieu stood as the Liberal candidate at the resulting by-election. This time his margin of defeat was over 8,000 votes and this was to be Mallalieu's last attempt to return to parliament as a Liberal. In 1945, partly due to the influence of his brother Joseph who was elected that year as a Labour MP, Lance Mallalieu joined the Labour Party. He was elected as Labour MP for Brigg at a by-election in 1948, where he sat until his retirement in February 1974.

Lloyd George Objectors

The events of 1915 to 1918 had created and solidified the split between the followers of Asquith and those of Lloyd George. Asquith, the more cool, aloof and intellectual of the two leaders, aroused strong loyalties in some quarters and despair and frustration in others. However, he did not arouse the intense feelings which Lloyd George provoked. Liberal MPs who were antagonistic towards Asquith were not motivated to leave the party solely on the issue of personalities. However, Lloyd George was a controversial enough figure for his passionate, devious and quixotic personality alone to be a reason for some to leave the party. There is also a practical reason why this was the case. For the duration of Asquith's leadership of the party up to 1926, his detractors always had Lloyd George present as a leader-in-waiting and source of solace. After Asquith's death, the Lloyd George detractors had no such alternative spiritual or potential leader to turn to within the party.

Rhys Hopkin Morris was probably the most virulent parliamentary opponent of Lloyd George – and that from a fairly strong field of contenders. Morris's first foray into politics was as a supporter of the Asquithian candidate, Llewelyn Williams, who lost to Ernest Evans in the 1921 Cardiganshire by-election. Evans had been Lloyd George's private secretary. This was one of four consecutive elections in the constituency, where the only candidates were Liberals. In 1922 Morris himself took up the fight and contested the seat at five consecutive elections. He was defeated by Evans at the 1922 election. The Liberals had reunited by the 1923 election and Evans, as a sitting MP, had been adopted as the party's official candidate. As Morris was determined to oust Evans, his only avenue of approach for the 1923 election was as an independent Liberal. Morris defeated Evans in 1923 and in 1924 he was re-elected unopposed. Once in parliament, Morris continued his opposition to Lloyd George, voting against his chairmanship of the Parliamentary party in 1926 and again, as the only objector, in 1929. Morris held Cardiganshire until he resigned to become a Metropolitan Police Magistrate in 1932. He returned to parliament for the neighbouring seat of Carmarthen in 1945, capturing the only seat to be lost by Labour at that election. His death in 1956 occasioned the by-election at which the Lloyd George family reaped their revenge on Morris's legacy, when Megan Lloyd George was returned to parliament under her new, Labour, colours. While Morris had effectively left the Liberal Party to stand against the official Liberal candidate, he always remained a Liberal, even if of the independent variety. However, two other Lloyd George detractors – William Wedgwood Benn and Mackenzie Livingstone – defected from the Liberals to the Labour Party because of their personal dislike of Lloyd George.

William Wedgwood Benn served as a Liberal whip from February 1910 to May 1915. In this role he had close contact with Lloyd George, whom he initially admired, but later came to despise, after the Marconi Scandal. Two days after being commissioned to form a government, Lloyd George telegrammed Benn, by then serving at the seaplane base at Port Said: 'Will you accept the post of joint whip with Talbot [.] urgently need [your] help [.] you can render greater s[ervice] to war here now by serving in new government'.[122] Benn appears to have been Lloyd George's first, and, at that stage, only, choice as the Liberals' chief whip to serve alongside the Unionists' nominee Edmund Talbot. Benn did not reject the offer out of hand, and believed that a better position could even come his way. His first instinct was to consult his close friend Reginald McKenna to find out how his former colleagues were responding to the unexpected changes in the administration. The same day, 8 December 1916, Benn wired McKenna: 'Invited chief whip ignorant you[r] position decide loyalty to you urge[nt]'.[123] To be sure of getting the advice he most needed, Benn also telegrammed his father the following day: 'offered chief whip consult McKenna urgent'.[124] McKenna's reply sealed Benn's decision: 'Asquith and all h[is] late liberal colleagues are absent from ne[w] government'.[125] This was all that Benn needed to know and that day he replied to the Prime Minister: 'deeply grateful but prefer remain here godspeed new government'.[126] Benn's father, clearly still considering the possibility that his son might join the government in some senior capacity, suggested that: 'offer of office other th[an] c[hief] w[hip] may come if s[. . .] chief friend advises [. . .] acceptance'.[127] Having talked to McKenna, Benn Senior eventually came to the conclusion: 'nothing worth accepting'.[128] The advice which Benn received was far from impartial, and his decision was influenced more by personal feelings than by the interests of the country, or of the Liberal Party. McKenna was one of Lloyd George's keenest critics (see Chapter 4) and probably the least likely of all the former Liberal ministers to have transferred his allegiance to the new prime minister. He and Benn's father also concluded that on a purely personal level, Benn 'would not be happy as Chief Whip'.[129] On the basis of this advice (and, it appears from the surviving records, this advice alone), Benn rejected the post of joint chief whip.

This one decision, perhaps above all others, could have changed the course of Liberal Party history. Had Benn accepted the position of chief whip and remained in the post, he could have provided a vital link between the Asquithians and the Coalition Liberals. He would then also have prevented Freddie Guest, probably the single most divisive figure in the disintegration of the party, from holding the post.[130] Instead, Benn continued his military career. In 1918 he refused to support the Coalition Liberals, but was elected for Leith against Coalition Conservative and Labour opposition. He looked forward to the demise of the coalition and the end of Lloyd George's premiership, gloating that there were 'plenty of heroes getting ready to dance on his corpse'.[131] Freddie Guest made sure that Lloyd George was in no doubt about this, writing to his chief about 'the evident fact that the Independent Liberals (inspired by Hogge and Benn) would not accept *any* terms of reunion'.[132]

Although Benn had a strong instinct for social reform from his knowledge of East End conditions as MP for Tower Hamlets from 1906 to 1918, it was not a foregone conclusion that his dissatisfaction with the Liberal Party would result in his joining Labour. As the Lloyd George Coalition was crumbling, Benn had even harboured thoughts of an alignment between the Asquithians and the Conservatives. He saw Bonar Law and said that he hoped that he was arranging 'a new Coalition with the Wee Frees' and would introduce a little 'ginger' into that 'effete' group.[133] There must have been a strong temptation for Benn to go in this direction: his closest parliamentary colleague, Reginald McKenna, eventually took this path. The tone of the correspondence between the two suggested a very strong bond of friendship and allegiance, with McKenna's writing to his 'beloved Wedgwood' and signing off 'Ever your affectionate R. McK'.[134] Further influence came from Benn's brother Ernest, who announced his intention of supporting the Conservatives. Benn held a fairly poor opinion of the Labour Party when it was in power in 1924, commenting in his diary that 'The Labour Party accept our help in the House, but . . . abuse us in our constituencies . . . making no attempt whatever to carry out the programme they advertised'. This deterred him from leaving the Liberals for the time being, although the thought had crossed his mind as early as February 1924. However, at that time he saw 'no point in abandoning the Party at this moment'. Benn remained in the Liberal Party while Asquith was still nominally the leader, but he had a realistically low expectation for the Liberals' performance at the 1924 election, seeing it as the 'suicide of the Liberal Party. [But] Perhaps it is better boldly to commit hara kiri than to await senile decay'. The result was even worse than he had imagined. After the election, at which Asquith lost his seat but Benn retained his, Benn went to the party meeting at the Reform Club, ready to oppose any move by Asquith to anoint Lloyd George as his successor in the Commons. He was unsure how much support he would get, but he had prepared a statement and was poised to deliver it:

> I thought the moment had arrived, and recapitulated my points mentally. Not a single word, however, about Ll.G . . . I felt like an anarchist with a bomb in his hand who learns that the route of the Royal procession has been altered.[135]

Instead, Benn resorted to a campaign against Lloyd George by telephone and in the press; having a letter published in the *Daily News*, offering the opinion: 'The people have no confidence, and rightly so, in Mr. Lloyd George.'[136] He received the support of George Thorne and McKenzie Livingstone, but confided that newspaper comment on his letter was 'universally critical and hostile', while letters from Leith showed very considerable differences of opinion. Benn visited his Leith constituency and noted the 'intense gloom' among Liberals and a 'steady almost overwhelming slide' to Labour. In the Commons he recorded the change of atmosphere: 'The relations between ourselves and Labour have completely changed. In place of the pin pricks and suspicions of the last parliament, there is a very warm feeling of friendship.' Benn organised a dinner for dissident Liberals opposed to Lloyd George including Thorne, Trevelyan Thomson, Percy Harris, Mrs Hopkin Morris (but not her husband, Rhys), Livingstone, Kenworthy and Crawfurd, at which Trevy Thomson raised the question as to 'whether or not we were an Opposition Party: a strange question to be raised in the Liberal Party under a Tory Government'. Relations with his constituency Liberal association declined after Benn sent them an open letter saying that he did not support Lloyd George as party leader. In February 1926 he was subject to a vote of censure by his local party. After the General Strike, Benn drafted a letter declaring Lloyd George 'unfit for leadership'. Kenworthy was unwilling to sign this because he was sympathetic to Lloyd George over the strike. Benn noted ruefully that the Parliamentary Liberal Party was being asked to pass a public vote of censure on Asquith, who had for forty years 'stood by Liberalism, not always, perhaps, going fast or far enough, but always down the straight road'. He asked what common ground there was between himself and Guest who had 'pleaded' for unity.[137] Ironically, Kenworthy, who usually opposed Lloyd George, supported him on the Strike, but still defected to Labour in October 1926, while Benn remained in the Liberal Party until the following January. In the meantime, Kenworthy had resigned his seat and won it back under Labour colours in the resulting by-election. Benn, a man of principle, felt that he would be honour-bound to resign his seat, if he too were to defect. The problem for Benn was that Leith already had a Labour candidate in place, whereas Kenworthy had not had a Labour opponent in any of his four previous elections in Hull. Benn resigned his seat, accepting that he would have to wait for another opportunity to return to the Commons. He wrote to his constituency Liberal association:

> The Country needs above all, an alternative to Conservatism. On which side Mr. Lloyd George's Party will use its strength after the next Election is not known. I firmly believe therefore that the Labour Party provides the only ... alternative ... This decision involves the honourable obligation to resign my seat. I have always considered that obligation as being unconditional; it has never been part of any bargain. The choice of a candidate rests with the Leith Labour Party ... Whoever is selected to advance the Labour Cause will have my goodwishes and support.[138]

Benn wrote sadly to Asquith, 'the only leader I have ever had',[139] and received the baleful reply: 'I regret more than I can say the decision which you have persuaded yourself to take.'[140] The Leith by-election, held on 23 March 1927, was won by Ernest Brown for the Liberals, but with a much reduced majority – down from over 5,000 to just 111. Benn had to wait until the following year to find an opportunity to stand for Labour; winning a comfortable by-election victory at Aberdeen North in August 1928, following the death of the sitting Labour MP. He held the seat with an increased majority in 1929 and joined MacDonald's second cabinet, as Secretary of State for India. On the formation of the National Government, Benn parted company from MacDonald; going down to a massive defeat at the hands of his Conservative opponent in Aberdeen North at the 1931 election. Benn eventually returned to the Commons in 1937 and, in 1942, was elevated to the Lords as first Viscount Stansgate. Having served as an air commodore in the Second World War, he was appointed Secretary of State for Air in the 1945 Labour Government. Benn's principles had led to his political career being disjointed, but nonetheless he achieved high office and served as a minister until the age of nearly seventy. He was taken ill in the House of Lords while waiting to speak, at the age of eighty-three, and died the following day. However, his political influence was to continue, as his death was the catalyst for a campaign by his Labour MP son, Tony, which led to the 1963 Peerage Act, allowing the renunciation of hereditary peerages.

Mackenzie Livingstone sat for the Western Isles as Liberal MP from 1923 to 1929, having previously narrowly lost twice in Inverness at the hands of a sole Coalition, then National, Liberal opponent. After Asquith's 1924 defeat, Livingstone, a strong supporter of his defeated leader, had tried to prevent Lloyd George's taking on the party leadership, proposing that 'until Mr. Asquith returns to the House of Commons or until the end of the session the Chief Whip do act as Chairman at the Party Meetings'.[141] In the Commons, Livingstone was a close associate of Kenworthy and Benn. By the time of the 1929 election, the latter two had left the Liberals, but Livingstone had stayed. Despite having a solid majority and having tolerated Lloyd George's leadership and policies for the preceding three years, Livingstone withdrew as a candidate for re-election less than a month before the 1929 election declaring:

> I have decided with great regret not to seek re-election . . . The chairman of the Parliamentary party has given to the country a definite pledge . . . to reduce unemployment in the course of a single year to normal proportions without adding one penny to the national or local taxation. I am . . . in complete sympathy with the policy of alleviating the bitter hardships of unemployment . . . but the promise given is one with which I am quite unable to associate myself, for I have grave doubts as to the possibility of its fulfilment . . . It may be that in the future an opportunity presents itself for further service.

Livingstone's resignation came as a total surprise to his local party, who regarded him as having 'dropped a bomb' into the Liberal camp. The constituency Liberal association responded by urgently asking party headquarters for the names of potential candidates who had to be 'in full sympathy with Mr. Lloyd George's policy and loyal to the party leader'.[142] Their wish was not entirely fulfilled. Thomas Ramsay, the defeated 1922 National Liberal candidate for Glasgow Shettleston was drafted in. He won the seat in 1929 and held it in 1931. However, on the formation of the National Government, he did not follow Lloyd George's lead; instead following Simon. Despite his veiled reference to an opportunity for 'future service', Livingstone never sought re-election under any party colours. However, he continued to be a thorn in the side of the Liberal Party, writing to *The Times* on 2 November 1929:

> The humiliation of the Liberal Party continues. It is once more being offered for sale to Mr. Lloyd George ... There is one step now clearly necessary to those who still claim the name of Liberal, and that is to sever all connexion with the present leadership of the party and to refuse to participate in a fund whose sinister origins can bring no credit to the party.

Livingstone became a supporter of National Labour and was knighted during the National Government, in 1933. He was not the only former Liberal to find his way into National Labour, and to be rewarded with a title or office.

MacDonald Supporter Careerists

The MacDonald Supporter Careerists tended to have successful careers outside politics and were not very party minded, or politically principled. They were influenced by their friendship with Ramsay MacDonald, flattered by his approaches and willing to take office under his leadership. In return they received rewards.

Sydney Arnold was elected as Liberal MP for Holmfirth (later Penistone) at a by-election in June 1912. He did not vote on the Registration Bill in 1915, but he opposed conscription and became increasingly out of step with the Liberal Party, to the point of becoming 'fanatically hostile' in his opposition to the Military Service Bill.[143] However, he stood again in the 1918 general election and was one of only four Liberal War Policy Objectors who retained their seats as Liberals. In 1921 Arnold resigned his seat on health grounds and the following year he joined the Labour Party, where he came to have a significant influence on policy through his relationship with MacDonald. Arnold did not stand again for the Commons, but was given a peerage on

12 February 1924 and served as parliamentary under-secretary for the Colonies in the first Labour Government. He accompanied MacDonald on a nationwide speaking tour leading up to the 1929 election. He was appointed Paymaster General in 1929, but resigned in March 1931, due, again, to ill-health. His influence over MacDonald was waning and Arnold felt neglected. Kenworthy observed the breach and afterward explained that Buxton, Ponsonby and Arnold all thought that they were in MacDonald's confidence and all were disillusioned. The Arnold case was typical. Arnold was considered 'the confidant ... and made no enemies. There was no breach, no quarrel'. MacDonald simply 'dropped' Arnold.[144] On the formation of the National Government, Arnold parted company from MacDonald. Later in the 1930s he became alienated over Labour foreign policy, which he thought made war more likely and he resigned his Labour Party membership in March 1938. However, the other MacDonald Supporter Careerists all followed MacDonald into the National Government.

By mid-November 1915 **Richard Denman** had fallen out with his local Liberal constituency association in Carlisle, where he had sat since January 1910. They passed a vote of no confidence in him and resolved to find an alternative candidate.[145] It was reported in the national press that the prominent UDC member and 'peace crank M.P. for Carlisle, has obtained a commission in the Royal Artillery'.[146] Denman did not contest his seat in 1918, but his war objections did not end his relationship with the Liberal Party. He stood again as a Liberal candidate in 1922 in Newcastle-upon-Tyne West and also in 1923, when he was invited back to re-contest his old seat of Carlisle, but finished bottom of the poll. During the Labour Government's first period of office he was Liberal candidate for Mid-Cumberland, but he later explained that the action of the Liberal Party in helping to 'turn out' the Labour Government ended his connection with his party, and that soon after that he joined the Labour Party.[147] At the 1924 election, he wrote to the local press to assert that 'the Liberal policy meant a determination at once to substitute a Conservative for a Labour Government. To that policy neither I nor thousands of other Liberals could be accessories. I could only fight as an Independent and my offer in that matter was not accepted'.[148] In December 1924 he explained that he had concluded that the Liberal Party's powers of 'preventing both Protection and Socialism, are exercised at the undue cost of hindering the fulfilment of its own positive aims'. 'My own conception of Liberalism forbids me to remain a member of a party more effective in prevention than in positive achievement.'[149] Denman served as Labour, and later National Labour, MP for Leeds Central from 1929 to 1945. He hesitated over supporting the National Government in 1931, but decided that he would give his backing, although he regretted 'more deeply than you will imagine a temporary severance from those whose fellowship in politics I have valued so highly. They will never find me in any other party'.[150] Denman's brother, the third Lord Denman, remained loyal to the Liberal Party throughout his career.

Ernest Lamb was another Liberal MP who left the Commons in 1918, but who then reappeared as a Labour peer in the 1930s. Lamb sat for Rochester, being elected at his first attempt in 1906 and retiring from the House of Commons at the 1918 general election. He appeared on Labour platforms in the 1924 and 1929 elections. He was elevated to the peerage in January 1931 and also followed MacDonald into the National Government, where he was much more active than some of his other co-defectors. Lamb took on the role of Paymaster-General from November 1931 to December 1935, although he had had no previous ministerial experience.

The most high-profile of the MacDonald Supporter Careerists was **William Jowitt**. He was a highly capable and ambitious lawyer, but in politics even he accepted that he lacked conviction. He was insecure, indecisive and sensitive. With nine older sisters, and a vicar for a father, Jowitt relied on external guidance when making major decisions. His first term in parliament was as Liberal MP for Hartlepool from 1922 to 1924. Even during this time his party allegiance seemed malleable. In March 1924 Jowitt wrote to Spears that if he were a voter in the Abbey Division, Churchill would almost certainly have his vote, but that he was 'dependent to such a large extent on the goodwill of the Labour voters in my constituency that I cannot express publicly what I have expressed privately to you'.[151] Less than a year later Jowitt was seeking reassurance and direction from Wedgwood Benn, who was then pondering his own defection. Benn recorded in his diary that Jowitt was 'tortured to know what to do'; 'he wants to join the Labour Party, but is afraid it would affect his briefs'.[152]

Jowitt lost his Hartlepool seat in 1924, but his request to fight Preston as a Liberal at the next election was granted and he was duly elected there in May 1929. However, he had already been sounded out two years earlier by his close friend Ramsay MacDonald about serving in a future Labour Government. Immediately after the 1929 election MacDonald asked Jowitt to serve as Attorney-General. After a painful interview with Lloyd George, Jowitt accepted. He received severe criticism from the bar and from all parties, and he and his wife were ostracised. Jowitt resigned his seat, causing a by-election, which he won under his new party colours on 31 July 1929, without any

Liberal opposition. He thus became the last of only three defectors who resigned his seat on changing party (all defectors to Labour) – the others being Benn and Kenworthy. The Liberals were therefore deprived of Kenworthy's Hull Central and Jowitt's Preston seats, as these defectors retained their old constituencies for Labour. Benn had not re-contested Leith and the by-election had been won by the Liberals, but with a much reduced majority. Even after Jowitt had made his decision to transfer to Labour, he continued to obsess about his lack of convictions. He wrote to Lord Buckmaster, pouring out his self-doubt, almost to the exclusion of commiserating with Buckmaster, who had just suffered the death of his daughter: 'I have tried for once to shew courage & unselfishness – I've funked it previously . . . I was feeling utterly wretched . . . I am much too sensitive to pretend I didn't mind.'[153] Jowitt confided: 'I could have wished the request to serve had never been made.'[154] Jowitt was once more tortured with indecision over the National Government. In the opinion of his friend Kenworthy, when the election of 1931 was called Jowitt should immediately have rejoined the Labour Party. For days he hesitated, commenting: 'My heart is in politics . . . I shall never be happy outside the House of Commons; and I know I have no future with the Tories'. Kenworthy believed that Jowitt 'just lacked the ultimate courage'. In the 1931 election, Jowitt did eventually stand as a National Labour candidate, for the Combined English Universities, although he had previously advocated the abolition of the university franchise. He was expelled from the Labour Party and defeated at the election. Jowitt, by his hesitation, also compromised his relationship with MacDonald, who temporarily adopted 'freezing tactics' towards him.[155] Reflecting on his situation in November 1931, Jowitt wished he had had 'some convictions'.[156] A year later MacDonald put pressure on the Conservative Party to find a seat for Jowitt, but without success. Jowitt tried to be re-admitted to the Labour Party before the 1935 election, writing to Lansbury to ask for re-instatement to the list of eligible candidates. Lansbury replied that the 'movement is more suspicious of middle class and professional people than ever before, but there is a real friendly feeling towards you and some others in some quarters though strong opposition in others . . . I do not think MacDonald Snowden Thomas and some others could or would come back'.[157] In 1936 Jowitt was readmitted to the Labour Party and in October 1939 he was re-elected in an unopposed by-election. He went on to reach the Lord Chancellorship in 1945 and to receive an earldom – his legal abilities outweighing his weak convictions.

George Croydon Marks, an engineer by profession, sat as a Liberal MP for Launceston, subsequently Cornwall North, from 1906 as 'generally a silent member', never making 'an outstanding speech'. After his eighteen years in the House of Commons ended in defeat in 1924, he provided a behind-the-scenes link between the Liberal Party and Ramsay MacDonald, with whom he had developed a close personal friendship. According to his biographer, after the election on 30 May 1929, Marks had a 'change of heart and he surprised many of his friends and former colleagues' by announcing that he was leaving the Liberals and joining the Labour Party. Without making any connection between the two events, the biography explains that 'on 11 July 1929 it was announced that Marks had been 'elevated to the Peerage on the recommendation of the new Prime Minister'.[158] It would be hard to imagine that the two events were unconnected, especially in view of the fact that the recipient had to confirm his willingness to accept the peerage. Marks justified himself to his local paper, using Jowitt's actions as a precedent:

> I can see no reason at all why Liberals of my way of thinking should remain outside in an impotent position when they could possibly be of great assistance in giving to Mr. MacDonald the support that he needs ... What Mr Jowitt has done is quite consistent with his attitude as a progressive Liberal ... I believe that the differences between Liberals of my way of thinking and the members of Mr. MacDonald's present Ministry are very slight.[159]

Marks was introduced to the Lords on 18 July 1929 by Lords Parmoor and Arnold. He accompanied MacDonald on a visit to Washington and Toronto in October of that year and, after their return, continued to act as a link between MacDonald and members of the Liberal Party. Marks remained loyal to MacDonald, literally to the bitter end and was there to meet MacDonald's body when it was returned to Plymouth, after his death at sea in 1937.

Willoughby Dickinson was an old Etonian barrister, elected in the 1906 Liberal landslide, for St Pancras North. He was an outspoken advocate of women's suffrage. He held the seat until his defeat in 1918, when he faced a Coalition Conservative opponent who claimed that, had Dickinson been a 'wholehearted supporter' of the Coalition Government, he would have withdrawn in his favour; but he found it impossible to do so after Dickinson voted against the government in the Maurice Debate.[160] Dickinson made one further attempt to regain his old seat as a Liberal in 1922, but he slipped to the bottom of the poll. Dickinson was elevated as a Labour peer in January 1930, and followed MacDonald on the formation of the National Government. He only ever played a very limited role in the upper house, speaking around twice a year. This was in sharp contrast to his frequent interventions during his period in the Commons, where he made over eighty speeches in his last year. Dickinson introduced Lamb to the Lords, when Lamb was created Lord Rochester the year after his own elevation, although Lamb had been a member of the Labour Party for six years before Dickinson had joined.

It is hard to discern anything other than personal advancement, in one form or another, as the motivating factor behind the defections of the MacDonald Supporter Careerists. Jowitt was the most able of the group, but even he, in common with all the others, almost certainly achieved, through defection, recognition beyond that merited by his talents. A personal attachment to Ramsay MacDonald opened up the opportunities, but in many cases that relationship did not endure.

Rightward Drift Objectors

The Rightward Drift Objectors were Liberal MPs and former MPs who objected to Clement Davies's leading the Liberal Party in a perceived rightward direction from the late 1940s to the mid-1950s. The first and most independent-minded of the Rightward Drift Objectors was **Tom Horabin**. Horabin was the Radical-Liberal victor in a bitterly contested by-election in July 1939. In four of the five pre-war by-elections of 1939 contested by the Liberals, including North Cornwall, the Liberals' share of the vote had actually increased, giving a (later to be extinguished) glimmer of hope to the beleaguered party.[161] During the war, Horabin was among a small minority of MPs prepared to criticise the government's policies in the Commons, despite his personal admiration for Churchill. This alienated Horabin from the Liberal leadership, but aligned him with Clement Davies, then on his way from the Liberal Nationals via a period as an independent before he re-joined the Liberals in 1942. By 1943 Davies's views were radically left-wing and he even went as far as proposing the formation of a new radical party, which he intended to lead, in opposition to Churchill.[162] Davies and Horabin developed a close working relationship and earned Violet Bonham Carter's opinion of them as 'lunatics and pathological cases'.[163] Davies and Horabin were associated with the Radical Action Group, along with Richard Acland, before his departure to Common Wealth. Acland's father had sat for North Cornwall until his death, which had occasioned the by-election, at which Horabin had been elected. In October 1944 Horabin published a book *Politics Made Plain: What the next general election will really be about* – a radical anti-Conservative polemic, urging an electoral arrangement between the Liberals, Labour and Common Wealth. Horabin's views placed him well to the left of Liberal thinking at the time, but they were not significantly divergent from Lloyd George's industrial policies of 1929. The 1945 election swept away all the leaders of the Liberal Party – Sinclair, Beveridge and Harris. Horabin and Davies were among the twelve survivors and Davies emerged as party leader. He appointed Horabin as chief whip. Ironically, in view of the later defections of the Rightward Drift Objectors, Davies set out a direction for the party, which former leader Sinclair considered to be dangerously close to 'outflanking Labour on the left'.[164] Perhaps this initial position raised false hopes among the more left-wing Liberal MPs, but as political reality set in, Davies appeared to move the party's position closer to that of the Conservatives. This was partly a reflection of the order in which Labour policies were enacted. Davies supported many of Labour's early nationalisation plans but, on pragmatic organisational grounds, opposed the nationalisation of the steel industry. This effectively moved the Liberal Party's position from one supporting Labour to one allying themselves with the Tories.[165] This was not the only practical reason why Davies appeared to move the party in a rightward direction. As the next general election approached, Davies was concerned to avoid contests with Conservatives wherever he could. Davies had a difficult task balancing the competing demands from the left and right wings of the party – and all the MPs could readily be categorised on one or other wing, rather than in the centre. In a small, polarised party liable to veer off in a different direction if given a hard enough tug on the tiller, individual MPs were tempted to flex their muscles. Davies was a weak leader in a difficult situation. He admitted that his position was one of 'almost supine weakness for if I give full expression to a definite course of action that at once leads to trouble and a threatened split'.[166] Horabin was not the first defector to leave the party under Davies's leadership. Gwilym Lloyd-George had been in the process of moving towards the Conservatives, almost by stealth since 1945 (see Chapter 4). However, Horabin's was the first leftward departure under Davies's tenure. There was no great personal rupture. Horabin resigned as chief whip in March 1946, writing to Davies that a whip 'is expected to be seen and not heard, and that is not in accordance with my temperament'. Lady Rhys-Williams, wife of Liberal defector Rhys Williams (see Chapter 4) and head of the Liberal Party's Publications and Publicity Committee resigned her post in protest at Horabin's increasingly left-wing pronouncements. In October 1946 Horabin wrote again to Davies, this time announcing that he would leave the Liberal Party, to sit as an independent Liberal. Just over a year later, in November 1947, he joined the Labour Party, writing to Attlee that 'there was no place . . .

for any party standing between ... Labour ... and the Tory Party'.[167] Once inside the Labour Party, Horabin gravitated to their left and was a signatory to the 1950 *Keeping Left* pamphlet. He did not want to fight against his Liberal former colleagues by contesting North Cornwall for Labour, so at the 1950 election he stood in Exeter, losing and ending his political career. Ironically, had Horabin remained in North Cornwall, his Liberal opponent would have been Dingle Foot, who later also defected from the Liberals to Labour in protest at the rightward drift.

Horabin's departure was an individual act, not coordinated with any of his colleagues. The other defections by the Rightward Drift Objectors did display signs of collusion and attempts, generally unsuccessful, at coordination. Horabin was also the only one of the Rightward Drift Objectors to defect whilst still in the Commons; the others had lost their seats before they defected.

Geoffrey Mander, a member of the family which owned the eponymous paint business, sat as Liberal MP for Wolverhampton East. From 1832 to 1945 the seat had only had four MPs – all Liberal, the last of whom was Mander, elected in 1929. It was one of the last urban Liberal strongholds. However, in 1945 the seat fell to Labour. Early in his parliamentary career, Mander had been approached by MacDonald, who had asked him: 'Are you coming over?' Mander's reaction at the time was that 'the question astonished me as I had no intention of deserting'. However, after Mander lost his seat in the 1945 Liberal debacle, his attitude changed and he felt that it became necessary for many Liberals, if they wished to remain in active politics, to decide which party they should join, advising:

> For a Right Wing Liberal the choice was easy, if they could describe themselves as Conservative, Tory, National Liberal Conservative, Liberal National Conservative, National, or any other combination of the words, with complete sincerity, but Liberals of the Left had no such engaging variety of adjectives to choose from. They had to be Labour and nothing else if they joined the Party.[168]

Between his defeat and his announcing his adherence to Labour in June 1948, Mander was wooed by the local Conservative Party with the offer of their standing aside in his favour, if he would adopt a hybrid party label, containing 'Liberal' and 'Conservative' or 'Unionist'. However, after a meeting of the East Wolverhampton Liberal Association in November 1947, Mander confirmed that he would not fight under any other name but Liberal.[169] Once this potential avenue of return to parliament had been closed off, Mander announced that he was joining Labour, commenting: 'when I joined the Labour Party, I did not find it necessary to alter in any way my view of politics. [I] had always found myself in general sympathy with its objectives'.[170] Sympathy was certainly not what Sinclair felt, when he heard a rumour of Mander's impending defection: 'A silly ass wrote to me the other day that you were joining the Labour Party! If the noise of my answering rocket should by any chance reach your ears, don't for a moment suspect me of taking him seriously!'[171] Mander's defection, once confirmed, did cause a rupture with Sinclair. Mander did not contest any further elections. In common with Richard Acland, Mander left his home at Whitwick Manor near Wolverhampton to the National Trust.

Of all the Liberal MPs since 1910, **Edgar Granville** was the most prolific defector and the longest-lived; he reached his hundredth birthday two days before he died.[172] Granville was elected as a Liberal in 1929, for Eye, became a Liberal National in 1931, returning to the Liberals in 1945 after a spell as an independent, only to defect to Labour in 1952, after he had lost his Commons seat. After being ennobled as a Labour peer, he continued his litany of defections in the Lords, leaving the Labour Party in the mid-1970s to sit as a crossbencher. Granville, together with Emrys Roberts and Megan Lloyd George, became increasingly at odds with Clement Davies during the 1945 to 1951 parliaments. On one occasion, Granville, Roberts and Lloyd George even voted against a Liberal Party amendment, to which all three had actually put their names. Granville justified their actions by arguing that the Liberal motion was being used as a 'cat's paw' by the Conservatives to bring down the Labour Government. Granville, Roberts and Megan Lloyd George all lost their seats at the 1951 election; perversely strengthening the position of Davies as leader of the Liberal Party, as his three harshest critics were removed from the parliamentary party. After his defeat, Granville quickly moved to join Labour, in January 1952, much to the chagrin of Megan Lloyd George, who was not consulted before his defection. Granville's change of party allegiance was smoother than that of most defectors, partly because he encouraged his local association only to operate for the six months before each polling day. He therefore had a fairly free hand to take his own political positions, without referring back to a committee during the course of each parliament. Granville stood in his old seat of Eye, for Labour, in the1955 general election. The Liberal vote slumped from 36.1% to 11.8%, while the Labour vote rose from 23.3% to 43.2%, suggesting that Granville received a large personal vote; he was only 889 votes short of beating the Conservative candidate. Granville made one further attempt to regain Eye, in 1959, but his margin of defeat widened. In 1967, he was elevated to the House of Lords by

Harold Wilson, and initially sat as a Labour peer, before becoming a cross-bencher during the 1970s.

David Lloyd George had predicted in 1938 that his son, Gwilym, would go to the right and his daughter, Megan, to the left. The two siblings waited until after their father's death before changing parties, but they did fulfil their father's prediction. **Megan Lloyd George**'s character contrasted strongly with that of her brother. While Gwilym was conciliatory and diplomatic, Megan was outspoken, robust, disorganised and bore grudges. She had persuaded Gwilym not to go to their father's second wedding (to Frances Stevenson). Like Granville, Megan Lloyd George was a Liberal MP from 1929 until her defeat in 1951. She sat for Anglesey. As a defensive tactic, to try to maintain her loyalty, Davies appointed Megan Lloyd George Deputy Leader of the Liberal Party in January 1949. The party had managed without a deputy leader before her appointment, and the size of the party (ten MPs) hardly warranted the additional position. The appointment was less than successful: on accepting the position, Lloyd George advocated that the party should adopt radical policies and shed 'our right wing'.[173] In her mind, the 'right wing' probably included her party leader. In 1951 Megan Lloyd George's radical group, the parliamentary remnant of Radical Action, was engaged in inconclusive talks with Labour MPs about a possible mass defection of radical Liberals to Labour.[174] Although she lost her seat in the 1951 general election, Lloyd George waited until April 1955 before defecting to Labour. She contributed to Labour's general election campaign that year, but did not stand herself. Her defection had been encouraged by Philip Noel-Baker, a Labour MP, with whom she had a long-term affair. Another factor weighing on the situation was that Megan was the only female Liberal MP at the time when there were few female MPs in the Commons – the majority of them being Labour members. Megan had therefore developed strong social links within the Labour Party. In November 1956, Rhys Hopkin Morris, one of then only six remaining Liberal MPs, died. Megan Lloyd George was adopted by Labour to stand in Carmarthen, the seat which Morris had held. Morris had been an outspoken critic of Megan's father throughout his parliamentary career, including his being the only MP who had dissented when David Lloyd George was proposed for the re-election to the party leadership in 1929. The selection of Megan Lloyd George to stand for Labour, in this previously Liberal-held seat, generated much animosity within her former party. A song including the line 'Lady Megan is a traitor' was later sung at Liberal Party conferences.[175] Megan Lloyd George won the Carmarthen by-election in February 1957 and held the set until her death in May 1966 – having been re-elected in the general election of that year, but having played no part in the campaign due to her suffering from terminal cancer. Megan's defection had deprived the Liberal Party of its last member of the Lloyd George family. However, the transfer was not a total success from her point of view. Noel-Baker broke off his relationship with Megan after the death of his wife and Megan was never entirely happy in her new party, where she did not play a prominent role and did not receive the hoped-for ministerial office in the 1964 Labour Government.

Within the Liberal Party Megan Lloyd George had been close to Dingle Foot, and there had been plans for Foot, Lloyd George and others to make a mass defection to Labour. However, Lloyd George had pre-empted the move by announcing her own defection, without coordinating her transfer with the others. Like Megan Lloyd George, **Dingle Foot** came from a prominent Liberal Family. His father Isaac sat as a Liberal MP and his brother John became a Liberal life peer. Another brother, Hugh, was also given a life peerage after serving as a diplomat. The third brother, Michael, became leader of the Labour Party. Dingle Foot was elected as Liberal MP for Dundee in 1931 and sat until his defeat in 1945. He made two further unsuccessful attempts to re-enter the House of Commons as a Liberal – in 1950 and 1951, in North Cornwall, despite the intense mutual dislike between Foot and party leader Davies. Although his close alliance with Megan Lloyd George failed to result in a concerted defection between them to Labour, Foot did coordinate his defection with Wilfrid Roberts, jointly writing with Roberts to Gaitskell in 1956:

> We have decided to join the Labour Party ... the Liberal leaders and members of Parliament have appeared incapable of pursuing any consistent theme save that they have shown fairly constant preference for voting with the Conservative Party. Indeed, since 1951 they have presented ... the extraordinary spectacle of a Liberal Parliamentary Party giving general support to a Tory Government ... It is merely an indication of the general drift to the right.[176]

Foot then followed in Megan Lloyd George's footsteps by returning to parliament as a Labour MP at a by-election in 1957 – in his case at Ipswich. Unlike Lloyd George, Foot's career did initially prosper within the Labour Party. Foot was appointed Solicitor-General in 1964, but he resigned over the Labour Party's policies on Rhodesia in 1967. In 1970 he lost his seat, after an election campaign in which he was clearly out of step with the Labour Party, particularly over the party's commitments to immigration restrictions. Even at the 1957 Ipswich by-election, Foot's views had stayed essentially Liberal; he supported the Common Market in principle, home ownership and House of Lords reform. Foot was always a radical, and never really a socialist. It is doubtful if he ever felt at home in the Labour Party. In 1976, Foot took as the theme for his one publication, *British Political Crises, the Collapse of the Liberal Party*, calling it the 'principal tragedy of British politics in modern times'.[177]

Wilfrid Roberts was the one former Liberal MP who did coordinate his defection with Foot. Roberts won Cumberland North for the Liberals in 1935, in the absence of a Labour opponent. He held the seat in a straight fight with a Conservative in 1945, by a wafer-thin margin of 198 votes. Roberts would have been Sinclair's choice as chief whip, had Sinclair retained his seat and the party leadership in 1945.[178] Roberts had a reasonable claim to the party leadership in 1945 – having served for ten years as a Liberal MP and having been Sinclair's parliamentary private secretary, while the latter was serving as Secretary of State for Air in the wartime coalition. Instead, Clement Davies was chosen. The fact that seven of the twelve Liberal MPs elected in 1945 sat for Welsh seats may well have been the decisive factor in favour of Davies, the Montgomeryshire MP. Also, as Davies was a much older candidate (Davies was sixty-one compared to Roberts' forty-four), this probably meant that the younger MPs saw Davies only as a short-term stand-in leader, who would create an opportunity for a successor in the not-too-distant future. Roberts therefore had reason to feel overlooked for preferment. His political views encouraged his association with the other disaffected left-wingers Megan Lloyd George and Edgar Granville. Roberts lost his seat in 1950 and joined Labour at the same time as Dingle Foot, in July 1956. Roberts contested Hexham for Labour in 1959, but was unsuccessful and played no further part in national politics.

For the Rightward Drift Objectors, their very defection caused the party to move to the right, by removing the more left-wing members. The departure of the Rightward Drift Objectors by 1956 marked the end of any pattern of defections from the Liberals to Labour. In over half a century since then only two other MPs have defected from the party to Labour: one was an inward defector from Labour only four years previously, Paul Marsden (see Chapter 6); the other was Bill Pitt, in 1996.

Bill Pitt was the first Liberal-SDP Alliance by-election victor, in October 1981. In fact the Alliance was one stop on a political journey which took Pitt from the Conservatives, via the Alliance to Labour. He was chairman of the South Norwood Young Conservatives during 1959/60, but joined the Liberal Party in the 1960s. He first stood as a

Liberal candidate in February 1974 in Croydon North West – the seat which he would eventually win at the 1981 by-election. His adoption for the by-election was resisted by the SDP, but Pitt was selected and won the seat. However, the row over the candidature presaged serious rifts right up to the leadership of the Alliance. At the following general election Pitt lost his seat to the Conservatives by a margin of over 4,000 votes. Reflecting later on the situation, Pitt observed that in 1981 'we knocked the Tories off their perch' and boasted that we had 'gone home to prepare for government'. 'Just under two years later, the Tories regained the seat and the government had not been budged an inch, in fact it took another 14 years to get rid of them. Byelections are more often than not protests, not declarations of future intent.'[179] Pitt's defection was low key; he was then out of parliament and his party leader at the time was not even aware of it until thirteen years later.[180] In 1987, Pitt stood against the Conservative Jonathan Aitken in Thanet South, under the Alliance banner. The 1992 election was a repeat contest with Aitken, but Pitt, standing for the Liberal Democrats dropped from second to third place. In November 1996, disillusioned with the party, Pitt resigned as chairman of the Thanet South Liberal Democrat Association and joined the Labour Party.[181] Still determined to unseat Jonathan Aitken, Pitt campaigned for Labour in Thanet South and saw his old adversary defeated by a swing of 15% to Labour. Pitt was the last defector from the Liberals/Liberal Democrats to Labour between 1910 and 2010.

In December 1910, when the Liberal Party was in power, cohesive and with Labour as its junior partner under the Gladstone-MacDonald Pact, the likelihood of a large number of defections from the Liberals to Labour had seemed very remote. Yet, in total forty-seven Liberal MPs and former MPs made this move in the ensuing century, with forty-five of them transferring between 1918 and 1956; Pitt and Marsden were the two outlying later examples. For over half of the Liberal MPs and former MPs who defected to Labour, their move was not a success. Some of the dissatisfaction can be attributed to the difficulty for the former Liberals of assimilating themselves socially into Labour circles, where a culture of trade unionism, strict party discipline, dogged commitment in adversity and, in many cases, poverty, predominated. Many of the former Liberals, generally from wealthy professional backgrounds, found it difficult to make friends with, and to be trusted by, their Labour colleagues. Of the forty-five who had made the transition to Labour by 1956, twenty-four (53%) either left the Labour Party or became seriously dissatisfied with their new party.[182] Two (Alden and Garro-Jones) defected back to the Liberals; two defected on to the

Liberal Nationals (Ellis Davies and Alexander); five became National Labour and did not return to the Labour Party (Denman, Lamb, Marks, Dickinson and Livingstone); eight became independent or independent Labour (Money, Ponsonby, Trevelyan, Arnold, Acland, Granville, White and Wedgwood); seven remained in the Labour Party but were seriously dissatisfied (Scott, Foot, Fletcher, John, Outhwaite, Malone and Noel-Buxton). As most of the defectors had been motivated to transfer their allegiance by the problems of the Liberal Party, rather than the attractions of Labour, the level of later discontent was, perhaps, not surprising. However, the experiences of the Liberal defectors to the Conservatives contrast strongly with this, as Chapter 4 reveals.

Notes

1 Simon to Lincolnshire, 2 December 1926, quoted in Hart 'Decline', p. 103.
2 Excludes Independent Labour candidates, includes Lib-Lab candidates as Liberals.
3 *Daily Herald*, 3 and 4 July 1912.
4 Harris, Sally, *Out of Control: British Foreign Policy and the Union of Democratic Control, 1914–1918* (University of Hull Press, 1996), pp. 27–9.
5 MacDonald had inherited the income from his late wife's trust fund.
6 Marquand, David, *Ramsay MacDonald* (Cape, 1977), pp. 169, 206 and 227.
7 Webb diary, 22 April 1914, quoted in Swartz, Marvin, *The Union of Democratic Control in British Politics during the First World War* (Clarendon, 1971), p. 19.
8 C.P. Scott memoranda, 3 and 4 September 1914, quoted Swartz, *UDC*, p. 29.
9 *Webb diaries, 1912–24*, quoted Cline, Catherine Ann, *Recruits to Labour* (Syracuse University Press, 1963), p. 9.
10 Draft letter Trevelyan to Bichnell, n.d., quoted Morris, A.J.A., *C.P. Trevelyan: Portrait of a Radical* (Blackstaff, 1977), pp. 126–7.
11 *Nation*, 2 October 1915, quoted Johnson, Matthew, 'The Liberal War Committee and the Liberal Advocacy of Conscription in Britain, 1914–1916', *Historical Journal* (2008): 51, 399–420.
12 Also Charles Lyell, Liberal MP for Edinburgh South, resigned after being wounded and died in 1918.
13 MacDonald diary, 9 September 1917, MacDonald Papers, National Archives, Kew.
14 Ponsonby to Trevelyan, 30 March 1918, quoted Swartz, *UDC*, p. 203.
15 MacDonald diary, 27 June 1917 and 27 December 1917.
16 Pelling, H., 'Labour and the Downfall of Liberalism' in Pelling, *Popular Politics and Society in Late Victorian Britain* (London, 1968), p. 120.

17 Bentley, Michael, *The Climax of Liberal Politics: British Liberalism in Theory and Practice, 1868–1918* (Edward Arnold, 1987), p. 124.
18 Dutton, David, *A History of the Liberal Party* (Palgrave, 2004), p. 55.
19 Hart, 'Decline', pp. iv and 92.
20 *Brighouse Echo*, 27 November 1914, quoted in Morris, *Trevelyan*, pp. 128–9.
21 Trevelyan to Ponsonby, 22 November 1914, Ponsonby Papers, Ms Eng. hist. c.661/134, Bodleian Library.
22 Handwritten note, Trevelyan, n.d., c.667/176–7, Ponsonby Papers.
23 Trevelyan to Robert Trevelyan, 15 November 1917, quoted Morris, *Trevelyan*, p. 139.
24 *Leeds Mercury*, 30 November 1918, p. 5, col. c.
25 Notes, Trevelyan, October 1915, quoted Morris, *Trevelyan*, p. 133.
26 Trevelyan, Charles, *From Liberalism to Labour* (Allen & Unwin, 1921), pp. 19–26.
27 Trevelyan to MacDonald, 6 January 1924, RMD/1/14/79, 23 February 1931, RMD/1/14/81 and 19 February 1931, RMD/1/14/80, MacDonald Papers, John Rylands University Library, University of Manchester.
28 MacDonald diary, 22 February 1931.
29 Unsent draft, MacDonald to Trevelyan, 28 February 1931, RMD/1/14/83, MacDonald Papers.
30 Morris, A.J.A., 'Trevelyan, Sir Charles Philips, third baronet (1870–1958)', *Oxford Dictionary of National Biography* (hereafter ODNB).
31 Trevelyan to Ponsonby, 7 November 1931, c.672/116, 28 August 1918, c.667/87–8, 12 November 1915, c.663/159, Ponsonby Papers.
32 Robertson to Ponsonby, 27 March 1915, c.662/50–2, Ponsonby Papers.
33 Gulland to Ponsonby, 17 August 1915, c.663/36, Ponsonby Papers.
34 Ponsonby to Gulland, 29 August 1916, c.665/16, Ponsonby Papers.
35 Ponsonby to Robertson, 10 January 1917, c.666/15–20, Ponsonby Papers.
36 MacDonald diary, 14 April 1918.
37 MacDonald to Ponsonby, n.d., c.667/103, Ponsonby Papers.
38 Jones, R.A., 'Ponsonby, Arthur Augustus William Harry, first Baron Ponsonby of Shulbrede (1871–1946), ODNB.
39 Draft Ponsonby to MacDonald, 27 August 1931, c.672/100, Ponsonby Papers.
40 *The Times*, 18 December 1914.
41 Outhwaite, R.L., *The Land or Revolution* (Allen and Unwin, 1917), p. 1.
42 *Wiltshire Gazette*, 5 December 1918, p. 7, col. c.
43 *Hansard*, 5 July 1915.
44 *Leeds Mercury*, 4 December 1918, p. 8, col. a.
45 Dutton, David, 'One Liberal's War: Richard Durning Holt and Liberal Politics, 1914–1918', *Journal of Liberal Democrat History*, 36 (2002): 6.
46 Whitehouse to Lloyd George, 16 September 1915, LG/D/1/2/20, Lloyd George Papers, Parliamentary Archives.
47 UDC pamphlet, quoted Dowse, Robert, 'The Entry of the Liberals into the

Labour Party 1910–20', *Bulletin of Economic Research*, 13(2), November 1961: 83.
48 *Doncaster Chronicle*, 22 November 1918, p. 2, col. g and p. 3, col. f, 6 December 1918, p. 3, col. e and p. 8, col. d and 13 December 1918, p. 3, col. a.
49 Lees-Smith to press, June 1919, DLS/1, Lees-Smith Papers, University of Hull.
50 John to Simon, 15 January 1916, 1564, E.T. John Papers, National Library of Wales.
51 John to Evans, 15 January 1916, 1561 and 4 November 1918, 2022, E.T. John Papers.
52 John to Williams, 4 November 1918, 2025, E.T. John Papers.
53 Daunton, Martin, 'Money, Sir Leo Chiozza (1870–1944)', ODNB.
54 Money, Leo, *The Triumph of Nationalization* (Cassell, 1920), p. vii.
55 Money to Lloyd George, 14 November 1918, LG/F/35/2/86, Parliamentary Archives.
56 Unpublished autobiography, Money, ADD 9259/1, University Cambridge Library, pp. 298–320.
57 Money to Lloyd George, 11 December 1933, enclosing letter to Home Secretary, 8 December 1933, LG/G/14/10/22, Parliamentary Archives.
58 Nicholls, Mark, Introduction to Chiozza Money Papers, Cambridge University Library.
59 Morris, *Trevelyan*, p. 131.
60 Wedgwood, C.V., *The Last of the Radicals* (Cape, 1951), pp. 88–158.
61 Dowse, 'Entry of the Liberals into the Labour Party', p. 84.
62 Shawcross, *The Times*, Obituary, 28 May 1948, p. 7, col. f.
63 *The Times*, 19 March 1921, p. 4, col. d, 14 June 1921, p. 5, col. g and 29 July 1922, p. 4, col. b.
64 *The Times*, 4 December 1934, p. 11, col. b.
65 *Crewe and Nantwich Observer*, 14 October 1922, p. 5, col. d.
66 Malone, letter to *The Times*, 26 July 1919, p. 8, col. b.
67 *Walthamstow, Leyton and Chingford Guardian*, 6 August 1920, p. 5, cols d–e.
68 MacCallum Scott diary, 1928, 10 January 1928, Ms Gen 1465/25, MacCallum Scott Papers, University of Glasgow Library Special Collections.
69 Communist Party of Great Britain, www.cpgb.org.uk, accessed 6 September 2008.
70 Cook, C., *A Short History of the Liberal Party, 1900–97* (Macmillan, 1998), p. 85.
71 *The Times*, 31 July 1923, p. 6, col. g.
72 *Newcastle Weekly Chronicle*, 17 October 1931, p. 7, col. a, *Evening Chronicle*, 19 October 1931, p. 5, col. a and 21 October 1931, p. 6, col. b.
73 Jones to Davies, 18 October 1934, Ellis Davies Papers, 28/15.
74 Jones to Davies, 23 December 1934, Ellis Davies Papers, 28/16.
75 Among them Acland, Richard, *Unser Kampf* (Penguin, 1940).

76 Acland to Lloyd George, 12 February 1944, LG/G/1/3/14, Lloyd George Papers.
77 Bennett, G.H., 'The Wartime Political Truce and Hopes for Post War Coalition: The West Derbyshire By-election, 1944', *Midland History* (1992): 118–35.
78 Two others, Bill Pitt and Paul Marsden, defected after 1956.
79 Griffiths, C.V.J., 'Buxton, Noel Edward Noel-, first Baron Buxton (1869–1948)', ODNB.
80 Anderson, Mosa, *Noel Buxton, A Life* (Allen & Unwin, 1952), pp. 103–6. 'Charlie' could refer to his brother, Charles Roden Buxton, or to his friend, Charles Trevelyan, both of whom made the same move before Noel Buxton.
81 Kenworthy, Joseph, *Sailors, Statesmen: and Others* (Rich and Cowan, 1933), p. 283.
82 MacDonald diary, 30 June 1918, 7 July 1918 and 12 April 1919.
83 Webb, *Our Partnership,* quoted Matthew, H.C.G., 'Haldane, Richard Burdon, Viscount Haldane (1865–1928)', ODNB.
84 Haldane, Richard Burdon, *An Autobiography* (Hodder & Stoughton, 1929), pp. 287.
85 Matthew, quoting Sommer, D., *Haldane of Cloan* (1960), 352.
86 Haldane to Asquith, 16 January 1922, MS.5915.133, Haldane Papers, National Library of Scotland.
87 Addison to Lloyd George, 14 July 1921, LG/F/1/6/30 and Lloyd George to Addison, 14 July 1921, LG/F/6/31, Lloyd George Papers.
88 Isaac to Addison, 18 December 1922, quoted Hart, 'Decline', 201.
89 Henderson to Addison, 13 November 1923, c.203/27 and Addison to Henderson, 19 November 1923, c.203/20, Addison Papers, Bodleian Library, University of Oxford.
90 *New Leader*, 30 November 1923, c.203/101, Addison Papers.
91 *Liverpool Evening Express*, 21 November 1923, c.203/29, Addison Papers.
92 MacDonald to Addison, 24 November 1923, c.203/80, Addison Papers.
93 Lloyd George to Addison, 13 May 1937, LG/G/4/11, Lloyd George Papers.
94 Owen, Frank, *Tempestuous Journey* (Hutchinson, 1954), pp. 684 and 691.
95 Cooper, Kathleen, 'The Political and Military Career of Major-General J.E.B. Seely, 1868–1947', Southampton, M.Phil., 2001.
96 Scott to Paterson, 23 November 1922, MS Gen 1465/420, MacCallum Scott Papers, University of Glasgow Library Special Collections.
97 Scott diary, 6 February 1924 and 18 October 1924, MS Gen 1465/15, MacCallum Scott Papers.
98 Scott to Pethwick Lawrence, 16 November 1924, MS Gen 1465/423, MacCallum Scott Papers.
99 Scott to Asquith, 29 November 1924, *The Times*, 6 December 1924, p. 24, col. c.
100 Scott to MacDonald, 5 December 1924, MS Gen 1465/378, MacCallum Scott Papers.

101 Scott diary, 29 December 1924, 11 January 1925, 16 January 1925, 18 December 1925 and 26 December 1925.
102 Spero to Asquith, *The Times*, 23 April 1925, p. 12, col. g.
103 Kenworthy, *Sailors*, pp. 148, 160 and 213.
104 Kenworthy to Collins with attached letter to Chairman of Central Hull Liberal Association, 23 October 1926, LG/G/5/1/12, Lloyd George Papers.
105 Kenworthy, *Sailors*, pp. 220–2.
106 Kenworthy to Lloyd George, 23 October 1926, LG/G/31/1/44, Lloyd George Papers.
107 *Manchester Guardian*, 25 October 1926, LG/H/234, Lloyd George Papers.
108 Kenworthy, *Sailors*, 281–9.
109 *Buchan Observer*, 14 May 1929, p. 6, col. b, 8 October 1929, p. 5, col. b and 20 October 1931, p. 2, col. d.
110 *The Times*, 6 November 1929, p. 14, col. g, 9 October 1952, p. 6, col. f and 28 September 1960, p. 18, col. c.
111 Bulmer-Thomas, I., 'Fletcher, Reginald Thomas Herbert, Baron Winster (1885–1961)', ODNB.
112 Barnes to Guest, 21 November 1919, LG/F/21/4/21, Lloyd George Papers.
113 Draft letter [probably Guest], 12 Downing St, for Lloyd George to Barnes, 29 November 1919, LG/F/21/4/23(a), Lloyd George Papers.
114 Unnamed newspaper report, n.d., LG/F/168/2/11, Lloyd George Papers.
115 Barnes to Hogge, 21 November 1919, LG/F/21/4/21(a), Lloyd George Papers.
116 *Newcastle Weekly Chronicle*, 19 October 1935, p. 7, col. a.
117 Barnes, Harry, *The Slum: its Story and Solution* (King, 1931).
118 Stocks, M., *Ernest Simon of Manchester* (Manchester University Press, 1963), pp. 61, 76 and 124–5.
119 Morris-Jones diary, 21 July 1930, quoted Dutton, David, *Liberals in Schism* (Tauris, 2008), p. 22.
120 Hyde, H. Montgomery, *Strong for Service* (Allen, 1968), pp. 108–17.
121 Janner, Greville, *To Life!* (Sutton, 2006), 4–5; *Leicester Mercury*, 26 July 1945, p. 7, cols b–c.
122 Lloyd George to Benn (part missing), 8 December 1916, ST/24/1/1, Stansgate Papers, Parliamentary Archives.
123 Benn to McKenna, 8 December 1916, ST/24/1/5, Stansgate Papers.
124 Benn to his father, 9 December 1916, ST/24/1/6, Stansgate Papers.
125 McKenna to Benn, 10 December 1916, ST/24/1/2, Stansgate Papers.
126 Benn to Lloyd George, 10 December 1916, ST/24/1/7, Stansgate Papers.
127 Benn's father to Benn, 11 December 1916, ST/24/1/8, Stansgate Papers.
128 Benn's father to Benn, 16 December 1916, ST/24/1/9, Stansgate Papers.
129 McKenna to Benn, 31 December 1916, ST/24/3/1, Stansgate Papers.
130 Guest succeeded Primrose, who was chief whip for less than three months, after Benn's rejection.

131 Benn diary, 14 March 1922, Stansgate Papers.
132 Memorandum, Guest to Lloyd George, 13 March 1919, LG/F/21/3/9, Lloyd George Papers.
133 Benn diary, 20 March 1922.
134 McKenna to Benn, 31 December 1916, ST/24/3/1, Stansgate Papers.
135 Benn diary, 11 March 1924, 19 February 1924, 8 October 1924, 10 November 1924 and 13 November 1924.
136 *Daily News*, 14 November 1924.
137 Benn diary, 20 November 1924, 26 October 1925, 25 November 1925, 2 December 1924, 16 December 1924 and 16 February 1926.
138 Draft letter, Benn to Munro, n.d., probably January 1927, ST/85/1, Stansgate Papers.
139 Benn to Asquith, 4 January 1927, ST/85/3/251, Stansgate Papers.
140 Asquith to Benn, 11 February 1927, ST/85/3/252, Stansgate Papers.
141 Livingstone to Collins, 27 November 1924, LG/G/5/1/7, Lloyd George Papers.
142 *Stornoway Gazette and West Coast Advertiser*, 3 May 1929, p. 5, col. e and 10 May 1929, p. 5, col. a.
143 Guest to Lloyd George, 8 March 1919, LG/F/3/5, Lloyd George Papers.
144 Kenworthy, *Sailors*, p. 283.
145 *Carlisle Journal*, 16 November 1915, temporary box no 1, folder E, Sir Richard Denman Papers, Bodleian Library.
146 *Daily Express*, 1 December 1915, temporary box no 1, folder E, Denman Papers.
147 Denman, election address, May 1929, temporary box no. 1, folder F, Denman Papers.
148 Denman to *Mid Cumberland and Westmorland Herald*, 21 October 1924, temporary box no. 4, folder 4(5), Denman Papers.
149 Denman to *Carlisle Journal*, 8 December 1924 (wrongly dated 1944), temporary box no. 5, folder 4(8), Denman Papers.
150 *The Times*, 11 September 1931, p. 12, col. g.
151 Jowitt to Spears, 10 March 1924, quoted Hart, 'Decline', p. 233.
152 Benn diary, 27 January 1925.
153 Jowitt to Buckmaster, 11 June 1929, JOW/1/3, Jowitt Papers, Parliamentary Archives.
154 Jowitt to Somervell, 10 June 1929, JOW/1/3, Jowitt Papers.
155 Kenworthy, *Sailors*, pp. 282–3.
156 Legg, T.S. and Legg, M-L., 'Jowitt, William Allen, Earl Jowitt (1885–1957)', ODNB.
157 Lansbury to Jowitt, 24 September 1935, JOW/1/4, Jowitt Papers.
158 Lane, Michael, *Baron Marks of Woolwich* (Quiller, 1986), pp. 114–22.
159 *Cornish Times*, 21 June 1929, p. 8, col. c.
160 *The Times*, 10 December 1918, p. 10, col. e.
161 Reynolds, Jaime and Hunter, Ian, 'Liberal Class Warrior', *Journal of Liberal Democrat History*, 28 (2000): 18.

162 Davies to his son, Stanley, 3 November 1943, C/1/16, Clement Davies Papers, National Library of Wales.
163 Pottle, Mark, *Champion Redoubtable: The Diaries and Letters of Violet Bonham Carter 1914–45* (Weidenfeld & Nicolson, 1998), 294.
164 Sinclair to Samuel, 9 August 1945, SAM/A/155/11, Samuel Papers, Parliamentary Archives.
165 Labour MPs Alfred Edwards and Ivor Bulmer-Thomas defected to the Conservatives over the issue.
166 Davies to Murray, 11 May 1950, J/3/26, Clement Davies Papers.
167 *The Times*, 21 March 1946, p. 4 and 19 November 1947, p. 2.
168 Mander, autobiographical notes, B/4, Mander Papers, National Trust, Whitwick Manor.
169 Minutes, East Wolverhampton Liberal Association, 7 November 1947, B/5, Mander Papers.
170 Mander, autobiographical notes, B/4, Mander Papers.
171 Sinclair to Mander, 15 May 1947, B/3, Mander Papers.
172 The oldest of all the Liberal MPs since 1910 was Theodore Taylor, who never defected. He lived to 102 years of age.
173 Wyburn-Powell, A., *Clement Davies: Liberal Leader* (Politico's, 2003), p. 175.
174 Egan, Mark, 'The Grass-roots Organisation of the Liberal Party, 1945–64', Oxford, D.Phil. (2000), p. 179.
175 Conversation with author, David Alexander, 18 December 2006.
176 Roberts, Foot and Hopkins to Gaitskell, *The Times*, 10 July 1956, p. 10, col. d.
177 Foot, Dingle, *British Political Crises* (Kimber, 1976).
178 Sinclair to Samuel, 9 August 1945, SAM/A/155/11, Samuel Papers.
179 Pitt to *Guardian*, 27 May 2008, p. 29.
180 Interview, Ashdown, 10 September 2009, in which the author broke the news to Ashdown.
181 *Guardian*, 5 November 1996, p. 2.
182 Others such as Jowitt were also temporarily seriously dissatisfied.

4
Liberal defectors to the Conservatives

> Trevy Thomson ... raised the question as to whether or not we were an Opposition Party: a strange question to be raised in the Liberal Party under a Tory Government.[1]

This chapter considers all the defectors who left the Liberal/Liberal Democrat Party to join the Conservatives during the hundred years covered by this study. The defectors are studied by grouping, according to their reasons for defection, as described at the end of Chapter 2. Figure 2.3 gives an overview of the membership of each grouping.

No Liberal defectors went to the Conservatives between December 1910 and October 1922. The leftward-headed War Policy Objectors, discussed in Chapter 3, had begun to part company from the Liberal Party even before the formation of the Asquith Coalition and primarily because of their severance from the party at constituency level. Although the Lloyd George Coalition caused great resentment among sections of the Liberal Party, no Liberal MP had defected from the party as a direct result of the Lloyd George Coalition by the time of its demise in October 1922.

However, the Lloyd George Coalition did have serious indirect effects on the future outflow of defectors from the Liberals, for two reasons. First, the electoral consequences of the split in the Liberal Party damaged its performance and cost it seats. Many constituencies were left with a Labour candidate unchallenged by any Liberal. Secondly, Coalition Liberals had the opportunity to establish working relationships with Conservatives, and this led to moves for fusion of the two parties.

Bonar Law supporters – Third Coalitionists

The first of the defectors to the Conservatives made their moves in 1922. In contrast to the majority of the former Liberals who went to the Conservatives, the first two – Reginald McKenna and Ronald Munro-Ferguson (Viscount Novar) – were anti-coalitionists. They were to become the first of eight Asquithians to defect to the Conservatives.[2]

Reginald McKenna was offered, and negotiated about, the position of Chancellor of the Exchequer under two Conservative prime ministers – Bonar Law and Baldwin. McKenna had already served as Chancellor in the Asquith Coalition, and in the process, some Liberals argued that he had defected ideologically from Liberalism by his introduction of the McKenna Duties in 1915.[3] His adherence to the Asquithian wing of the Liberal Party was not in doubt during the war. He was an opponent of conscription, but on economic grounds, rather than pacific. On the ethics of conscription he made no comment. McKenna became an implacable adversary of Lloyd George and the coalition – more the expected background of a defector to Labour than to the Conservatives. Lloyd George complained to Beaverbrook that he had 'only to make a proposal for McKenna to oppose it'. McKenna regarded Lloyd George as a kind of 'pest in council – never helpful, always running down other people's departments'.[4] McKenna's closest friend in the Liberal Party was Wedgwood Benn, whom he had advised not to serve under Lloyd George. McKenna had also withdrawn his own services, telling Benn:

> My beloved Wedgwood . . . I am glad to be relieved of responsibility . . . I had a meeting of my Executive and found the most perfect good feeling. As yet there is no candidate against me . . . Ever your affectionate R. McK.[5]

McKenna fought, but lost, his seat in 1918, coming third behind the Labour victor and a Coalition Conservative. After the war no cabinet was large enough to contain McKenna and Lloyd George. Lloyd George believed that the antipathy arose when McKenna was appointed temporarily to succeed him at the Treasury and that the possibility of his return made McKenna a 'bitter enemy'. McKenna, according to Lloyd George, divided his colleagues into those he liked and those whom he viewed with distrust, suspicion or jealousy. This made him a source of weakness and distraction. His was the 'most active personal element in the disintegration of the Asquith Coalition.'[6] However, Ramsay MacDonald had been told later in the war that Lloyd George had offered the Foreign Office to Asquith and office to McKenna, but they had declined.[7] McKenna, instead, took up a directorship, then later the chairmanship, of the Midland Bank. After the fall of the Lloyd George Coalition, but before the 1922 election, possibly in the hope of establishing an alliance with the Asquithian Liberals, Bonar Law offered McKenna the chancellorship. His friend Benn had earlier discussed a possible alliance with Bonar Law. McKenna engaged in specific, documented, publicly debated, but ultimately abortive negotiations to serve as Chancellor of the Exchequer in a Conservative Government. Thus, although McKenna never acknowledged that he made a political defection, his actions can be construed otherwise. Even after his retirement, McKenna continued to call himself a 'Liberal'; but to the charge of trading with his political enemies he did not offer the defence that the Liberal Party had left him, not he the Liberal party. He was certainly judged by others at the time to have changed party allegiance. After his first appearance on a Conservative platform three weeks before the 1922 election, the South Edinburgh Unionists wrote eagerly to say that reports of McKenna's appearance at a City of London Conservative & Unionist Association meeting had been 'read with very great interest here. [We wonder] whether you would be prepared ... to come forward for the constituency'.[8] And a Liberal former admirer complained:

> [M]y political idol has fallen!!! I find it impossible to believe you have abandoned ... Liberal principles [by] appearing on a ... Tory platform ... you 'have backed the wrong horse'.[9]

McKenna argued that he did not intend to serve as a Conservative minister, instead seeing himself as a 'technical man called in to do a job of work.'[10] McKenna claimed to have no intention of being absorbed into the Unionist Party and, if by taking office under Bonar Law, he had helped to form a third coalition, the party which he would have brought to it would have been a party of one. In December 1916 Lloyd George had persuaded Balfour to become a 'living bridge' over which the Tory ex-ministers from the first coalition could 'march with dignity' into the second. McKenna could have constituted a bridge for the Liberal ex-ministers from the first coalition to join a third. The 'latest and greatest of all coalitions' claimed the jesting Edwin Montagu: 'Reggie McKenna and the Tory Party'.[11] However, in the event, McKenna declined the offer of the Exchequer in 1922, as he doubted that Bonar Law would win the election. He did not contest a seat himself at that election. Baldwin issued the second invitation when he became prime minister in 1923, and McKenna was prepared to accept it under certain conditions. One was that he needed time to recover fully from a bout of paratyphoid. Another, which proved to be a stumbling block, was that McKenna wanted to be returned to parliament at an unopposed by-election for a Conservative seat. Baldwin was still temporarily covering the Exchequer himself, but wanting to relinquish the post. Eventually McKenna wrote to Baldwin conceding that his conditions were unlikely to be met:

> When you invited me ... to join your Government ... we both hoped that a seat ... would be available without the arduous labours of an ordinary by-election ... I understand ... that no vacancy of the kind ... is likely to occur ... I have no option but to beg you to release me from my conditional promise to accept the office.[12]

McKenna's reasons for not accepting appear contrived. Hoare had even offered that if there was any difficulty in finding an opportunity for McKenna 'I am always prepared to drop out or to fit in'.[13] Hoare presumably had in mind relinquishing his safe seat at Chelsea, in return for a peerage. Baldwin missed the opportunity to persuade the diehards to find McKenna a seat. Sir Frederick Banbury, one of the two Conservative MPs for the City of London, refused to retire. One after another all Conservative electoral doors were closed against him.[14] Another complication was that, even had Banbury resigned, there was no guarantee of an unopposed election. As the press observed, in any 'election in which he stood there would have been sure to be against him an Independent Conservative candidate, who would probably have on his platform Mr Austin [sic] Chamberlain ... and not improbably Mr Lloyd George'.[15] To some extent, McKenna was being used by the Conservatives who were less keen on the Lloyd George Coalition, to keep out some of the pro-Lloyd George Coalition Conservatives, such as Austen Chamberlain. In the end, McKenna's health, his success at the bank and his distaste for the personality-driven aspects of politics led him to focus on his business career. He never returned to politics and came to be regarded by some as a prime minister-manqué. In reality, he was a highly skilled technical expert with business acumen and wealth, but limited in his political skills and following. Although they were very different in personality, the career of McKenna displayed similarities to that of John Simon. Both objected to conscription on practical rather than moral grounds, both were highly regarded for their professional expertise but did not gather a loyal political following, both eventually fell out with Lloyd George and sought office for themselves under a different political regime.

Munro-Ferguson was close to Asquith and Grey and also to Haldane, who was briefly engaged to his sister. Although married into an aristocratic family, Munro-Ferguson was short of money and became keen to pursue an imperial career, after his service in the Commons since 1886 appeared to have peaked at the level of junior whip. In February 1914 Munro-Ferguson accepted Asquith's offer of the governor-generalship of Australia. He remained in Australia until 1920, being created Viscount Novar on his return. He seized the opportunity to renew his official career (and increase his earnings) when his friend Bonar Law became Prime Minister in 1922. He served as Secretary of State for Scotland from October 1922 to January 1924. Novar's personal loyalty was displayed when he was the only member of the cabinet wholeheartedly to support Bonar Law in the row over American debt. As Novar later wrote:

> B.L. told the Cabinet he would resign rather than agree. I was his only supporter, which became very plain at a meeting of members of Cabinet, without the P.M. . . . when I opposed Baldwin, alone, the rest supporting him.[16]

Baldwin dispensed with Novar's services when he formed his second administration in November1924. Novar acknowledged his opportunism in a letter to Baldwin after his omission from the new administration:

> I only joined the Conservative Party in 1922 and I only did so then because I thought . . . that everyone should back Mr. Bonar Law and you in your efforts to bring the Coalition to an end and to keep out the Socialists . . . I recognise that my original nomination was due to the friendship of Mr. Bonar Law and not to party claims.[17]

Baldwin cast around for a diplomatic reason for not having re-engaged Novar's services, but the best that he could offer was: 'It was with real regret that I was unable to avail myself of your services . . . I have always felt it a weakness not to have the Scottish Secretary in the Commons.' Novar added a hand-written note at the bottom, 'This is weak but his best line of argument. The reasons were quite different . . . I don't trust Mr B!'[18] Novar's defection was opportunistic and limited in objectives and, within these parameters, it was largely successful. Partly due to his absence from British politics during his time in Australia, Novar had not cultivated a loyal following from within the Liberal Party and his defection was inconsequential in terms of encouraging colleagues to take his lead.

Fusionists

For those Lloyd George Coalition Liberals who found their Conservative colleagues to their liking between 1918 and 1922, and, perhaps more importantly, those who found former Conservative voters supporting them, the possibility of creating an enduring link between the parties was very attractive. 'Fusion' was the term used at the time for a scheme to merge the Coalition Liberal and Unionist supporters of the Lloyd George Government at all levels. Lloyd George wanted to implement it to provide himself with a permanent base, from which to repel the threat of Labour. The Fusionists centred on the Guest brothers and their cousin, Winston Churchill.[19] Of the five Guest brothers, four – Ivor, (Christian) Henry, (Frederick) 'Freddie' and Oscar (Montagu) – served as Liberal MPs, and all defected from the party. The fifth brother, Lionel was a member of the London County Council, but not in parliament. The Guest brothers not only shared political allegiances, but also constituencies. Henry and Freddie were both sometime MP for Bristol North, Dorset East and Plymouth Drake. Ivor also sat for the Plymouth seat. Freddie failed in his first three attempts to enter parliament and was unseated for election expense violations following his fourth contest. His brother Henry stepped in, won the East Dorset by-election caused by Freddie's expulsion and kept the seat warm until Freddie was returned again in December 1910. Churchill and the Guests co-ordinated many of their political activities.[20] They had all been Conservatives who had defected to the Liberal Party in 1904, in support of free trade.

Freddie Guest was the key figure in the Liberal War Committee and had acted on his own advice, offering himself for service. After being invalided out of the army he was appointed coalition chief whip in March 1917. At best, Guest had been Lloyd George's third choice. Wedgwood Benn turned down the job on 10 December 1916. Lloyd George had then urgently cast around for an understudy, but none was immediately available. In near-desperation, he decided to offer the role to Neil Primrose, a trusted colleague, but one who had other ambitions:

> My dear Neil, I am very anxious that you should at least for a short time ... take the chief Whipship. I know you prefer the Labour job ... but I am asking you this as a real favour ... I promise ... that it will only be temporary.[21]

Primrose, although politically well-positioned as the son of a former Liberal prime minister (Rosebery) and married to the great-great-grand-daughter of a Conservative prime minister (Derby), was not the ideal alternative for chief whip: he had no wish to take on the job and was expecting to rejoin his regiment on active service. Primrose replied: 'My feelings against taking the position of Chief Liberal Whip are insuperable. I have neither experience nor inclination for the office, which is one which has no attraction for me.' Primrose suggested that Pringle take his place. However, such was the urgency and importance of the request, even Primrose's discouraging reply was not enough to deter Lloyd George, who extracted the concession from Primrose: 'In view of the urgency of your request ... I will fill the position ... on the understanding that you will relieve me of that office ... after a few months.' Primrose relinquished the job after only two and a half months and declined another post in order to rejoin his regiment; he was killed in action later that year.[22] Freddie Guest took up the role vacated by Primrose. While Benn's allegiance was strongly to the Asquithian wing of the Liberal Party, so he could have acted as a bridge between Lloyd George and the Asquithians, Primrose had taken a tactful middle course, writing after taking up the post: 'I most sincerely regret that Mr Asquith has at present no share in the Government'.[23] Guest, however, was extremely partisan in Lloyd George's favour. He was one of the few who actively worked for a split, and who was in a position to engineer it.[24] Guest was to become Lloyd George's fixer and fund-raiser, indulging in activities which brought the honours system into disrepute; eventually even alienating Lloyd George. After the Maurice Debate had emphasised the split within the Liberal Party in May 1918, the events leading up to the general election reinforced the divide. Guest shamelessly used his position to advance his own views, his friends and his family. He did not care much for the niceties of tact (or, for that matter, punctuation), writing to Lloyd George: 'Would you care to consider my brother Ivor for Paymaster General.'[25] Lloyd George did not care to, and appointed Sir John Tudor Walters instead. Despite Guest's efforts, there were some moves towards reconciliation after the 1918 election. Meetings of a joint committee to promote unity in early 1919 and the appointment of the non-couponed George Lambert as parliamentary chairman of the coalition Liberal group gave hopes in some quarters of a possible reunion. However, Guest rejoiced that the Wee Frees had had a 'very uncomfortable' time,[26] and he was instrumental in a turf war to claim front-bench seats for Coalition Liberals at the expense of the Wee Frees. He claimed gleefully to Lloyd George that negotiations with the Speaker over the allocation of seats would 'depose Maclean and Thorne from their indefensible usurpation of spokesmanship for Liberalism'.[27] Guest made his ambitions clear that: 'if the Coalition supporters, both Conservative and Liberal, hold together ... the Coalition will develop into an organised reality', so, he hoped, the Asquithians would 'be left high and dry, without any rank and file support'.[28]

The Guest brothers coordinated their careers, but the closest cooperation was between **Henry Guest** and his younger brother, Freddie. Henry was preceded and succeeded by Freddie in his first constituency of East Dorset, where he sat from June to December 1910. Henry then sat for Pembroke from December 1910 to 1918 – the only one of his four constituencies not also to have elected Freddie. Henry then sat for

Bristol North in 1922/23, where Freddie followed him in 1924. Henry's last constituency was Plymouth Drake, where he succeeded Freddie on the latter's death.

Oscar Guest consistently supported fusion, along with Freddie. The press began to comment on the new 'Centre Group', chaired by Oscar Guest, within which Coalition Liberals accounted for five of the thirteen members of the executive committee. However, of the fifty-two members present at its first meeting on 15 July 1919, only three were Liberals. In May 1919 Freddie Guest was able to tell Lloyd George about a 'movement of New Members towards the formation of a Centre Party'. By July 1919 Guest told Lloyd George about the latest developments: '[T]he Centre Party . . . have invited Winston to speak at [their dinner]. He has accepted, on the understanding that the movement, generally speaking, has your approval. I have assured him that this is so.'[29] Guest must have been pleased by the *Daily Mail*'s coverage of the moves towards fusion, when it recorded the inauguration of a new political party 'destined . . . to supersede the existing Coalition Liberal and Coalition Unionist groups and replace them by a permanent Combined Party'. It went on to explain that candidates would appear as 'Coalition' or 'Centre Party' candidates and that in the House of Commons 'there will be but two great parties – namely, the Centre Party and Labour . . . with a few extreme elements of Toryism and Bolshevism feebly represented . . . the old Asquithian Liberals will disappear both individually as members and as a party. Their only alternative to extinction would appear to be to throw in their lot with the new party'.[30]

Later that year, Freddie Guest helped to raise the temperature of ill-feeling within Liberalism surrounding the Spen Valley by-election, by urging the selection of a Coalition Liberal candidate, where no obvious contender was available. To stiffen his resolve to contest the seat, Guest wrote to Lloyd George that Simon's 'Invasion of the Division is a direct challenge to Coalition Liberalism and the Government'.[31] Eventually, after the preferred potential candidate had declined, the Coalition Liberals selected Colonel Fairfax, a character of 'manly bearing', but limited electoral appeal. Major Grant, appointed to report back to Coalition Liberal Headquarters, warned that Fairfax 'showed up badly in comparison [with Simon]; indeed his first appearance . . . was . . . a disaster, so much so that the next day our local supporters were in despair'. In the event, the by-election *was* a disaster for the Coalition Liberals, who managed to fall from the incumbent party to last place in the poll and, at the same time, alienate their Conservative allies. Grant issued a stinging report after the debacle, concluding that the 'very serious delay in securing a candidate irritated and alienated the

Conservatives [as did the] choice of such a "raw" candidate. [The] Whips should not appear on the scene unless and until a request is made [and] no action should be taken by Headquarters without the knowledge of the person on the spot'.[32] While the brunt of the attack was probably directed at William Edge, Guest's deputy, who had been 'helping' in the constituency, Guest's fingerprints were all over the master plan.

The Coalition Liberals' poor showing in post-war by-elections, culminating in the defeat at Spen Valley, added urgency and impetus to the moves to fusion. The Unionists reluctantly supported Lloyd George's proposals, but by 18 March 1920 the scheme was killed off by the Liberal coalitionists, many of whom wanted to keep open the possibility of reunion with the Asquthians. Among the coalition ministers, Mond, Montagu, Fisher and Shortt opposed the plan. Backbench feeling was even more strongly against fusion, and Lloyd George was forced to abandon it. The collapse of fusion meant that the Coalition Liberals were distanced from their Unionist colleagues. To make their positions more isolated still, several of them then deliberately undermined their tenuous relationship with the Asquithians. The Wee Frees, feeling that they were in the ascendancy after Asquith's victory in the Paisley by-election in February 1920, had organised a conference in Leamington Spa in May. One of their resolutions welcomed 'Asquith's return to the House of Commons and reaffirm[ed] its unabated confidence in him as Leader of the Liberal Party'. Another declined the invitation by the prime minister to enter into closer cooperation with the Conservative Party. Asquith was keen to portray himself as a leader with a future: a portrait painted at this time, now hanging in the Reform Club, shows Asquith holding a book, his finger marking a place near the middle, as though his story still had a long way to run. A group of senior Coalition Liberals, including Addison, Hewart, Macnamara, Kellaway, Edge and Ward, took the train to Leamington Spa and sparked a row with the Wee Frees at their conference. Amid scenes of chaos, the Asquithians shouted down the coalitionists. Addison was heard to denounce the 'sentence of excommunication' which had been passed on the coalitionists, before his group left, fired up with emotion, even claiming later that they had had 'an enjoyable time'.[33] But, in reality their provocative interruption had damaged the dwindling prospects for their party's recovery.

The collapse of the post-war boom and the forced curtailment of many of the coalition's most liberal policies, such as housebuilding, caused a steep decline in the popularity of the government and the prestige of its senior Liberal ministers. In April 1921, Lloyd George sidelined Guest to the position of Secretary of State for Air, a post well removed from party organisation. His relationship with his leader hereafter became increasingly remote. By 1922, Lloyd George was becoming expendable in the eyes of large parts of the Conservative Party and in October he was ditched. A hastily cobbled-together agreement on seats for the 1922 election between the Lloyd George Liberals and the Conservatives resulted in the emergence of 'National Liberal' candidates, as Lloyd George's supporters were labelled. Some salvaged their political careers through this last-minute concession, but the result of the election clearly put Labour ahead of the two arms of the Liberal Party combined, for the first time: Labour won 142 seats, while the combined total for the National Liberals and Asquithians only amounted to 116.

Although the campaign for fusion at a national level had failed, the pursuit of its objectives, by different means and under a different name, remained an ambition for several key National Liberals, notably Guest and Churchill. A local version was attempted in several constituencies, without official sanction. No Liberal MP had defected to the Conservatives during the life of the Coalition, but soon after the 1922 election a serious exodus began, often driven by local electoral circumstances.

It was the situation in Berwick-upon-Tweed which occasioned the start of the exodus of Coalition/National Liberals to the Conservatives. **Hilton Philipson** had been elected as the National Liberal MP for the constituency in 1922. The local press summing up the position: 'The Unionist Party . . . decided to support Mr Philipson, the National Liberal candidate . . . who . . . came into the fight . . . with the approval of the Unionist Party. The Duke of Northumberland one of the leading "Diehards" was present at the meeting.' However, a petition was heard on 25 April 1923 against Philipson on grounds of his having made a false return of election expenses and having exceeded the expenditure limits. The petition was successful and the election result declared void. Philipson's wife, Mabel, an actress, agreed to contest the resultant by-election; but as a Conservative candidate. She offered the opinion: 'There is not much difference . . . between the National Liberals, as a nominee of whom her husband sat, and the Conservatives who . . . adopted her as a candidate.' H.B. Robson appeared as a Liberal candidate. The National Liberals were split as to where their loyalties should lie between Mrs Philipson and Robson. Mrs Philipson won the by-election and claimed after her victory that 'in spite of an edict by National Liberals' Headquarters, I am certain that most National Liberals have been with me'.[34] She went on to serve as the Conservative MP until

1929, when she retired. However, Hilton Philipson was unsuccessful in the 1923 and 1924 elections (at nearby Wansbeck and Gateshead respectively), both of which he contested as a Conservative.

In 1923 **Arthur Evans** caused 'much commotion among National Liberals' after he was the only National Liberal to support the government in a division on the Finance Bill. At a garden party organised by members of his East Leicester National Liberal Association Evans said that he was returned as 'an anti-Socialist', but very often in the House of Commons the party asked him to vote in support of 'a Socialist measure'. He had refused to do so. On 27 July 1923 Evans wrote to Lloyd George: 'At the last General Election . . . I received the unanimous support both of the National Liberal and Conservative parties . . . and I gave definite pledges of support to the Conservative Government . . . I have found it most difficult, in fact, impossible, to vote as requested by the Whips of the National Liberal Party . . . I have decided . . . to ask for the Conservative Whip.'[35] Lloyd George replied: 'in order to keep your pledge to your constituents you are about to sever your connexion with the party as a member of which you were elected . . . I assume that you will follow all honourable precedent by affording them an opportunity of expressing an opinion on your change of party.'[36] Evans did not afford his constituents an immediate opportunity, but at the general election in December their opinion was negative: his Labour opponent won the seat. According to *The Times*, there were persistent rumours that Captain Evans's example might be followed by other members of the National Liberal Party, among whom George Roberts and Maurice Alexander were mentioned.[37] The report turned out to be wrong on several counts. Roberts had in fact been a Coalition Labour MP and former Food Controller, who became an Independent and eventually a Conservative, and Alexander followed a totally different trajectory (as described in Chapter 3) and went from National Liberal to Labour. Evans himself, however, did go on to be Conservative MP for Cardiff South at the 1924 general election.

The circumstances in Romford at the time illustrated another aspect of inter-party confusion which could also have occurred in other constituencies, although in the event it was an isolated example. The sitting National Liberal MP, Albert Martin, nearly became another defector. Martin had been chosen by the Conservatives and National Liberals as their Coalition, then National, Liberal candidate in 1918 and 1922. The Conservatives had therefore not fielded their own candidate in these elections. As the 1923 election approached and Liberal reunion was more or less enacted, the local Liberal association selected the former War Policy Objector David Mason as their candidate. Martin was expected to retire. The Conservatives had no candidate in place. The Tories decided to approach Martin to see if he would stand as the Conservative candidate, as he had voted 'most consistently with the Government'. The plan to approach Martin unravelled, though, when Martin 'collapsed . . . in a prostrate condition' on the 'verge of a breakdown'.[38] His poor health meant that he did not become a defector and did not contest that or any further election under any party label.

Another example of confusion caused by blurred party boundaries occurred in Scotland. **Walter Waring**, old-Etonian and former army officer, nicknamed 'Jumbo' by his family, was a tall man, with very decided, and not very liberal, views. He described the working classes as swine, who did not contribute to the public finance and claimed that politicians only pandered to them when they were seeking office.[39] Despite his views, Waring was elected as a Liberal MP in 1907. In 1922 he changed constituencies and became embroiled in a four-horse race (of which three were Liberals), for the seat of Berwickshire and Haddingtonshire, where the sitting National Liberal John Hope had been deselected on the eve of the election, but had refused to withdraw (see Chapter 5). The local press reported Waring's arrival on the scene, sporting the label of a National Liberal, but commenting that he was really a Conservative.[40] Waring won the 1922 contest, but the bitterness of the local battle spilled over into the 1923 election, when Waring defended the seat against a Labour and a Conservative opponent – the Conservatives clearly not having agreed that Waring was one of their number. A local Liberal commented ruefully, after Waring came bottom of the 1923 poll, that the election had resulted in the present of a strong Liberal seat to Labour.[41] Waring was defiant after the debacle, rejecting calls for a change of candidate and threatening to set up a new organisation. He claimed that the Liberal leadership was unaware of the realities of the Liberal reunion at grass-roots level.[42] After his 1923 defeat, Waring finally gave up on the Liberals (and they on him), and he flirted briefly with the idea of forming a new party. He floated the idea with the Duchess of Atholl (then, but not later, a loyal Conservative Party member), who did not see that there was any room for a new party, but believed that cooperation should be the aim.[43] Waring then supported Churchill (whose PPS he had earlier been) in the Westminster Abbey by-election, when Churchill was ambiguously poised on the fringes of the Conservative Party while trying to maintain a Liberal following (see pp. 107–8).[44] In return, Churchill tried to intervene to find a seat for Waring to contest with Conservative backing in the 1924 election, writing hopefully, 'Derby . . . is going to try to fix Dudley Ward and Waring in some Lancashire seats'.[45] In the event neither Ward nor

Waring stood in the 1924 election.[46] In his Liberal days, Waring had vigorously supported his party's land policies, giving them his 'hearty support'.[47] However, from his new Tory vantage point in 1925, Waring raged against the Liberals' land policies, trumpeting to *The Times* that *The Land and the Nation* 'must be held up to scorn as a piece of barefaced propaganda equalling, if not surpassing, the efforts of the Union of Socialist Republics.'[48] Even a sympathetic observer conceded that 'Waring stood alone. [H]e had an awkward instinct to mock at doctrinarianism which infuriated "serious" politicians and made him an impossible member of the Liberal Party'.[49] Waring's political career was truncated. He served as a Conservative member of the LCC from 1925 to 1928 and stood once more, unsuccessfully, for parliament as a Conservative at Wallsend in 1929; but he died suddenly in 1930 at the age of only fifty-four.

The interval between the failure of fusion in 1920 and the 1924 election had therefore seen the former Coalition Liberals Waring, Martin, Evans and Philipson in ambiguous political positions, not entirely of their own making. The 1924 election, the first fought after the Liberals had allowed Labour their first taste of office, saw a more numerous band of former Liberals deliberately choosing to perch precariously between the Conservative and Liberal Parties.

Constitutionalists

The term Constitutionalist gained prominence in 1924, when it was used, most famously, by Churchill, but also by a small group of other candidates. The aims of the Constitutionalists were similar to those of the Fusionists, and some of the groups' membership overlapped. Several former Fusionists, who had not already become members of the Conservative Party by the time of the 1924 election, including the Guests, Churchill, Moreing and Sturrock, joined with others to form the Constitutionalists. While the Fusionists were more strategic in their long-term ambitions to merge their branch of Liberalism with the Conservatives, the Constitutionalists were more short-term in their focus and primarily concerned with maximising their chances of victory at the next election, by avoiding a local Liberal-Conservative contest. The choice of the name Constitutionalist loosely fitted their political positions and highlighted their fears of an unbridled socialist government. The origins of Constitutionalism can be traced back to the theories of John Locke, that government should be legally limited in its powers and that its authority depends on its observing these limits. In Britain, with its uncodified constitution, the potential for government excess was certainly present in theory, but the record of the first, timid, respectable, safe and rather rule-bound Labour Government had already dispelled most people's fears on this score.

The first publicity for a putative Constitutionalist group had appeared in *The Times* in September 1920 in the form of a display advertisement inviting readers to attend a conference in London to 'help to carry out the preliminary organisation of the Constitutional Party'.[50] The contact given was Charles Higham, an export merchant and the Coalition Conservative MP for Islington South from 1918 to 1922. Nothing appears to have come of this initial venture. The term 'Constitutionalist' then appeared as an electoral label, used by **George Jarrett** in 1922. Jarrett was the one-armed former chief organiser of the Coalition National Democratic Party (NDP). In a letter to *The Times* in 1922, he described himself as a 'constitutionalist'. In 1922 Jarrett was nominated by both the National Liberal and Conservative associations in Dartford. He won in 1922 against Labour and Liberal opposition. In his 1923 election address Jarrett wrote: 'A year ago you honoured me by returning me ... without respect to party ... Upon the invitation of a joint meeting of Conservatives and Liberals, I seek renewal of the confidence which you placed in me ... Again I stand as the Constitutional Candidate.'[51] In 1923 he was defeated against only Labour opposition, his name having appeared on both the Liberal and Conservative Party official lists of candidates. Jarrett thus served only one year in parliament, in 1922/23, but was the first to do so as a Constitutionalist.[52] The final straw for Jarrett, which ended his association with the Liberals, appears to have been the Liberals' support for the first Labour Government. In February 1924, together with Algernon Moreing, he wrote to Churchill complaining about the difficult position into which they had been put by this and saying how they looked to Churchill for leadership.[53] Jarrett joined the Conservative Party before the 1924 election and unsuccessfully fought this and two later elections as a Conservative candidate, but was never re-elected.

Algernon Moreing was the son of Charles Moreing, a wealthy mining engineer. Moreing Senior had stood once, unsuccessfully, for parliament as a Conservative in Gainsborough in 1906. He did not stand again, possibly as a result of his being cited as co-respondent in a divorce case in 1910, after his alleged involvement with a woman named (rather inopportunely) Nesta Cocks.[54] Algernon Moreing was first elected for Buckrose as a Coalition Liberal in 1918. He was a strong advocate of fusion in 1920, and had written to Freddie Guest explaining the situation in his constituency: 'There is a strong demand amongst the people generally for the formation of a party combining

Tories and Liberals ... The Chairman of the Conservative Association would, I believe, be willing to join such a party.'[55] In 1922, Moreing changed constituencies and was successful as the National Liberal candidate for Camborne. The 1923 election in this constituency illustrated that Liberal reunion was less than total, as the only two candidates in Camborne in 1923 were both Liberals: Moreing and Leif Jones. Moreing was the nominee of the Lloyd George Liberals and the local Conservative Association and Jones was backed by the Asquithians. The United Liberal Committee in London, which had been created to assist in selecting candidates and to help bring the two wings of the Liberal Party together, declared itself neutral between the candidates, after it had failed to obtain local agreement. Jones was the winner of the 1923 contest, after which Moreing was to follow Churchill's lead in standing as a Constitutionalist at the 1924 election.

Winston Churchill tried on party names as others try on clothes. By 1922 he had already been a Conservative, a Liberal, a Coalition Liberal and a National Liberal. He had been an enthusiastic advocate of fusion and had considered calling the proposed new party 'The Constitutional Reform Party'. By the end of 1922 Churchill was out of parliament, having lost his seat at Dundee.

In May 1923, Churchill described himself (in private conversation with Conservatives) as 'a Tory Democrat'.[56] But the arrival of the 1923 election forced Churchill to abandon his oscillation over party labels, and he settled for the Liberal candidacy at West Leicester. He vainly hoped that he might have been spared a Conservative opponent, so that he could have had a chance of winning the seat, although it was, as Roy Jenkins observed, impossible to see why he should have thought this 'remotely likely'.[57] Clementine, so often more objective than her husband about his career, suggested: 'I am sure the old *real* Liberals will want you back but ... do not give them cause ... for thinking that you would like a new Tory Liberal Coalition ... if you were to lose a seat ... it would be better for you to be beaten by a Tory (which would arouse Liberal sympathy) than by a Socialist.'[58] Churchill's (temporary) rehabilitation within the Liberal Party was signified when in November 1923 his portrait, and that of Lloyd George, which had been banished to the cellars in 1921, was re-hung at the National Liberal Club. Churchill lost West Leicester to Labour and, like Jarrett and many others, was very unsympathetic towards the Liberal Party when it supported Labour after the 1923 election, commenting that some Liberal MPs 'will certainly co-operate with the Conservatives'.[59] When he was asked to stand again as a Liberal, Churchill replied that he would not be willing to fight the Conservatives. Caught between parties, Churchill was tempted to stand as an independent, when the Westminster Abbey by-election 'swooped' down upon him in February 1924. He believed that Grigg, Spears and McKenna, together with the Rothermere and Beaverbrook press, would support him. He was also convinced that Baldwin wanted him to be returned, and felt therefore that the local Conservative association might adopt him as their candidate, despite the fact that he was not even a member of their party. But the Westminster Conservative Association adopted Otho Nicholson as their candidate. Churchill decided that he would still contest the seat and Baldwin did not intervene. Churchill was variously described as a 'Constitutionalist' or as an 'Independent anti-Socialist'.[60] Guest helped Churchill to set up his campaign, and by 10 March all nine Abbey wards were being organised for Churchill by a Conservative MP. Churchill lost to Nicholson by just 43 votes, but he had performed the 'paradoxical feat of opposing an official Conservative . . . while moving himself in a more Conservative direction'.[61] After the Westminster near-miss, Churchill decided to improve his negotiating position with the Tories by gathering around him 'a distinctly Liberal block, ready to cooperate with the Conservative Party', and said that it was 'of great importance that the Conservative and Liberal wings in this matter should develop separately'.[62] Churchill envisaged that his followers would occupy the same position as the Liberal Unionists had in 1886, commenting: 'I am a Liberal who is working with the Conservatives in the same way as Joe [and] Hartington.'[63] He claimed that there were at least twenty Labour seats which could be won by Liberals, and only Liberals, if they were given Conservative support.[64] This helped Churchill persuade Baldwin to allow him to stand at the next general election as a 'Constitutionalist' with Conservative support. Baldwin agreed that Churchill would be found a safe Conservative seat in or near London, and if possible, a seat for which there was no Liberal candidate. They agreed that, at this stage, Churchill would not join the Conservative Party. As the 1924 election approached, Churchill negotiated with the Unionist Central Office to arrange for a raft of 'Constitutionalist' candidates to be given a clear run by the Conservatives. He claimed that his co-conspirators were Guest, Grigg and Seely and that the deal would cover '25 or 27 candidatures'.[65] This report turned out, as the plan unfolded, to be wide of the mark, in terms of both numbers and personnel. However, a crucial part of the strategy fell into place on 5 August 1924, when the chairman of the Epping Conservatives wrote to Churchill to ask if he would allow his name to go forward as a candidate for the seat.[66] He did; but there was a flaw to the plan, as there was a Liberal candidate also in the field.

One of Churchill's key allies in the Constitutionalist venture was **Hamar Greenwood**, who had been Churchill's parliamentary private secretary between Greenwood's first election in 1906 and his loss of his seat in January 1910. Brought up in Canada, Greenwood had strong Imperial leanings. He was brother-in-law to the arch-Imperialist Conservative MP, Leo Amery.[67] Greenwood was re-elected in December 1910 and rose to be a tough and controversial Chief Secretary for Ireland. He lost his seat in 1922 and failed to be re-elected the following year. By 1924, he was exploring alternative avenues back to the Commons. He ruled out an invitation from Central Cardiff Liberal Association, saying that: 'the best way to defeat Socialism . . . is . . . to unite in common action. These views must preclude . . . nomination . . . where there is already a Conservative and a Socialist candidate in the field'.[68] Greenwood wrote to Lloyd George: 'I understand that you . . . sanctioned the [Cardiff] invitation, and I must thank you for this . . . I have never altered in my view that the interests of the Home Country and the Empire were best served . . . by the closest co-operation between the two old parties'.[69] A more suitable opportunity for Greenwood's re-election came when the Unionist MP for East Walthamstow announced his retirement in late September 1924. An arrangement was reached for Greenwood to stand there as a Constitutionalist, unopposed by the Tories. Greenwood, however, was, like Churchill and Moreing, opposed by a Liberal. Greenwood's Liberal challenger – named Heffer – goaded him over his record in Ireland, describing him as 'a political hermaphrodite . . . not blue or red or orange, but black and tan'. Heffer argued, countering the Constitutionalists' claims that the withdrawal of his own candidature would make a present of the seat to Labour. He claimed that Greenwood had tried to persuade Liberal headquarters to have him 'retired'.[70] Although Greenwood, Churchill and Moreing went into the election facing Liberal opponents, the other Constitutionalists managed to avoid this.

Considerably less strident in his anti-Socialist views than most of the others who became Constitutionalists was **John Leng Sturrock**. Sturrock was first elected as Coalition Liberal MP for Montrose in 1918, being re-elected in 1922 and 1923. Making his moderate views clear, he wrote after the 1923 election:

> Are the . . . unemployed to be left out of the calculations [?] . . . Theirs is a cruelly hard case . . . Baldwin and the remnant of his party, are bankrupt . . . If . . . MacDonald desires to form a Government he is entitled to do so.[71]

After the formation of the first Labour Government, and while serving as a Liberal MP, Sturrock publicly questioned his party's continued survival, writing to *The Times*, speculating what would happen 'when the obituary of the Liberal Party comes to be written, as come it may'.[72] In 1924 Sturrock moved south to contest North Tottenham as a Constitutionalist, where he received Liberal and Conservative support.[73]

Henry Cairn Hogbin was first elected to parliament in 1923, for Battersea North. Standing as a Liberal, he had beaten his only opponent – Shapurji Saklatvala – who was standing as a Labour-Socialist candidate.[74] In 1924 Hogbin again faced only Saklatvala, but by this time the two men had both changed party labels: Hogbin stood as a Constitutionalist and Saklatvala as a Communist, having been denied his earlier Labour support. Thus the 1924 Battersea North contest had the unusual feature of having no Liberal, Labour or Conservative candidate. If ever there was a contest where Constitutionalism was given an unfettered opportunity to pit its virtues against its antithesis, this was it. Hogbin made this issue prominent in his campaign, putting the question of the constitution in the forefront of his address and claiming that the great question was 'whether you will have Constitutional Government . . . or submit to the forces of revolution and disorder'.[75]

By background, **John Ward** had little in common with most of the other Constitutionalists. He had little formal education, working initially as a navvy and only learning to read as a teenager. In 1886 he joined the Social Democratic Federation and three years later he founded the Navvies' Union. Ward represented Stoke in parliament from 1906, initially as a Lib-Lab member. He had refused to sign the Labour Representation Committee constitution in 1903, and was elected without their endorsement. He therefore faced repeated Labour opposition. Although the Liberal Party always claimed him as one of their members, Ward stood as a Constitutionalist in 1924. He was ill and did not take an active part in that year's election campaign, but there was a joint campaign of Liberals and Conservatives and trade unionists on his behalf.

In 1924, nine of the ten Staffordshire seats had straight fights between Labour and one other challenger. In seven of these nine, the Conservatives faced Labour, without Liberal intervention. In the remaining two – Stoke and Burslem – Labour's challenger fought under the Constitutionalist banner. Ward contested the Stoke seat and **William Allen** fought Burslem. Allen was a barrister and had been a Liberal MP from 1892 to 1900. The term 'Constitutionalist' was not used in the local press and no party was mentioned on the front of Allen's 1924 election address.[76] The address had very little policy content, but was moderately anti-Labour in tone, and made no mention of the

Conservatives, or of any party leader at all, but Allen did declare that he had 'accepted the invitation of the Liberal Association to become a Candidate.' However, Allen was generally included in national lists of Constitutional candidates, and is described as such by Craig.

(John) Hugh Edwards was the author of *three* biographies of Lloyd George and a supporter of the 'Young Wales' Movement of the 1890s. Before the First World War, Edwards was notorious for his anti-socialist campaigning. He initially sat for Mid Glamorgan (renamed Neath) from December 1910 until his defeat in 1922. He then stood in Accrington in 1923, where he was elected as a Liberal. In 1924 he again stood for Accrington, this time as a Constitutionalist, with support from the local Liberal and Conservative associations. He was received with 'great cordiality' at the Accrington Central Conservative Club and was unanimously adopted as the candidate. He pledged 'that he would never lose an opportunity of voting against Socialists' and claimed that he had done so 'even to the annoyance of the heads of his own party' and that he had 'stuck to the Conservatives on all occasions' since the last election.[77]

Thomas Robinson used the label Constitutionalist for his campaign in Stretford in 1924, where he was the sitting MP. From his first election in 1918 to his retirement in 1931, he was elected as the result of a local Liberal-Conservative pact. He had stood under a variety of labels, generally variations on 'Independent Free Trade and Anti-Socialist', although he was always claimed by the Liberal Party as one of their members. Robinson's 1924 election address was strongly anti-Labour in tone. He put himself forward, saying: 'Once more I seek your support as an Independent, Constitutional and Anti-Socialist Candidate.'

Abraham England was another Lancashire MP who was elected as the result of a local pact between the Liberals and Conservatives, and who stood as a Constitutionalist in 1924. Robinson and England, although adopting the Constitutionalist label in 1924, were therefore effectively just continuing a pre-existing local arrangement. England claimed he had 'been no Party hack ... I am anti-nothing ... If you examine my record for the last Parliament you will probably be astonished to find the number of votes I gave to the Labour Party. I have never let Party influence any vote'.[78] However, he was one of ten Liberal MPs who had defied the party whip and voted against putting Labour into office, following the 1923 election. As a result, local Conservatives strongly supported England's candidature in 1924, some signing his nomination papers. The local press commented that: 'the support he will receive from [his Tory backers] will be even larger than in November last'.[79]

Table 4.1 *Electoral record of the 1924 Constitutionalists*

	1922 election	1923 election	1924 election
Churchill	lost v **SPP***, **Lab**, Lib, Com	lost v **Lab**, Con	**won** v Lib, Lab
Moreing	**won** v Lib, Lab	lost v **Lib**	**won** v Lib, Lab
Greenwood	lost v **Con**, Lab, Lib	lost v **Con**, Lab	**won** v Lib, Lab
Ward	**won** v Lab	**won** v Lab	**won** v Lab
Edwards	lost v **Lab**	**won** v Lab	**won** v Lab
England	**won** v Lab	**won** v Lab	**won** v Lab
Robinson	**won** v Lab	**won** v Lab	**won** v Lab
Sturrock	**won** v Lab	**won** v Lab	lost v **Lab**
Hogbin	lost v **Lab**, Lib	**won** v Lab	lost v **Comm**
Allen	not candidate	not candidate	lost v **Lab**

* Bold type indicates victor(s).

The Constitutionalists largely failed to coordinate their activities as a group in the approach to the 1924 election. A common theme of the Constitutionalists' election addresses was the absence of any mention of political parties or leaders whom they supported; only those opposed were mentioned. While the common enemy was clearly Labour, the stridency of the criticism varied from mild (in the case of Allen) to rabid (in the case of Moreing). Constitutionalist candidates only stood in England, nearly all in urban seats, mainly north-east of London and in Lancashire and Staffordshire.[80] The label Constitutionalist was not used by any candidate north of the border. However, an informal pact operated in most Scottish constituencies: only fifteen of the seventy-one Scottish seats had a Conservative and a Liberal candidate in 1924.[81] The Constitutionalist label was intended to operate as a coupon, with the aim of avoiding a split in the anti-socialist vote. It is clear why the Constitutionalists believed that this was crucial. As Table 4.1 shows, they had won nine of their eleven straight fights with Labour in the two previous elections, but only three of the ten contests where the anti-Labour vote had been split.

Seven of the ten Constitutionalists were successful at the 1924 election. This represented a net loss of one seat – Battersea North contested by Hogbin – when comparing seats where the same candidate contested the 1923 and 1924 elections. However, 1924 was a much more difficult election for candidates standing as Liberals and, had the Constitutionalists all stood under the Liberal banner, almost certainly fewer would have been elected. When comparing votes where the candidates contested the same seats as in 1923, the Constitutionalists achieved an average improvement of just under 2,500 votes.[82] Therefore, as a defensive electoral tactic, the Constitutionalist label achieved modest success, but it did not herald the arrival of a lasting new political creed or alignment.

The Constitutionalists were never really a party, and were not treated as such by the other parties. At the 1924 election, Ward, England, Edwards, Allen, Sturrock and Robinson had the backing of their local Liberal associations and faced only Labour opposition. Moreing, Churchill, Greenwood and Jarrett did not have the backing of their local Liberal associations, but only Churchill, Moreing and Greenwood faced Liberal opposition. Ironically, these three won their seats, while Jarrett lost in a straight fight with Labour.

Ward, Edwards, England and Robinson repeated their victories of 1923, in the same constituencies, with straight wins against Labour. The Constitutionalist label helped to ensure that there was no Conservative challenger in their constituencies, but the Conservatives had not contested any of these seats in the preceding two elections anyway. The position of Churchill, Greenwood and Moreing was somewhat different. They were seen to be closer to being Conservatives than Liberals by this stage, and their results can more reasonably be compared to that which a Conservative candidate would have achieved in the same constituency. Churchill's seat at Epping was essentially a safe Conservative seat. Walthamstow East, where Greenwood was elected, was a Conservative seat at the preceding three elections, but more marginal. Moreing's constituency of Camborne was a knife-edge marginal, where left and right had alternately won; however, the main contest recently had been between the two brands of Liberalism – Moreing as a Lloyd George Liberal, and Leif Jones as an Asquithian. In 1924, with a revival on the right and a Liberal decline, the seat would have been likely to swing to the more rightward contender, whatever the party label. So, overall, the Liberal Party was not deprived of any seats that it otherwise might have won, and the Constitutionalists as a group did not achieve any electoral advantage from their adopted party label. The real change was that Churchill, Greenwood and Moreing had secured their re-election as nascent Conservatives, as was soon to become apparent.

By the time of the 1924 election, the Constitutionalists' political paths were already diverging. After the election, the 'Constitutional Group' of MPs held a dinner at the Constitutional Club, which over fifty guests attended. However, the only Constitutional candidates to attend this were Churchill, Greenwood and Moreing. Freddie Guest was there too. Ward was invited but sent his apologies. Almost all the other attendees were figures from the Conservative Party. Churchill claimed at the meeting that although he 'and his Constitutionalist friends represented a very small group of members in the House of Commons ... They also, to some extent, represented a larger group of Liberal members, who had stood with Conservative support and who would certainly recognize that fact in the action which they would take in the new Parliament'.[83]

Ironically, it was in the announcement of its demise that the press finally accorded the Constitutionalists the status of a party. 'The Constitutional Party is no more', *The Times* reported only seven weeks after the 1924 election. 'It has always been difficult to calculate exactly how many members the party embraced, but the general impression after the election was that the correct total was seven ... then Mr. Churchill joined the Government and was classified as a Conservative, and the Liberals claimed Colonel England, Colonel Ward, Mr. Edwards and Sir Thomas Robinson, reducing the party to two, Sir Hamar Greenwood and Captain Moreing, who have both now agreed to accept the Conservative Whip.'[84]

The varied career paths of the Constitutionalists after 1924 illustrated that they were a loose grouping, whose main reason for their adoption of this label had been to avoid a three-cornered contest. Many of the Constitutionalists had military backgrounds and this may have led to their focus on achieving results, irrespective of the means. Churchill was appointed Chancellor of the Exchequer in the new Conservative Government and remained in parliament as a Tory until 1964, when he was nearly ninety years old, having served as prime minister twice. He always retained a benign attitude to the Liberal Party and tried to induce an Asquith and a Lloyd George into his administration in 1951 – Cyril Asquith declined, but Gwilym Lloyd-George accepted. Churchill also offered Clement Davies a coalition and a seat in cabinet, which he declined.

After taking the Tory whip in 1924, Greenwood served just a single further term in the Commons, but never returned to ministerial office. In 1929 he was elevated to the peerage, after which he served as honorary treasurer to the Conservative Party, being advanced to a viscountcy towards the end of his term. Moreing had won in 1924, but in 1929, in the last head-to-head contest between them, Leif Jones beat him. Moreing was by then described as a Conservative, and this was his last outing to the polls, having stood in five successive elections, each time under a different party label: Coalition Liberal in 1918, National Liberal in 1922, Liberal in 1923, Constitutionalist in 1924 and Conservative in 1929. Moreing's younger brother Adrian picked up the family political baton and sat as a Conservative for Preston from 1931 until his death in 1940, which caused the by-election at which Winston Churchill's son Randolph was elected unopposed.

Had Sturrock succeeded in 1924, he would have taken the Conservative whip. However, he retained a benevolent attitude towards the Liberal Party, warning that:

> Liberals ... represent an element not inferior, at least intellectually or patriotically, to what one may find in Conservative or Socialist ranks ... [T]elling Liberals to put their shutters up immediately ... is calculated to produce anything but an exact antithesis of what is desired ... Government supporters are unwise to indulge in an anti-Liberal vendetta.[85]

Hogbin endured the distinction of being the only Liberal MP ever to be defeated by a Communist. He was given one more opportunity to avenge his defeat at the hands of the left, and it was potentially an easy ride. He was selected to stand as the Conservative candidate at the Stourbridge by-election in 1927, caused by the death of the sitting Conservative MP, who had enjoyed a majority of just under 2,000 votes. Hogbin had by then changed his views on protection and declared that 'he was out whole-heartedly to protect our industries'. At a meeting a week before the by-election Hogbin arrived saying that he was 'all to pieces' and had come against the advice of his doctor.[86] His campaign suffered and he lost the election to Labour by a margin of over 3,000 votes, thus ending his political career.

Allen failed in 1924, but returned to parliament after a gap of thirty-one years, as the Liberal National MP for Burslem from 1931 to 1935.[87] After the 1924 election, England re-took the Liberal whip, but 'acknowledged the great help of the Conservative Party, who had given loyal support to a candidate not quite their own colour'.[88] In 1929 his election address said that he again offered himself as the 'Liberal Candidate'. However, he included a separate message from the local Unionists saying that they would not nominate a candidate and would again urge support for him. He supported the Liberal Nationals in 1931, but retired at the election that year. After the election when it appeared that there was no prospect of formal closer ties between the two parties, Edwards also re-took the Liberal whip in parliament. After his re-election with an increased majority, Ward rejoined the Liberal Party.

Robinson continued his ambiguous relationship with the Liberal Party for the rest of his parliamentary career until 1931. In 1929, he again had the support of both Conservatives and Liberals, but said that he 'acknowledged no party Whip in the House of Commons. He went there, not in the interests of any party, but in the interests of the nation.'[89] In a letter to the *Daily News* in 1929, he stated that he had been 'an Independent MP' since the Coalition was dissolved in 1922. 'Notwithstanding this', he said, 'my Liberal friends in the House of Commons generously continued to send me their whip which I have regarded as an act of courtesy. To prevent however any possibility of misunderstanding in the future on this point, I arranged that the sending of the whip to me should be discontinued in this Parliament'.[90]

Churchill had mentioned Grigg, Seely and Guest as his co-conspirators in the early stages of Constitutionalist venture. However, Grigg stood as a Liberal in 1924 and won his seat, although he did eventually defect, but not until in 1931 (see pp. 126–7). Seely was defeated at the Isle of Wight as a Liberal in 1924. He never stood again for the Commons and never defected, even during his fourteen years in the Lords, after his elevation as Baron Mottistone in 1933.[91] Freddie Guest was the only one of the Guest brothers to contest the 1924 election. On 15 April 1924 he had announced at a Liberal Party meeting that he had withdrawn from Stroud (the seat he had represented since the last general election), and that he had been offered a seat where he would have Tory support. He said that he was prepared to accept this, and wished to see the Liberal Party 'as a wing of the Tory Party'. Benn, who attended the meeting, was dismissive of his leader's response to Guest's announcement, noting that 'Mr A. followed . . . saying that we should all be in a stronger position' when we had come in touch with our constituencies (he is off to the Riviera tomorrow!) and that he was confident, convinced, etc, that the Party would be unimpaired, united, and anything else that begins with a u2'.[92] Guest's 1924 election address described him as the 'Liberal Anti-Socialist Candidate'. He was the official candidate of the local Liberal Association, but also received support from the local Conservative Association.[93] He did not describe himself as a Constitutionalist, but his campaign was conducted by a joint committee and he stated that he was prepared to support a Conservative Government under Baldwin's leadership. Guest won Bristol North in 1924 against only Labour opposition. After his re-election, his once very close relationship with Lloyd George continued to deteriorate. During the General Strike in 1926 Guest more or less blackmailed Lloyd George: 'we are not in sympathy with the attitude we thought you took in the House of Commons during the Strike . . . but . . . we are not prepared to see you censured . . . as long as you can give us certain assurances [including] that you have no intention' of allying yourself with the Labour Party.[94] In January 1929 the Western Counties

Liberal Association disaffiliated the Bristol North Liberal Association and established a new association, which adopted their own candidate – J.O.M. Skelton. However, shortly before the 1929 general election, the Liberal Parliamentary Party endorsed Guest's receipt of the whip and he received a letter of support from the Liberal chief whip. This did not mean that Guest had the wholehearted backing of the Liberal Party and, on the eve of the election, Lloyd George sent a letter to Skelton recognising him as the only official Liberal candidate in the constituency. The Labour candidate won the seat, Guest came second and Skelton last. After Guest's defeat in 1929, Churchill tried, unsuccessfully, to get Baldwin to give Guest a peerage, saying that he was a 'life long friend [and] in every way qualified for the House of Lords'.[95] Guest drafted a letter to Baldwin on 28 June 1929, asking to join the Conservative Party, but he waited another nine months before formally submitting his request.[96] Although Guest was not ennobled, he did return to the Commons as a Conservative at Plymouth Drake in 1931. Never one to waste time when it came to promoting himself, within four days of his election as a Conservative MP, Guest wrote to Beaverbrook, saying: 'I have heard rumours that Bobbie Monsell is anxious to obtain a post in the Government instead of carrying on as Chief Whip in the Tory Party. Do you think it is of any use for me to aspire to fill his chair?'[97] It was not. Guest sat at Plymouth until he died of cancer in 1937. True to the family tradition, his brother Henry, who had preceded him at East Dorset and Bristol North, succeeded Freddie as Conservative MP for Plymouth Drake at the by-election following his death. All of the Guest brothers ended up defecting to the right, as Oscar became Conservative MP for North-West Camberwell from 1935 to 1945 and Ivor (by then Viscount Wimborne) was to become the first President of the Liberal Nationals.

Lloyd George Policy Objectors

The Liberal Party after the 1924 election had been dominated by Lloyd George, although until 1926 Asquith was still nominally the party leader; but by then out of the Commons after his defeat at Paisley. Lloyd George was elected chairman of the shrunken group of surviving Liberal MPs. But even within this group, his support had been severely curtailed. Only twenty-six of the forty Liberal MPs elected in 1924 had voted for his chairmanship, seven voted against and the rest abstained. The seven objectors – Hopkin Morris, Benn, Livingstone, Kenworthy, Thorne, Thomson and Briant – were primarily motivated by personal antagonism to Lloyd George. Lloyd George had also by this time forfeited the once-fierce personal loyalty of Freddie Guest. The victorious Constitutionalists, who had retaken the Liberal whip – Robinson, Ward, Edwards and England – had also demonstrated that their adherence to the Liberal Party was not unconditional, especially if it were to be led in a leftward direction. In the 1924 parliament, the Liberal Party needed a distinctive policy agenda, around which the party could unite and campaign. Instead, an argument over policy did further – and lasting – damage to the party machine. To repair the party's finances after the third election in two years, the Liberal Million Fund was launched. But by late 1926 it had only raised around £80,000.[98] It became apparent that the existence of the Lloyd George Fund acted to dissuade potential donors, who believed that the party was already well financed. In reality, Lloyd George was holding back contributions until he knew the outcome of the debate on the proposals from his land inquiry committee. The party was therefore put under severe tension. Some members objected to Lloyd George's having such a pivotal role on policy-making, even though they were broadly supportive of the land proposals. Some Asquithians objected to Lloyd George personally, but in the interests of party unity and financial health wanted the proposals adopted. Others simply objected to the policies themselves – the most controversial being the Green Book, which advocated rural land nationalisation and the turning of farmers into 'cultivating tenants', supervised by county agricultural committees.

Chapter 3 considered the cases of three of the objectors to Lloyd George's chairmanship – Rhys Hopkin Morris, William Wedgwood Benn and Mackenzie Livingstone – who were motivated by their personal animosity to Lloyd George. However, another ten defectors left the Liberals between 1925 and 1931 due to their disagreement with Lloyd George's policies, although in some cases they retained a good personal relationship with Lloyd George. Maxwell Thornton left the Liberals, but he did not join another party.[99] David Davies, once a close colleague of Lloyd George's, also left the party to sit as an independent. The remaining eight Lloyd George Policy Objectors all went to the Conservatives.

Within two weeks of his election in November 1922, **Maxwell Thornton** had called a meeting of both wings of the Liberal Party to discuss reunion. Between seventy and one hundred members attended. There were no repeats of the Leamington showdown of May 1920, but the debate was inconclusive.[100] Thornton resigned from the party in December 1925, a year after his two-term tenure at Tavistock had ended in defeat. It was the culmination of his annoyance at intra-party dissent, a drift on his part to the right and his objection to Lloyd

George's land policy. Thornton wrote to Asquith announcing his secession from the Liberal Party, regretting 'the renewal of quarrels' in the party and believing that the issue had become that 'between Socialism and those who are opposed to Socialism ... To coquet with Socialism ... by the proposed nationalisation of the land ... seems to be a peculiarly dangerous experiment'.[101] Thornton was especially opposed to the land policy, as he represented a rural constituency where he could see the Conservatives gaining votes at the Liberals' expense on the issue. This was the final straw which caused Thornton to sever his links with the Liberal Party. He never contested another election for any party.

David Davies, grandson of the famous industrialist 'Top Sawyer', jointly inherited with his two sisters an estate valued at over £2 million when he was eighteen. In 1906 he was elected unopposed as Liberal MP for Montgomeryshire – the nearest thing to a continually Liberal-held seat anywhere in the country.[102] With a Cambridge education, significant wealth and a safe seat, David Davies was well positioned to show independence of mind. He did, diverging from his party's line over Ireland, tariffs and church disendowment. Some local Tories viewed him as a potential defector in their direction. In the event, he never migrated to the Conservatives, but he did fall out with the Liberal Party towards the end of his parliamentary career. In the Great War he reached the rank of lieutenant-colonel, raised a new battalion and experimented with unconventional weapons, before being recalled to London to be appointed Lloyd George's parliamentary private secretary in June 1916. At this stage their personal rapport was very close. The relationship continued to prosper when Lloyd George became Prime Minister; with Davies acting as one of his closest advisors. However, by June 1917 the two were at loggerheads. Davies had persisted in his role as 'candid friend' to the point that he began to irritate and offend Lloyd George who, unfairly in view of his earlier wartime record, virtually accused Davies of cowardice, writing: 'it is a scandal to force men of doubtful fitness into the fighting line when others whose physical efficiency is beyond question are shirking under powerful protection ... your wealth is your shield ... you can render better service to your country as a soldier'.[103] In 1918 Davies was issued with the coupon, but repudiated it: he could afford to, as he faced no opposition at that or any of the elections from December 1910 to 1924. By 1926, Davies's objections to Lloyd George had been compounded by the General Strike, the Lloyd George Fund and the land proposals. Davies hoped to receive the nomination of his constituency association to fight the 1929 election as an Independent Liberal, with a free hand to oppose

Lloyd George's Green Book. Although he had significant support in the constituency, it was not 'whole hearted' in the meaning of the term which Davies wanted to apply – 'unanimous' and totally unfettered. He withdrew his candidature, but tried to exert an excessive influence over his successor, Clement Davies, who won the seat as a (nearly-wholehearted) Lloyd George supporter in 1929: even he had doubts over the land proposals.[104]

The eight Lloyd George Policy Objectors (see Table 4.2) who went to the Conservatives were important politicians in terms of ability, influence and wealth. Significantly, they included several politicians who had been personally close to Lloyd George; in several cases they retained a fondness and respect for him even after they decided to leave the Liberal Party. The loss of these figures – Alfred and Henry Mond, Edward Hilton Young, Courtenay Mansel, Cyril Entwistle, Samuel Pattinson, Albert Illingworth and Edward Grigg – represented a serious loss of talent to the Liberal Party. Alfred Mond, Illingworth and Grigg had been Coalitionists, and Young had crossed over to join them. By background, they were all barristers, company directors or journalists; in several cases they practised more than one of these professions. Five of the eight later sat as Conservative MPs; one was already a peer, and the other two stood unsuccessfully as Conservative parliamentary candidates. Alfred Mond and his son Henry acted in concert over their defections, but the others all made independent decisions to leave, although there had been meetings of like-minded objectors to Lloyd George and his policies during the 1924 parliament.[105]

Alfred Mond was from a wealthy Jewish industrial background and used his business skills in a 'blunt, direct, rather blustering' way, to achieve his political objectives.[106] He served as First Commissioner of Works and later as Minister of Health in the Lloyd George coalition governments between 1916 and 1922. Although reflecting that he had 'worked in perfect loyalty and comradeship with Conservative colleagues' in the Coalition, he was strongly opposed to fusion and keen to see a Liberal reunion.[107] Always ambitious, even between his 1923 defeat, when he lost his seat at Swansea, and his return at a by-election in August 1924 for Carmarthen, he wrote to Asquith: 'If by any chance in my absence you ... form a Government ... I would very much like [to be] Chancellor of the Exchequer'.[108] Mond's previously productive relationship with Lloyd George broke down over the land proposals. Mond explained his doubts about the land campaign at length in a letter to Lloyd George in September 1924.[109] Although the proposals were modified, Mond remained totally unsympathetic to them, as he explained to Asquith in January 1926:

Table 4.2 *Lloyd George Policy Objectors defecting to Conservatives*

Defector	Date of defection	Parliamentary status at defection
Alfred Mond	Jan 1926	in Commons
Henry Mond	Jan 1926	former Lib MP, later Con MP
Hilton Young	Feb* 1926	in Commons
Cyril Entwistle	Feb 1926	former Lib MP, later Con MP
Courtenay Mansel	March 1926	former Lib MP, later Con cand
Samuel Pattinson	May 1929	former Lib MP
Albert Illingworth	April 1930	in Lords
Edward Grigg	Feb 1931	former Lib MP, later Con MP

* Young left the Liberals in February 1926 and joined the Conservatives that June.

> The unity which we have striven for ... has ... never been achieved, and all efforts to revivify and reorganize the Liberal forces have been rendered hopeless by the introduction by Mr. Lloyd George of a land policy ... To this policy in any shape or form I am absolutely and unalterably opposed ... I have ... decided that the only course for me to take is to sever my lifelong connexion with the Liberal Party and ... join the ... Conservative Party.[110]

The land policy was the cause of problems between Mond and Lloyd George, but their personal relationship turned very sour. Lloyd George's anti-semitic riposte that Mond 'like another notorious member of his own race, had gone to his own place', embittered the dispute.[111] Mond believed that the 'hindrance to Lloyd George's greatness [was] that he cannot bear a man who has the instincts and code of a gentleman near him for long. It gives him an inferiority complex'.[112] Benn bemoaned the latest spat, commenting that Lloyd George's 'vulgar taunt ... is the sort of thing that drives all decent-minded people away from the Party'.[113] Mond had little ideological difficulty in reconciling himself to a future in the Conservative Party. His biographer believed that the war had 'turned him from a free trade radical into an ardent nationalist; the Liberal had become a Conservative or an Imperialist in thought if not in deed'. Two further considerations weighed in Mond's mind. There was the opportunity for personal advancement, as revealed in a letter from Baldwin: 'When you told me that you wished to join our Party ... you said that you would like to go to the House of Lords ... I ... consented to submit your name in June ... though ... I thought it would be wiser to defer it in your own interests.'[114] Mond, eager to milk the opportunity for all it was worth, reminded Baldwin that he had asked for the rank of viscount. Not only was Mond's eventual reward merely a barony, but there was also a delay in Baldwin's fulfilling his part of the bargain at all, due, ironically, to the introduction of the Honours Prevention of Abuses Act, which had been enacted in the wake of Lloyd George's earlier perversion of the system. Baldwin did not want to risk suspicion over Mond's motives for joining his party: Mond was eventually created first Baron Melchett, in 1928. The other consideration, divined, probably correctly, by Lloyd George, was that Mond 'did not like the thought of his son's career being in the arctic regions of Liberalism'.[115]

Henry Mond, although close to his father politically, was very different in personality. While Alfred was an industrialist of 'forbidding personal bearing', Henry was an aspiring poet who set up a ménage à trois with the writer Gilbert Cannan and the artist Gwen Wilson, who eventually became his wife.[116] Henry was elected as Liberal MP for the Isle of Ely at his first attempt in 1923, but, as with so many of his cohorts, lost his seat the following year. He was therefore out of parliament when his father defected, but Henry, as usual, followed faithfully in his father's footsteps. Two days after his father resigned from the Liberal Party, Henry followed suit. In a letter to Asquith he gave as his reasons not only his disagreement with Lloyd George's rural proposals, but also his disillusionment with the party's 'incessant and degrading squabbles, and the petty internal dissensions'. Henry made a brief return to the Commons, winning the East Toxteth by-election for the Conservatives in March 1929, but only sat until December 1930, when he inherited the peerage on his father's death.

(Edward) Hilton Young was an Eton-educated barrister and journalist by profession: his first writing was published when he was nine – on his family's printing press. He later became assistant editor of the *Economist*. After being injured while serving in the Navy in 1918, he had his right arm amputated and had to learn to write with his left hand; his handwriting from then on had, perversely, a childish appearance. Young had been returned unopposed at a by-election in Norwich in 1915, a two-member constituency, during his absence on war service. He held his seat as a Liberal in 1918, but was perplexed to find himself counted as a Coalition Liberal, despite his original intention of standing as an Asquithian.[117] He did formally transfer his allegiance to the coalition during the parliament and served as Financial Secretary to the Treasury from 1921. He became increasingly close to Lloyd George, and on the collapse of the coalition in 1922 wrote to him asking to be 'associated with you in whatever action you may take'.[118] He held his seat in 1922 and after the election was appointed chief whip of the Lloyd George Liberals. However, contrary to the general Liberal tide, he was defeated in 1923, only to regain his seat in 1924. Young, who had been returned in harness with a Conservative at Norwich, came to be seen as a somewhat suspect member of the Liberal Party.[119] Young defended himself, saying that in Norwich, which 'returns two members, the seats were contested by two socialists, a conservative, – and myself. I recommended electors to give their second vote to the Conservative'. Young was also involved in detailed discussions with Freddie Guest about his attempted two-whip arrangement, suggesting that it would allow him to 'come to the party meeting, [but] he would probably not vote on any division about leadership'. After his defeat at Norwich in 1923, Young had still been fondly attached to Lloyd George, gushing: 'I shall account my association with you ... as one of the greatest goods for me that political life could bring. Nothing can ever affect the gratitude that I feel for the privilege of that association.' However, only months later, his gratitude for the privilege of the association had severely diminished: due to what Young considered to be Lloyd George's socialist policy direction. He warned Lloyd George about his disaffection over the land inquiry committee, saying that he could 'claim no practical acquaintance with agricultural conditions ... but I have ... fundamental misgivings about the proposed policy'. On the last day of 1925 Young wrote to Lloyd George:

> My heart, as you are I think aware, could not be in the landcampaign ... the more I stand back and see things from afar, the more I reluct from any approximation to agreement with the present labour party. If I am a liberal at top, it is because I am an individualist at bottom: and for an individualist, the Labour party is an Untouchable.

Six weeks later his views had crystallised. He wrote again to Lloyd George, saying that the scheme was 'fundamentally at variance with anything I can support ... If the party commits itself to this programme, that will not, of course, compel me to join the Conservative party; but it may compel me to sever my formal association with the Liberal ... party'.[120] Young wrote to Asquith less than a week later to formalise the break:

> The ... policy for ... rural land ... has made it necessary for me to consider my position in relation to the party ... I find myself with deep regret compelled to sever my connection with the present official Liberal organisation, and to act independently ... I desire to be allowed to express to you my great personal regard.[121]

Lloyd George clearly retained a fondness and respect for Young, saying that he would be 'a real loss to the Party ... and personally I shall miss your loyal comradeship ... I sincerely regret your severance from the Party, but I cannot without challenge pass by the implication ... that you and Mond alone are standing by Liberal principles'.[122] After four months as an independent, Young officially joined the Conservatives, in June 1926. He continued to sit for Norwich until the 1929 election, when he moved to Sevenoaks, where he was elected as a Conservative, with a large majority. In November 1931, having been returned unopposed, he became Minister of Health in the National Government. In this role he was responsible for slum clearance and rehousing and so became intimately involved in interventionist urban land policy. His 1935 Housing Act was the first to set standards of accommodation and provide for their enforcement. Young retired from politics with a peerage, as first Baron Kennet, in June 1935, but lived for a further twenty-five years.

Uncouponed, and challenged by a National Liberal in 1922, **Cyril Entwistle** held his seat at Hull South West from 1918 to 1924. He had been an advocate of reunion and had discussed the situation with Lloyd George in early 1923, although Lloyd George had found the terms proposed unacceptable, commenting afterward that 'He was prepared to go a long way in the way of conciliation [but] he would not crawl on [his] belly'.[123] After being defeated in 1924 by a Conservative, Entwistle was still keen to continue his political career. The prospects for his return to parliament as a Liberal looked bleak: he was out of sympathy with Lloyd George and his policies. On 1 February 1926, objecting to Lloyd George's land reports and dismayed by the continuing party squabbles, Entwistle left the Liberals and went straight to the Tories. He wrote to Asquith: 'the Liberal Party seems more concentrated on internal dissensions than on endeavouring to inform politics with the spirit of Liberalism. The conduct and aspirations of the present Government have satisfied [me that I] should associate [myself] with the Conservative Party'.[124] At his second attempt, Entwistle was returned to the Commons as the Conservative MP for Bolton in 1931 and sat until his defeat in 1945.

Courtenay Mansel, another of the Asquithians who defected to the Conservatives, had the unusual distinction of having succeeded twice to the same baronetcy. He inherited the title in 1892, relinquished it to his uncle who turned out not to have been illegitimate and then re-inherited it on his uncle's death in 1908. Mansel was a major landowner in Carmarthenshire, but took a rather unenlightened view of relations with the workers, arguing that there should not be a limit of forty-eight hours work per week and that negotiations should be left to 'master and man'.[125] Although retaining links with Carmarthenshire Liberalism, Mansel was elected for Penryn and Falmouth in 1923. He was defeated at the 1924 election. Following this, he was offered the chance to replace Alfred Mond as Liberal prospective candidate for Carmarthen.

However, he declined, saying that the Green Book was 'a political document I cannot reconcile with the fundamental conception of Liberalism ... I can put no confidence in an edifice ... based on ... Socialism'.[126] In March 1926, Mansel followed Mond into the Conservative Party, writing to *The Times* about the land policies:

> Lloyd George's restless activities are ... suggestive of ... the activities of the London street-breaker ... No sooner is a piece of road completed at great expense than it is torn up again, and the *disjecta membra* are again exposed. Both proceedings surely are destructive, wasteful, and unworthy of modern civilization.[127]

When Mond was finally ennobled in 1928, Mansel was chosen as the Conservative candidate for the resulting Carmarthen by-election. In a tight three-way contest, won by the Liberals, he came third. He repeated this performance in his final election, when he stood as the Conservative candidate for the University of Wales in 1929. As with Young (and later Grigg), Mansel retained a personal respect for Lloyd George even after the parting of their ways. Mansel wrote to Lloyd George at the time of the Carmarthen by-election to say that although 'in my v. humble scope, & unhappily for me, from a deep & instinctive conviction, opposed to your policy, I have never failed to recognise the claims of the greatest orator of the age, (fatally gifted!).'[128]

Samuel Pattinson was the brother of Robert Pattinson, and brother-in-law of Richard Winfrey, both Liberal MPs who remained loyal to the party. Samuel Pattinson was elected at his third attempt as Liberal MP for Horncastle in 1922 and sat until he was defeated by a Conservative in 1924. He was an Asquithian and an admirer of Bonar Law. Pattinson, described as a 'rough diamond' and 'a bit of a bruiser', lived at the Russell Hotel, when in London, where his brother and several other MPs also stayed. They had a reputation for getting up to pranks, including swapping a colleague's room while he was out, so that he came back to confront the new unsuspecting occupant on his return.[129] Soon after his defeat in 1924, Samuel Pattinson announced that he would not contest Horncastle again and there were rumours that he was about to join the Conservatives. However, he waited until May 1929 to announce his conversion, condemning Lloyd George's unemployment policies. His defection, and particularly its timing and reasons, were rather awkward for his brother, who was contesting Lincoln as a Liberal. Samuel Pattinson told his local newspaper that he admired Baldwin for the manner in which he managed the General Strike and that he should not give his vote to any supporter of Lloyd George's unemployment policy. 'I do not think it is a practical proposition and it is unworkable from a financial and other points of view.'[130] Pattinson's brother probably suffered no worse a fate than he would have, had his brother remained loyal to the party: he came bottom of the poll in Lincoln, as had his predecessor Liberal candidate for the seat, and in fact he slightly increased his share of the vote. Samuel Pattinson never contested a seat as a Tory and retired from national politics.

The next Liberal to defect over Lloyd George's policies was also one of two brothers who were both Liberal MPs. **Albert Illingworth** was the elder brother of Percy Illingworth, Liberal chief whip from 1912 until 1915, when he died after eating a bad oyster. Albert Illingworth served as a Liberal MP from 1915 to 1921, when he was raised to the peerage, having served as Lloyd George's Postmaster General from 1916 to 1921. Albert was almost as unfortunate at picking employees as his brother had been at picking crustaceans. The by-election resulting from Illingworth's elevation was won for Labour by one of his own farm labourers.[131] Albert's wife then had an affair with another of her husband's former employees. She wrote an incriminating letter to her lover, which fell into Illingworth's hands. Illingworth decided immediately to divorce her. He confronted his wife, who tried to allay her husband's wrath by saying that she had not committed adultery 'very frequently'.[132] The next day he filed his petition and saw nothing more of his wife until the petition came to court. Illingworth's abrupt ending of his marriage was echoed in the manner of his departure from the Liberal Party in April 1930. By then he was a director of the National Provincial Bank and the Ford Motor Company. Illingworth wrote to Salisbury, the Conservative leader in the Lords: 'As I am unable to support the present policy of the Liberal Party I have decided to leave them, and if you have no objection I should like to join the Conservatives.'[133] *The Times* reported Illingworth's 'revolt'.[134] As well as his new political allegiance, Illingworth also remarried the following year: both new alliances lasted until the end of his life in 1942.

The last of the Lloyd George Policy Objectors to defect to the Conservatives was **Edward Grigg**, in February 1931. While Albert Illingworth *was* the brother of Percy Illingworth, Edward Grigg was *not* the brother of Percy Grigg, although they both served in the same administrations in the Second World War and the 1945 Caretaker Government. Edward Grigg was a journalist with *The Times* before the Great War. After returning as a lieutenant-colonel, Grigg was appointed private secretary to Lloyd George. To the traditional loyalties required for the post, he added an intense personal admiration for his chief, which blinded him to all criticism.[135] Grigg's situation was similar to that of Young. Grigg was 'imposed' on Oldham, another two-member constituency, in 1922.¹³⁶ He stood 'heart and soul' for Lloyd George with, as Grigg described him, a 'delightful old gentleman of 70 who is a Unionist but a strong co-operator. We have the same agent and the same platform and attend the same meetings'. When, in the event, Grigg was elected alongside a Labour candidate he called it 'only half a victory as my Unionist colleague failed to get in'. Grigg was re-elected in 1923 and went on to be one of the Liberal survivors of the 1924 election, after which he commented: 'We shall be a chosen few in the House of Commons and I am not sure that a more suitable destination for us would not be in glass cases in the South Kensington Museum.'¹³⁷ Grigg had still hoped in 1924 that the Liberal Party would 'go forward on a Liberal Imperialist line', but warned that 'if the Party ... does not do so, I shall probably end by dissociating myself from it'.¹³⁸ On 27 May 1925 Grigg wrote (presumably) to Lloyd George, but addressing him as 'My dear P.M.', to say that he had decided to accept the offer of the Governorship of Kenya:

> [T]he work ... will be much preferable ... to sitting beside Runciman in the House and feeling tied up with horrible blighters like him ... we shall get no further ... till ... the Wee Frees have ... been swallowed up by the Socialists. Their one idea at present is to stiletto you ... but you are ... stuck full of arrows and none the worse for it!¹³⁹

Lloyd George replied: 'I shall miss you in the House.'¹⁴⁰ Grigg left the Commons in 1925 to take up his post in Kenya, where he served until 1930. Grigg and Lloyd George remained on friendly terms, even when Grigg eventually wrote in February 1931, after his return from Kenya, to finalise his split from the Liberal Party:

> You are evidently going left – with a vengeance, which I quite understand – and most of the Liberal Party with you. You will know, from what you know of me, that I cannot go that way. It is, I suppose, at bottom a matter of temperament ... I wish it were not so, but it is ... on the personal side, I hate this parting of the ways and will always regard you, not merely as the greatest man in our public life today (which is not saying much) but as one who saved the Empire ... I shall not – like some others – go back on it. Yours still (in all but politics).¹⁴¹

Grigg re-entered the Commons as National Conservative MP for Altrincham at a by-election in June 1933 and sat until 1945, when he was created Baron Altrincham. He held a series of ministerial appointments during the war, culminating in his posting as Minister Resident in the Middle East from November 1944 to May 1945. Grigg was to be the last of the Lloyd George Policy Objectors to defect from the Liberals, but the party was probably only spared further losses because Lloyd

George himself was to depart the leadership, and even, temporarily, the party.

Protection Convert Industrialists

In addition to the Liberals who left the party over their disagreement with Lloyd George's policies, there were also three other defectors who left, primarily because they changed their views on protection. These three were industrialists, who also served in the Commons, but who saw government policy through the prism of their business interests (see Table 4.3). They were willing to sacrifice political principles for commercial advantage.

Table 4.3 *Protection Convert Industrialist defectors*

Defector	Date of defection to the Conservatives
Henry Cowan	1923
Albert Bennett	1924
Walter Forrest	1930

Henry Cowan was involved with the firm of Parkinson Cowan, manufacturers of stoves and meters, eventually becoming chairman. He was a man of 'decided opinions' and he never hesitated to press them for fear of the consequences. Compromise was not in his nature and he made enemies.[142] In 1922 he was defeated as the Coalition Liberal MP for Aberdeenshire and Kincardineshire East by his only opponent, the Liberal, Frederick Martin, who later defected to Labour (see Chapter 3). Less than a year later, in October 1923, Cowan himself defected to the Conservatives. In a letter to *The Times* on 30 October 1923 he announced his conversion to tariffs:

> As one who ... accepted, under pre-war conditions, the policy of Free Trade, I looked to Liberalism for a solution ... only to find that ... there is nothing constructive in the proposals put forward by either of the groups into which the party is now divided ... I am prepared to support the Unionist programme ... under such changed conditions as exist today.[143]

Cowan wrote to the East Aberdeenshire Liberal Association: 'I have not deserted my leaders, but they have deserted me ... At the last election I was criticized ... by members of the Liberal Party, for the consistent support which I gave to the Safeguarding of Industries Bill ... The step I am taking to-day is not therefore, in any way inconsistent with the views I then placed before the electors.'[144] Adopted as Conservative candidate for North Islington at the 1923 General Election, Cowan said that his own views were the 'views of the orthodox Unionist Party'. Before the 1922 election the Unionists had invited him to stand under their auspices, but he was pledged as a Coalition Liberal. When the Coalition disbanded he had come to believe that the old policies were 'no good'.[145] Cowan's 1923 election address stressed the importance he put on protection: 'Free Trade is an experiment which ... has failed because other nations have refused to adopt it.' Cowan was successful and sat as a Conservative MP from 1923 to his retirement in 1929.

Albert Bennett had extensive business interests in South America, where he had been Controller of Propaganda in the Great War. He had stood unsuccessfully as an Asquithian Liberal in Chippenham in 1918, before being elected to serve a single term at Mansfield in 1922. He lost the seat in a straight fight with Labour in 1923. By the 1924 election, Bennett, who had lost confidence in free trade and in the Liberals for supporting a Labour Government, had been adopted as Conservative candidate for Central Nottingham. In his 1924 election address he blamed the increase in unemployment on the repeal of the McKenna duties and the Safeguarding of Industries Act and claimed that:

> Socialist Government ... is sufficient to frighten Capital away ... I appeal especially to patriotic Liberals to put their country first and to vote ... Conservative ... The General Council of the Trades Union Congress ... state that this Election is ... to be treated ... as a Constitutional Rebellion. It is the first time that 'rebellion' has been advocated at a General Election.

Bennett was successful as a Conservative in 1924 and in defending the seat in 1929. He was appointed Deputy Treasurer of the Conservative Party in 1928. However, on 14 January 1930 Bennett announced that he would not seek re-election and that, 'owing to pressure of business' as a result of the depression, he wanted to retire from parliament as soon as possible. Although, Bennett was keen to leave parliament quickly, he wanted to ensure a smooth transition to a Conservative successor. However, the transition did not progress as Bennett hoped. The chosen official Conservative candidate was not enthusiastic enough about Baldwin's industrial programme for the liking of some local Conservatives and a rival protectionist candidate came forward. Bennett had to postpone his departure until the threat of a split Conservative vote had been overcome. Eventually, Bennett's designated successor pledged himself to the full Baldwin programme, the protectionist prospective candidate withdrew and the Conservatives held the seat.

Walter Forrest was a Yorkshire woollen manufacturer. He was elected as a Coalition Liberal for Pontefract in 1919, but he was defeated in 1922. For the 1923 election he changed constituencies to Batley. Against the national trend, he was unsuccessful at this attempt, but won in 1924, losing it again in 1929. After his defeat, Forrest's politics drifted to the right. In January 1930 he offered to help Beaverbrook with his Empire Crusade.[146] That autumn Forrest was (rather inconsistently) describing himself as 'an old Liberal, a supporter of Lord Beaverbrook's and ready to stand as an official Conservative candidate'.[147] He was invited to contest the Shipley by-election for the Conservatives, but was concerned that his views were still not right-wing enough:

> Do you suppose Lord Rothermere will put up a Candidate? I expect he would certainly do so, if the official Conservative were backward in his Imperial policy. But should I decide to stand I feel, in view of my forward attitude on this question . . . he could at the least hold off in this case . . . Of course, I could not stretch my views to his.[148]

Forrest considered the offer carefully, taking into account the fact that the seat had been held by Labour since 1923, and then wrote back to Beaverbrook to decline.[149] The eventual Conservative candidate won the by-election with a majority of 1,665, and held the seat at the following general election. On 31 March 1931, Forrest wrote to Baldwin officially asking to join the Conservative Party and saying that his belief in free trade had 'gradually weakened' and that it was his conviction that the 'well-being of the nation demanded safeguarding at home and the widest possible extension of inter-Imperial trade'.[150] Later, he became identified with the Liberal National Party, and was a member of the National Executive, and Treasurer, of the Liberal National Council, but he did not seek re-election to parliament.

These three Protectionist Convert Industrialists arrived at their decision to defect from the Liberals to the Conservatives on the basis of the policies which they believed were in the best interests of their companies. Their views were focused onto short-term issues, as would have been demanded by their shareholders. Their perspective was little influenced by party loyalty or any other political considerations. Alfred Mond, who had already transferred his allegiance to the Conservatives over his objection to Lloyd George's land policies (see pp. 120–2), also became a leading advocate of tariffs and worked with Beaverbrook on the Empire Crusade.

Faux Fusionists

After the 1924 election, although the Constitutionalists had effectively disbanded, there persisted several cases where Liberal MPs, such as

Freddie Guest, Hilton Young and Edward Grigg, tried to ride two horses – Liberal and Conservative – exploiting an ambiguous relationship between the two at constituency level. Another who considered this delicate balancing act was **Louis Spears**. General Spears was a man of many parts – including French, English, German, Irish and Jewish. Despite a change of name from Edward Spiers to Louis Spears, of residence from France to England, of career from soldier to politician, of wife from Mary Borden (the author) to Nancy Maurice (daughter of the General of the 1918 debate fame), a consistent theme in Spears's life was his admiration for Churchill. This constancy though, led to another change, from Liberal to Conservative. Spears entered parliament unopposed in 1922 for Loughborough. The seat had previously been represented by Oscar Guest, who did not contest the election. Spears' election address stated: 'I stand as a National Liberal, ready to co-operate with the Conservative Party.' Almost immediately after the election Spears offered to give up his seat in order that the defeated Churchill could return to the Commons, to which Churchill replied: 'It is splendid proof of yr friendship [but] the Whips will find me a seat if I wanted one.'[151] Spears narrowly held his seat in 1923, but, soon after, compromised his position in the constituency by supporting Churchill (by then no longer a Liberal and facing a Liberal opponent) in the Westminster by-election, later writing to Churchill: 'I wd have given my right hand to get you in.'[152] The neighbouring Liberal MP dissociated himself from Spears's position, writing: 'I'm sorry I can't support you at Loughboro' ... I understand you have offered to support Mr. Winston Churchill against the officially nominated Liberal candidate.'[153] Spears's support for Churchill meant that it was 'impossible to get any financial support whatever' in Loughborough at the 1924 election.[154] Spears used the labels Liberal and, elsewhere Anti-socialist, at that election, but did not call himself a Constitutionalist and was opposed, as in 1923, by a Conservative. Spears's 1924 election address went into elaborate detail on his anti-socialist credentials, but ended up appearing more anti-Conservative in tone, because of his frustration at facing a Conservative opponent. He warned: 'A vote for the Tory Candidate may let the Socialist in.' In fact the votes for the Tory candidate let the Tory candidate in, and Spears fell to bottom of the poll. Despite Spears's annoyance at the Conservative Party over his 1924 defeat, within a matter of weeks he was actively negotiating his entry into their party. Regardless of the fact that Churchill had by then accepted the post of Tory Chancellor of the Exchequer, Spears still toyed with the idea of following his mentor's tortuous path into the same party. Instead of making a direct move, Spears considered standing again in

Loughborough, but as an Independent with Conservative support. His idea was quickly despatched as 'sheer madness'.[155] Spears then attended two interviews in December 1924 at Conservative Party headquarters, where he agreed unconditionally to join the party, but to wait until his return from an impending trip to America to announce his defection.[156] The letter announcing Spears's conversion appeared in The Times on 4 May 1925. However, Lloyd George was able to avenge his party's loss. At the Bosworth by-election of 1927, Spears contested the seat for the Conservatives. The Liberal, William Edge, won and Spears came last, in the formerly Conservative-held seat. After his defeat, Spears complained that 'Edge has been spending at least £10,000 of Lloyd George's money in the division, and thirty paid organisers have been at work on his behalf for many months.'[157] Spears managed to lose another Tory seat in 1929, when he was defeated at Carlisle. He did eventually return to the Commons, when he took Carlisle in the more favourable circumstances of 1931. He held the seat until he was again defeated in 1945. Spears was a courageous and many-faceted character, but not an electoral asset to any political party. He only won two contested elections of the seven which he fought, even though on every occasion he was fighting for the incumbent party.

Rhys Williams and his wife Juliet both had ambiguous, and inaccurately represented, relationships with the Liberal Party. Rhys Williams declared himself a Lloyd George supporter, writing to his leader in 1919: 'I do not think you need any assurances of my wholehearted allegiance, which, as you know, has been lifelong.'[158] Guest embellished the facts, referring to non-existent battles against the Asquithians, when he wrote to Lloyd George: 'I feel sure that you would not wish to forget . . . the gallant fight that Rhys Williams successfully made for us in the Banbury Division against the Asquithian hosts.'[159] In fact, Rhys Williams was elected three times for Banbury, but each time he was not opposed by an Asquithian, nor indeed by any other opponent at all. He was first returned without a contest at a by-election in September 1918, was unopposed in the 1918 general election and faced an unopposed by-election on his appointment as Recorder of Cardiff in June 1922. The Times reported that he was 'Never a keen party politician, [and that] he was content to drop out of Parliament when the Lloyd-George [sic] Government fell'.[160] However, in 1922 he did stand again, unsuccessfully contesting Pontypridd as a National Liberal. The inaccuracies and ambiguities continued. In March 1931, while Lloyd George was leader of the Liberal Party, there was a by-election at Pontypridd. Rhys Williams, still claiming to be a Liberal, appeared on the Conservative platform to oppose the Liberal candidate, because he believed that he was part of a pact to assist the socialists. As a self-proclaimed 'lifelong Liberal', Williams said he 'deplored the methods that had been adopted by those Liberals who still obeyed the orders of the official headquarters ... there were tens of thousands of Liberals who, like himself, detested this policy, and, like Sir John Simon, were tired of tactics'.[161] Williams's argument about assisting the Labour candidate was not supported by the evidence. At the last election the Labour candidate had gained more votes than the combined totals of the second-placed Liberal and the last-placed Conservative. The absence of a Liberal candidate at the by-election would almost certainly have resulted in an even larger margin of victory for the Labour candidate. In 1938, when the Labour victor of the 1931 Pontypridd by-election died, Williams's wife stood unsuccessfully as a National Liberal candidate in the by-election. However, she later reappeared as the (unsuccessful) Liberal candidate in Ilford North in 1945. However, by 1947 Lady Rhys Williams appears to have been back on the Conservative side of the fence: in February that year she was used as conduit for Churchill to approach Violet Bonham Carter for the Liberals about the possibility of a pact between the Liberals and the Conservatives. Nothing came of these confidential proposals and in 1951 Clement Davies publicly rejected a formal offer of a coalition with the Conservatives. Neither Rhys Williams nor his wife therefore ever won a contested election and their track record of loyalty to their parties, to their leaders and to their friends made them somewhat risky associates. They both appear to have taken a fairly consistent path along the boundary of the Liberal and Conservative Parties, which at different stages placed them in the orbit of Lloyd George, Simon and Churchill.

Robert Munro's departure from the Liberal Party was imperceptible at the time, and he never publicly announced that he had joined any other party. However, the facts demonstrate that he was indeed a defector, as he served as a Liberal MP from 1910 to 1918 and then as a Coalition Liberal until 1922, but in 1945 he was a member of the (Conservative) Caretaker Government. Munro served as Secretary for Scotland from 1916 to 1922 and by taking office had incurred the displeasure of his fellow Scottish Liberal MPs, none of whom would agree to serve as his parliamentary secretary.[162] He incurred considerable further displeasure in other quarters by his actions in the post. He took tough action over industrial unrest, including banning meetings, suppressing newspapers and sending troops and tanks to Glasgow. Aware that his unpopularity could affect his re-election prospects, Munro wrote to Lloyd George to check that his 'acceptance of the office of Secretary for Scotland should not ... prejudice my claims to judicial preferment'.[163] Munro was concerned about his career and his finances, and by 1922 could see little prospect on either count for him within the sphere of politics. Timing his departure rather neatly, he wrote to Lloyd George on 1 September 1922:

> It seems to me that I have come to the parting of the ways. If I had a private fortune or a . . . business – which I have not – I should prefer to remain in political life. But when I reflect on the financial condition in which I should be if I lost office, I am really alarmed . . . And therefore with great reluctance to leave politics and to leave you . . . I feel I must prefer my claim to the vacant [judicial] office.[164]

Munro accepted a judicial appointment and resigned his seat, which was still vacant at the time of the 1922 election. Writing his (rather opaque and sketchy) memoirs in 1930, Munro was keen to distance himself from all political parties: 'I have no right – and, indeed, no desire nowadays – to meddle in party politics.'[165] After he accepted a barony, as first Baron Alness, in June 1934, he moved to London and began a new parliamentary career, 'keeping away from party concerns'.[166] He was not listed as a Liberal or Liberal National in the 1939 Liberal Yearbook. Munro was appointed government spokesman on Scottish Affairs in the House of Lords from May 1940 to 1945, although this did not imply an alliance to any particular party. However, his appearance in the (Conservative) Caretaker Government as a Lord in Waiting in 1945, confirmed that he had changed his political alliance. Munro's defection was similar to that of Gwilym Lloyd-George, in that it was almost imperceptible at the time and difficult to date exactly, but with the opportunity of hindsight, it had most assuredly occurred.

Gwilym Lloyd-George's easy-going personality made him a congenial and flexible colleague in many delicate situations – and he saw many, from war service in the trenches to the Suez Crisis. Gwilym Lloyd-George (he alone among his family added a hyphen to his surname) was treated as something of a 'trophy politician' at several stages in his career. He had little political ambition[167] and went into politics 'because that was what my father wanted me to do'.[168] His name and family connections made him a valuable catch, but he was considered by colleagues as a down-to-earth 'fully paid-up member of the human race'.[169] He was elected for Pembroke in 1922 and served as a junior Liberal whip after the party's reunion in 1923, until he was defeated in 1924. He sat on the board of the *Daily Chronicle* during his absence from the Commons for the duration of the 1924 parliament. He was also a sometime trustee of the Lloyd George Fund. He returned to the Commons in 1929, at the same time as his sister Megan's first election. Gwilym Lloyd-George was appointed Parliamentary Secretary to the Board of Trade in the National Government, but served for only two months, resigning in November 1931. He was co-opted back into the same role by Chamberlain in 1939, despite most Liberals' supporting Sinclair's refusal to join the administration. Clement Davies later felt that Gwilym 'had drifted towards the Conservatives since 1939'.[170] Gwilym served as a minister throughout the war and stayed on in the 1945 Caretaker Government, with Alness (Munro). Gwilym Lloyd-George's defection from the Liberals was low-key, almost imperceptible at the time and probably the least dramatic of all the Liberal defections. At the beginning of the 1945 parliament, the Liberal chief whip furnished copies of the Liberal whip to Gwilym Lloyd-George and to several other independent members so that they might be informed of the business schedule of the House. So, while Gwilym Lloyd-George could thus truthfully say that he 'took the Liberal whip' until it was withdrawn in 1946, this referred only to the document, and not to the party discipline.[171] In 1945, after Sinclair's defeat, Gwilym Lloyd-George had been offered the leadership of the Liberals and, at about the same time, the leadership of the Liberal Nationals, but he declined both. Clement Davies was appointed Liberal leader instead and wrote to his predecessor, Sinclair, in 1950 bemoaning that 'Gwilym . . . has caused us a tremendous lot of worry'.[172] Gwilym Lloyd-George's 1950 election address described him as the 'Joint Liberal-Conservative Candidate . . . adopted by both Associations as their joint candidate . . . I hope I may be spared to serve you'. The Conservatives believed that Lloyd-George would have 'a hard fight to retain his seat' in 1950. There was 'a committee co-ordinating the Liberal and Conservative Associations, but the election campaign was hampered by a Conservative Constituency chairman who was 'past it', a 'lazy' Conservative agent and a Liberal agent who did not 'believe in canvassing'.[173] There was also 'the usual difficulty wherever the [Conservative] Party supports a Liberal'.[174] Part of this difficulty was that 'a section of Liberals who [did] not support his joint candidature [were] coming out into the open . . . suggesting that a Liberal candidate should be put forward'. In the event, Lloyd-George lost the seat in a straight fight with Labour. His prospects for the following election looked even worse: within two months, the local Liberals adopted a candidate of their own – 'without any consultation', as the local Conservative association grumbled. However, from the Liberal Party's point of view, they were not involved in any on-going relationship with the local Conservatives. This made a three-cornered fight almost inevitable.[175] Lloyd-George felt that he had been 'shockingly treated by treacherous Liberals' and the local Conservatives felt 'pretty sure' that Dr Pennant, the new Liberal candidate, would prove to be a 'Clem. Davies candidate in disguise'.[176]

It was clear that Pembrokeshire was a lost cause as far as any Liberal-Conservative cooperation was concerned, but the Tories still wanted to adhere nationally to a policy in which 'no action must be taken which would improve the prospects of the Labour Party' and where 'every effort must be made to secure friendly co-operation with the Liberals'.[177] Despite Conservative Central Office's considering that 'even ... Conservative supporters ... were impressed by the contrast between [Labour's 1950 victor] Donnelly and Gwilym Lloyd-George's virtual neglect' of Pembrokeshire,[178] the Conservative Party offered Lloyd-George a safe seat for the 1951 election in Newcastle North, where he 'was very much Central Office's candidate'.[179] The seat had had a troubled history as far as the Conservative Party was concerned. The long-serving Tory MP Sir Nicholas Grattan-Doyle had held the seat since 1918 and wanted to retire and hand the seat to his son, under the protection of the electoral truce during the Second World War. The plan was foiled when Sir Cuthbert Headlam, also a Conservative, decided to contest the seat and successfully persuaded Conservative Central Office not to acknowledge the younger Grattan-Doyle as the official candidate. Headlam won the seat and was accepted as the official Conservative MP, thus effectively disenfranchising the original local Conservative association. Headlam served until 1951 and his retirement created the vacancy for which Lloyd-George was selected. Lloyd-George had no prior connection with Newcastle North and only visited the constituency about once per month, where his activities were confined to 'staying at the larger country seats', which was commented on 'very bitterly'.[180] However, he did win the seat in 1951. Lloyd-George's career reached a peak as Home Secretary in Churchill's ministry in 1954, after earlier posts as Minister of Fuel and Power and Minister of Food. He was retained by Eden, but left the government with a viscountcy when Macmillan took over in January 1957.

When Gwilym Lloyd-George had resigned as Parliamentary Secretary to the Board of Trade in November 1931, his successor was **Leslie Hore-Belisha**. In many other respects too, Hore-Belisha's career followed that of Gwilym Lloyd-George – from the Liberals to the Tories via a period of ambiguous party status, a spell in the Caretaker Government and finally membership of the Conservative Party. Both also served in the Great War, reaching the rank of major and both were involved with the press during the 1920s. However, in terms of personality the two were very different. Lloyd-George – criticised by his own father for 'indolence'[181] and described by Violet Bonham

Carter as 'a floating kidney'[182] – contrasted strongly with the driven, ambitious and self-publicising Hore-Belisha. Hore-Belisha had lost his father at the age of one, and had to overcome the then disadvantage of being Jewish. Hore-Belisha was first elected as a Liberal MP in 1923, for Plymouth Devonport, and was one of only a handful of Liberals in southern England to survive the 1924 election. Despite changing party status, he held the seat until 1945. Initially an Asquithian, Hore-Belisha had then transferred his allegiance to Lloyd George. When Mosley founded the New Party in 1931, although he failed to attract the open support of more than a handful of prominent people, others, including Hore-Belisha let him understand that they were with him 'in spirit'.[183] However, later that year Hore-Belisha had joined the Liberal Nationals and this led to his first ministerial appointment, when he succeeded Gwilym Lloyd-George. From here, his career followed a steep upward trajectory – Financial Secretary to the Treasury in 1932, Minister of Transport in 1934, culminating in his appointment as Secretary of State for War in 1937. However, in January 1940 he was removed from the War Office by Chamberlain, and resigned from the cabinet, rather than accepting an alternative post. Many senior army officers disliked his radical approach to strategy, and he had little support from the political establishment because of his Jewish and Liberal background.[184] Hore-Belisha's career never regained its earlier heights. He spent the Second World War out of office and he resigned from the Liberal National Party in 1942, to sit as a 'National Independent' MP. On the formation of the Caretaker Government, Churchill recalled Hore-Belisha for a last nine-week ministerial stint as Minister for National Insurance. In the 1945 election, Hore-Belisha faced only Labour opposition, in the person of Michael Foot, who played upon his opponent's unclear party status, mocking: 'We do not know to which party Mr Hore-Belisha belongs ... I propose to fight this election on the assumption that he is a Tory. If he has any objection perhaps he will tell us.'[185] Hore-Belisha's adoption had been endorsed by Devonport Conservative Association as well as by the National Liberals. Foot won. A month after the 1945 election Hore-Belisha wrote to the Chairman of the Devonport Liberal National Association, stating that he had decided to join the Conservative Party, explaining: 'It now emerges clearly from the general election that it is under the aegis of the Conservative Party that the opposition to Socialism ... must be rallied.'[186] Hore-Belisha made one unsuccessful attempt to return to the Commons as a Conservative in Coventry South in 1950, before being given a peerage in 1954. He died suddenly at the age of sixty three, while delivering a speech as leader of a parliamentary delegation to France.

While several politicians were happy to let ambiguity cloud their exact political status, most at least were not dishonest. However, this was not always the case and there were examples of deliberate attempts to mislead voters. **George Wadsworth** won Buckrose as a Liberal in 1945, taking the seat from the Conservatives by 949 votes, in the absence of a Labour contender. In 1950 he faced Labour and Conservative opponents in the revised constituency of Bridlington, losing heavily to the Conservatives. After having difficulty finding a candidate, the Hillsborough Conservative and Liberal Association in Sheffield unanimously decided to recommend Wadsworth for adoption as their prospective candidate on 12 March 1951.[187] At the 1951 General Election all the Conservative candidates for the Sheffield seats were designated 'Conservative and Liberal' including Wadsworth. Other Yorkshire Area candidates were variously described as 'Conservative and National Liberal', 'National Liberal and Conservative', or 'Conservative and Unionist'.[188] Two of seven Sheffield Conservative candidates were expected to face Liberal opponents, but not in Hillsborough: all had Socialist opponents. Hillsborough had form in the misrepresentation of its candidates. Wadsworth's predecessor had been Sir Knowles Edge, who had fought and lost in 1950.[189] After his adoption in 1949 as the prospective Conservative-Liberal candidate for Sheffield Hillsborough, the Bolton Liberal Party – where Edge was still a member – had called on him to resign from the party after the executive passed a resolution stating that the Conservative-Liberal Association was an 'officially Tory-sponsored movement in direct opposition to the Sheffield Liberal Federation and in no way connected with, or officially recognized by, the Liberal Party'.[190] Wadsworth's 1951 election address was equally misleading:

> Do you desire wise, practical and efficient government which the Conservative Party, with the help of its Liberal Allies, can and will give[?] ... Mr. George Wadsworth was Liberal M.P. for Buckrose from 1945–1950. He is fighting this election as your Conservative and Liberal Candidate at the invitation, and with the support of, the fused constituency organisation of Conservatives and Liberals in Hillsborough.

The 'fused constituency organisation' was a blatant lie. Clement Davies took issue with Churchill over this type of misrepresentation. Davies was seriously concerned about the number of Conservative candidates using the word 'Liberal' in their party description: in addition to the National Liberals, there were candidates with many permutations of Conservative and Liberal or Liberal National and Conservative. Davies wrote to Churchill complaining: 'Is it so much to ask that the

Conservative Party should fight under its own name, or at least under a name which does not clash with that of another Party which is recognised throughout the world?' He cited examples of cases where local Conservative associations had dishonestly claimed to have merged with the local Liberals, in particular at Dunstable, North Angus and Torrington. Conservative tactics had included refusing Liberals admittance to meetings at which new associations with titles such as the 'United Conservative and Liberal Association' were established.[191] Davies's letter drew a predictably stinging response from Churchill:

> As you were yourself for eleven [sic] years a National Liberal, and in that capacity supported the governments of Mr Baldwin and Mr Neville Chamberlain, I should not presume to correct your knowledge of the moral, intellectual and legal aspects of adding a prefix or suffix to the honoured name of Liberal ... You and your friends do not seem to have any difficulty on the question of nomenclature with the Socialist Party. I have not heard, for instance, of any candidate who is standing as a Liberal-Socialist. The reason is, no doubt, that the two terms are fundamentally incompatible.[192]

The Conservative Party only stopped using titles including the word 'Liberal' in 1968, when the National Liberal Party was finally wound up.

Archibald Macdonald was the last defector to the Conservatives, in March 1971, since when no serving or former Liberal or Liberal Democrat MP has joined the Tories. Macdonald was one of that rare breed – a new Liberal MP at the 1950 election; the others being Jo Grimond in Orkney and Shetland and Donald Wade in Huddersfield West, where a local pact existed with the Conservatives. Wade was elected in the absence of a Tory opponent in return for the Liberals' not contesting the Eastern Division. Arthur Holt, the only new Liberal MP in 1951, was elected as a result of a similar arrangement at Bolton. Macdonald, in contrast to Grimond, Wade and Holt, only served a single term in parliament and was out at the 1951 contest. However, even Macdonald's short-lived tenure was a major Liberal achievement in the context of the times; and this was in spite of his relative lack of political experience. He was involved in the paint industry and had taken little part in politics before being adopted as the Liberal candidate at Roxburgh and Selkirk in 1944. He was not regarded by the party as a potential star and Lady Glen-Coats reported to Liberal Headquarters that she should have stopped his adoption as he 'retracted his financial offer, was defeatist and took a bad tone with the constituency officers'.[193] He was also described as a 'Right Wing Liberal' and at the same time 'disinclined to fight Labour'. Despite this unpromising start,

Macdonald came second in the 1945 election, only 1,628 votes behind the Conservative victor and in 1950 he overturned the Tory majority and won by 1,156 votes. After his defeat in 1951 Macdonald declined other opportunities to stand again, but initially remained active in the Liberal Party. In 1953 he was a member of the Radical Reform Group, which set out to counter the influence of the extreme free trade bloc within the Liberal Party. It supported government intervention to maintain full employment and social security, to regulate trade and to break up monopolies. Macdonald turned his focus to local politics, which he found more congenial, and he served as a Hampstead Borough Councillor and Liberal Group Leader from 1962 to 1965. However, only six years later, just before the Liberals' string of by-election victories, Macdonald left the Party and joined the Conservatives. He had been disillusioned with the policies being put forward by 'wild' Young Liberals. His conversion to Conservatism was not total, however, and he found himself out of step with their policies too.[194]

With a few exceptions, such as Archibald Macdonald, Liberal defections to the Conservatives were almost exclusively a feature of the period 1922 to 1931. Career opportunities (electoral and/or ministerial) were the central motivation of many of the defectors to the Conservatives, especially the Bonar Law Supporter-Third Coalitionists, the Fusionist, the Constitutionalists and the Faux Fusionists. In contrast to the defectors to Labour, the vast majority of those former Liberals who went to the right remained in their new political homes. Many adjusted their policy positions, for instance on free trade, but with backgrounds predominantly in the military, the professions and business there was little difficulty for the former Liberals to feel at home in the Conservative Party. All thirty-four of the defectors who joined the Conservative Party remained within that party.[195] Only a small number of the rightward defectors complained about their new party, but even they remained loyal to it. Courtenay Mansel, writing to Lloyd George who had told him that 'The Conservatives use you, & fling you aside', agreed with his old leader that 'as an under-dog, now securely muzzled, with bones and kicks ... I know from bitter experience that you said nothing but the truth'.[196] Decades later, Archibald Macdonald found himself in disagreement with some of the Conservatives' policies. But these complaints amounted to very little by comparison with the extensive dissatisfaction among the former Liberals who went to Labour. Perhaps, the ease of transfer of some of the former Liberals to the Conservatives begs the question as to whether they were ever truly Liberals. Some were; but others such as Mansel, Waring and the Guest brothers had at least some attitudes which were fundamentally at variance with Liberalism. The anger among many Liberals at their party's putting Labour into power in 1924 suggests that many had pro-Conservative leanings. While not sharing his political leanings, many of the rightward defectors would have concurred with Horabin's verdict that 'there was no place . . . for any party standing between . . . Labour . . . and the Tory Party'.[197]

Notes

1. Benn diary, 2 December 1924, Stansgate Papers, Parliamentary Archives.
2. The other former Asquithians who defected to the Conservatives were Cyril Entwistle, Courtenay Mansel, Samuel Pattinson, Albert Bennett, Leslie Hore-Belisha and Hilton Young. The last two were initially Asquithians, but transferred their allegiance to the coalition.
3. Outhwaite described the McKenna Duties in the Commons as 'A breach in the Free Trade system. We allow the enemy within our gates'.
4. McKenna, Stephen, *Reginald McKenna* (Eyre and Spottiswoode, 1948), pp. 256 and 283.
5. McKenna to Benn, 31 December 1916, ST/24/3/1, Stansgate Papers.
6. McKenna, *Reginald McKenna*, p. 285.
7. MacDonald diary, 17 November 1918, MacDonald Papers.
8. Paterson to McKenna, 25 October 1922, MCKN 9/17, McKenna Papers, Churchill Archives Centre.
9. Nicholas to McKenna, 29 October 1922, MCKN 9/17, McKenna Papers.
10. McKenna to Inchcape, 30 May 1923, MCKN 9/18/2, McKenna Papers.
11. McKenna, *Reginald McKenna*, pp. 9 and 318–19.
12. Draft McKenna to Baldwin, n.d., MCKN 9/18/1, McKenna Papers.
13. Hoare to Davidson, 25 August 1923, DAV/159, Davidson Papers, Parliamentary Archives.
14. *Daily News*, n.d., MCKN 9/18/2, McKenna Papers.
15. Newspaper cutting, unnamed, n.d., 28 August 1923[?], MCKN 9/18/2, McKenna Papers.
16. Novar to Rosebery, 16 January 1925, MS.10020.205, Munro-Ferguson Papers, National Library of Scotland.
17. Novar to Baldwin, 12 November 1924, MS.10020.203, Munro-Ferguson Papers.
18. Baldwin to Novar, 9 November 1924, MS.10020.202, Munro-Ferguson Papers.
19. The Guests' mother was the sister of Churchill's father, Randolph.
20. Freddie and Henry were in the Commons in 1917. Henry lost his seat in 1918, when Oscar was elected and Freddie re-elected.
21. Lloyd George to Primrose, 12 December 1916, LG/F/42/11/1, Lloyd George Papers.
22. Primrose to Lloyd George, 12 December 1916, LG/F/42/11/2, 13

December 1916, LG/F/42/11/3 and 2 April 1917, LG/F/42/11/7, Lloyd George Papers.
23 Primrose to *The Times*, 18 December 1916, p. 9, col. c.
24 Hart, 'Decline', 76.
25 Guest to Lloyd George, n.d. [probably August or September, 1919 after the death of Sir Joseph Compton-Rickett], LG/F/21/4/9, Lloyd George Papers.
26 Notes attached to Letter Guest to Lloyd George, 11 April 1919, LG/F/21/3/16, Lloyd George Papers.
27 Guest to Lloyd George, 3 April 1919, LG/F/21/3/14, Lloyd George Papers.
28 Guest to Mrs Lloyd George, 3 April 1919, LG/F/21/3/14a, Lloyd George Papers.
29 Guest to Lloyd George, 10 May 1919, LG/F/21/3/21 and 8 July 1919, LG/F/21/4/1, Lloyd George Papers.
30 *Daily Mail*, 16 July 1919, LG/F/21/4/6b, Lloyd George Papers.
31 Telegram Guest to Lloyd George?, n.d., LG/F/21/4/24(a), Lloyd George Papers.
32 Notes, Grant, 21 December 1919, LG/F/21/4/31(b) and 29 December 1919, LG/F/21/4/31(a), Lloyd George Papers.
33 Morgan, K., and Morgan, J., *Portrait of a Progressive* (Clarendon, 1980), p. 120.
34 *Berwickshire News*, 31 October 1922, p. 7, col. f, 3 April 1923, p. 4, col. b, 15 May 1923, p. 3, col. c, 29 May 1923, p. 5, col. c and 5 June 1923, p. 3, col. c.
35 *Leicester Daily Mercury,* 13 July 1923, p. 5, col. d and 31 July 1923, p. 7, col. d.
36 *The Times*, 1 August 1923, p. 7, col. c.
37 *The Times*, 31 July 1923, p. 6, col. g.
38 *Essex Times*, 17 November 1923, p. 3, col. c and 24 November 1923, p. 1, col. f.
39 Letter from Waring, 10 May 1914, GD372/54, Waring of Lennel Papers, National Archives of Scotland.
40 *Border Standard*, quoted *Berwickshire News*, 7 November 1922, p. 3, col. c.
41 Unnamed press cutting, n.d., letter, Macfarlane, 19 December 1923, GD 372/178, Waring Papers.
42 Waring to Young, 28 December 1923, GD 372/205/8, Waring Papers.
43 Duchess of Atholl to Clementine Waring, 28 December 1922, GD 372/137, Waring Papers.
44 GD 372/233/10, 14 January 1931, Waring Papers.
45 Churchill to Jackson, 12 October 1924, quoted Gilbert, *Churchill, Volume V*, p. 220.
46 William Dudley Ward had been defeated as a National Liberal in Southampton in 1922. He did not contest another seat for any party.
47 Waring, election address, 1923, GD 372/202, Waring Papers.

48 *The Times*, 24 October 1925, p. 15, col. f.
49 Brendan Bracken to *The Times*, 21 November 1930, p. 21, col. e.
50 *The Times*, 17 September 1920, p. 7, col. f.
51 *Gravesend and Dartford Reporter*, 18 October 1924, p. 4, col. e.
52 W. Harbison was also designated as a 'Constitutional and Democratic' candidate for Saffron Walden at the 1922 election. He was included on the official list of Liberal National candidates, but was not elected.
53 Moreing and Jarrett to Churchill, 5 February 1924, CHAR 2/132/29–31, Churchill Archives Centre.
54 J 77/1016/825, Family Division Records, 1910, National Archives.
55 Moreing to Guest, 31 March 1920, LG/F/22/25, Lloyd George Papers.
56 Riddell Diary, discussion Riddell and Horne, 30 May 1923, quoted Gilbert, *Churchill*, V, pp. 7–8.
57 Jenkins, Roy, *Churchill* (Macmillan, 2001), pp. 381–5.
58 Clementine Churchill to Churchill, n.d. [probably November 1923], quoted Gilbert, *Churchill*, V, p. 18.
59 Churchill to Bonham Carter, 8 January 1924, quoted Gilbert, *Churchill*, V, pp. 23–4.
60 *The Times* 3 March 1924, p. 12, col. d.
61 Jenkins, *Churchill*, pp. 388–90.
62 Churchill to Granville, unsent draft, [3] April 1924, quoted Gilbert, *Churchill, V Companion 1*, p. 138.
63 Churchill to Carson, 11 October 1924, quoted Gilbert, *Churchill, V Companion 1*, p. 219.
64 Birkenhead to Derby, 28 March 1924, quoted Gilbert, *Churchill, V Companion 1*, p. 39.
65 Churchill to Balfour, 11 October 1924, quoted Gilbert, *Churchill, V Companion 1*, p. 218.
66 Gilbert, *Churchill*, V, p. 43.
67 Notes on Greenwood, n.d. [1917 or later], LG/F/168/2/12, Lloyd George Papers.
68 Greenwood to Saunders, 4 October 1924, LG/G/8/9/1, Lloyd George Papers.
69 Greenwood to Lloyd George, 3 October 1924, LG/G/8/9/1, Lloyd George Papers.
70 *Walthamstow and Leyton Guardian*, 26 September 1924, p. 4, col. c, 17 October 1924, p. 5, col. b and 24 October 1924, p. 5, col. a.
71 Sturrock to *The Times*, 15 December 1923, p. 8, col. b.
72 Sturrock to *The Times*, 21 April 1924, p. 4, col. a.
73 *Montrose Review*, 17 October 1924, p. 7, col. c.
74 *Battersea Borough News*, 31 October 1924, p. 3, col. b.
75 *The Times*, 29 November 1923, p. 13, col. g.
76 *Staffordshire Weekly Sentinel*, 18 October 1924, p. 9, col. a.
77 *Accrington Gazette*, 18 October 1924, p. 3, col. a.
78 *Radcliffe Times*, 25 October 1924, p. 6, col. d.

79 *Radcliffe Times*, 18 October 1924, p. 4, col. b.
80 In addition to the former Liberal Constitutionalists, C. Loseby in Nottingham West, E. Doran in Silvertown, J. Davis in Consett and A. Fox-Davies in Merthyr Tydfil were listed in some newspapers as Constitutional candidates. Craig describes Loseby and Davis as Constitutionalists, but Doran and Fox-Davies as Conservatives. A. Hunter-Weston, sitting Conservative MP for Ayrshire and Bute, was also recorded as a Constitutionalist by *The Times*. Freddie Guest acted with the Constitutionalists, but did not use the label. George Jarrett had earlier used the Constitutionalist label, but in 1924 was a Conservative.
81 Excludes Dundee, a two-member seat, which had one Liberal and one Conservative candidate in 1924.
82 Aggregate increase or decrease in margins of victory or defeat from all the seats where the same candidate contested the seat in 1923 and 1924.
83 *The Times*, 4 November 1924, p. 16, col. c.
84 *The Times*, 17 December 1924, p. 14, col. c.
85 Sturrock to *The Times*, 18 February 1929, p. 8, col. d.
86 *County Express*, 29 January 1927, p. 5, col. e and 19 February 1927, p. 3, col. d.
87 Allen sat from 1892 to 1900 as Liberal MP for Newcastle-under-Lyme.
88 *Radcliffe Times*, 1 November 1924, p6, col. f.
89 *Stockport Advertiser*, 10 May 1929, p. 11, col. c.
90 Robinson to *Daily News*, 8 July 1929, quoted Craig, *Parliamentary Election Results, 1918–49*, p. 406.
91 Cooper, Kathleen, 'The Political and Military Career of Major-General J.E.B. Seely, 1968–1947', University of Southampton, M.Phil., 2001, pp. 200–2.
92 Benn diary, 15 April 1924.
93 Craig, *Parliamentary Election Results, 1918–1949*, 107, labels Guest 'Liberal' in 1924.
94 Guest to Lloyd George, 1 June 1926, LG/G/8/13/4, Lloyd George Papers, listing ten members of the 'Group' and ten 'likely supporters'.
95 Churchill to Baldwin, 4 June 1929, quoted Gilbert, *Churchill, V Companion 1*, p. 1474.
96 Guest to Baldwin, 14 March 1930, *The Times*, 24 March 1930, p. 9, col. b.
97 Guest to Beaverbrook, 30 October 1931, BBK/C/147, Beaverbrook Papers.
98 Douglas, Roy, *History of the Liberal Party, 1895–1970* (Sidgwick & Jackson, 1971), pp. 189–90.
99 *The Times*, 11 September 1928, p. 16, col. b.
100 *The Times*, 28 November 1922, p. 14, col. c.
101 *North Somerset Gazette*, 5 December 1925, p. 3, col. f.
102 Montgomeryshire returned a Liberal/Liberal Democrat MP at every election since 1880, except in 1979 and 2010.
103 Jones, J. Graham, 'The Peacemonger', *Journal of Liberal Democrat History*, 29 (2000/01): 16–18.

104 Interview Stanley Clement-Davies, London, 18 May 2002.
105 *The Times*, 28 January 1926, p. 14, col. g.
106 Jones, J. Graham, 'Sir Alfred Mond', *Dictionary of Liberal Biography*, ed. Brack, Duncan (Politico's, 1998) (hereafter DLB), p. 265.
107 *The Times*, 24 March 1922, p. 14, col. f.
108 Goodman, Jean, *The Mond Legacy* (Weidenfeld & Nicolson, 1982), pp. 124–6.
109 Mond to Lloyd George, 25 September 1924, LG/G/14/5/8, Lloyd George Papers.
110 Mond to Asquith, *The Times*, 26 January 1926, p. 14, col. c.
111 *The Times*, 27 January 1926, p. 14, col. e.
112 Goodman, *Mond Legacy*, p. 126.
113 Benn diary, 26 January 1926.
114 Baldwin to Mond, quoted Goodman, *Mond Legacy*, p. 128.
115 Goodman, *Mond Legacy*, pp. 124–6.
116 Greenaway, Frank, 'Mond family (per. 1867–1973)', ODNB.
117 Bentley, Michael, *The Liberal Mind 1914–1929* (Cambridge University Press, 1979), p. 77.
118 Young to Lloyd George, 19 October 1922, LG/F/28/8/18, Lloyd George Papers.
119 Seely declared that Young, by advocating the Tory cause, had kept him out of Parliament, Benn diary, 13 November 1924.
120 Young to Lloyd George, 20 May 1925, LG/G/10/14/17, 13 February 1926, LG/G/10/14/20, 20 November 1924, LG/G/10/14/16, 27 February 1924, LG/G/10/14, 26 August 1925, LG/G/10/14/18 and 31 December 1925, LG/G/10/14/19, Lloyd George Papers.
121 Young to Asquith, 19 February 1926, LG/G/10/14/21, Lloyd George Papers.
122 Lloyd George to Young, 23 February 1926, LG/G/10/14/22, Lloyd George Papers.
123 CP Scott diary, 8 March 1923, quoted Cook, C., *The Age of Alignment* (Macmillan, 1975), p. 95.
124 *The Times*, 2 February 1926, p. 14, col. d.
125 Wilson, *Downfall*, p. 233.
126 *The Times*, 6 March 1926, p. 9, col. f.
127 Mansel to *The Times*, 16 March 1926, p. 12, col. e.
128 Mansel to Lloyd George, n.d., LG/G/33/1/55, Lloyd George Papers.
129 CP Scott diary, 9 January 1924.
130 *Horncastle News and South Lindsey Advertiser*, 18 May 1929, p. 3, col. d.
131 The defeated Coalition Liberal candidate was Abraham England.
132 *The Times*, 30 October 1925, p. 5, col. d.
133 *Radcliffe Times*, 10 May 1930, p. 9, col. b.
134 *The Times*, 6 May 1930, p. 16, col. e.
135 Rose, Kenneth, 'Grigg, Edward William Macleay, first Baron Altrincham (1879–1955)', ODNB.

136 Jones, T., *Whitehall Diary*, Vol. 1, *1916–25*, 23 October 1922 (Oxford University Press, 1969), p. 217.
137 Grigg to Mond, 3 November 1924, quoted Hart, 'Decline', p. 256.
138 Grigg to Sinclair, 6 November 1924, quoted Hart, 'Decline', p. 256.
139 Grigg to Lloyd George, 27 May 1925, LG/G/8/11/6, Lloyd George Papers.
140 Lloyd George to Grigg, 28 May 1925, LG/G/8/11/7, Lloyd George Papers.
141 Grigg to Lloyd George, 16 February 1931, LG/G/8/11/9, Lloyd George Papers.
142 Obituary, *The Times*, 12 January 1932, p. 14, col. b.
143 *The Times*, 30 October 1923, p. 13, col. f.
144 *Buchan Observer*, 6 November 1923, p. 2, col. a.
145 *Islington and Holloway Press*, 24 November 1923, p. 3, col. a.
146 Forrest to Beaverbrook, 2 January 1930, BBK/B/148, Beaverbrook Papers.
147 Note of telephone call from Forrest, 17 September [1930?], BBK/B/148, Beaverbrook Papers.
148 Forrest to Beaverbrook, 18 September 1930, BBK/B/148, Beaverbrook Papers.
149 Forrest to Beaverbrook, 24 September 1930, BBK/B/148, Beaverbrook Papers.
150 *The Times*, 2 April 1931, p. 12, col. d.
151 Churchill to Spears, 18 November 1922, quoted Gilbert, *Churchill*, V, pp. 3–4.
152 Spears to Churchill, c.20 March 1924 after Westminster Abbey by-election, quoted Gilbert, *Churchill, V Companion 1*, p. 128.
153 Black to Spears, 11 March 1924, 1/43, Edward Spears Papers, Churchill Archives Centre.
154 Spears to Price, 9 November 1923, 1/280, Edward Spears Papers.
155 Packe to Spears, 4 December 1924, 1/261, Edward Spears Papers.
156 Spears to Packe, 17 December 1924, 1/261, Edward Spears Papers.
157 Spears to Churchill, 2 June 1927, quoted Gilbert, *Churchill, V Companion 1*, p. 1012.
158 Rhys Williams to Lloyd George, 24 November 1919, LG/F/18/3/34, Lloyd George Papers.
159 Guest to Lloyd George, 9 July 1919, LG/F/21/4/2, Lloyd George Papers.
160 Obituary, *The Times*, 1 February 1955, p. 10, col. d.
161 *The Times*, 10 March 1931, p. 16, col. c.
162 CP Scott diary, 30 January 1917.
163 Munro to Lloyd George, 16 December 1916, LG/F/1/7/1, Lloyd George Papers.
164 Munro to Lloyd George, 1 September 1922, LG/F/1/7/58, Lloyd George Papers.
165 Munro, Robert, *Looking Back: Fugitive Writings and Sayings* (Nelson, 1930), pp. 366–7.
166 Millar, Gordon, 'Munro, Robert, Baron Alness (1968–1955)', ODNB.
167 Interview, 3rd Viscount Tenby, London, 9 February 2004.

168 Unpublished autobiography, Gwilym Lloyd-George, MS 23671C, National Library of Wales.
169 Interview, Lord Allen of Abbeydale, 5 March 2004.
170 Davies to Sinclair, 28 November 1945, quoted Baines, Malcolm, 'The Survival of the British Liberal Party 1932–1959', Oxford, D.Phil. (1990), p. 67.
171 Rasmussen, Jorgen, *The Liberal Party: A Study of Retrenchment and Revival* (Constable, 1965), p. 11.
172 Davies to Sinclair, 6 January 1950 [mis-dated 1949], J/3/10, Clement Davies Papers, National Library of Wales.
173 James to Hay, 13 March 1950, quoted Baines, 'Survival', p. 76.
174 Report on Pembrokeshire Constituency, 7 July 1949, CCO1/7/542, Conservative Party Central Office Papers, Bodleian Library.
175 Constituency notes, Pembrokeshire, 8 November 1949, CCO1/7/542 and 2 May 1950, CCO1/8/542, Conservative Party Central Office Papers.
176 Howard Price to Charles Price, 3 May 1950, CCO1/8/542, Conservative Party Central Office Papers.
177 Meeting notes, Director General and Charles Price, 10 May 1950, CCO1/8/542, Conservative Party Central Office Papers.
178 Brooke to Central Office, 28 September 1950, CCO1/8/542, Conservative Party Central Office Papers.
179 Interview, 3rd Viscount Tenby London, 9 February 2004.
180 Partridge to Oliver, 12 April 1953, CCO1/8/542, Conservative Party Central Office Papers.
181 Morgan, K., 'George, Gwilym Lloyd-, first Viscount Tenby (1894–1967)', ODNB.
182 Pottle, Mark (ed.), *Daring to Hope: Diaries and Letters of Violet Bonham Carter, 1946–69* (Weidenfeld & Nicolson, 2000), p. 70.
183 Nicolson, H., *Diaries and Letters, 1930–39,* ed. Nicolson, Nigel (Collins, 1966), p. 66.
184 Tregidga, Garry, 'Leslie Hore-Belisha (1893–1957)', DLB.
185 *Western Morning News*, 9 June 1945, quoted Grimwood, Ian, *A Little Chit of a Fellow: A Biography of the Rt Hon. Leslie Hore-Belisha* (Book Guild, 2006), p. 202.
186 *Guardian*, 31 August 1945, quoted Grimwood, *Little Chit*, p. 205.
187 Note Urton to Thomas, 14 March 1951, CCO/1/8/189, Conservative Party Central Office Papers.
188 Yorkshire Area candidates and agents, 1951, CCO/2/2/6, Conservative Party Central Office Papers.
189 Son of former Liberal whip, William Edge.
190 Press cutting, unnamed, 20 October [1949], CCO/1/7/189, Conservative Party Central Office Papers.
191 Davies to Churchill, 23 January 1950, quoted Jones, J. G., 'Churchill, Clement Davies and the Ministry of Education', *Journal of Liberal Democrat History*, 27 (2000): 9.

192 *The Times*, 26 January 1950, p. 4, col. e.
193 Esselmont Papers, report on Macdonald, July 1944, quoted Egan, Mark, 'The Grass Roots organisation of the Liberal Party, 1945–64', Oxford, D.Phil., 2000, p. 88.
194 Reynolds, J. and Ingham, R., 'Archie Macdonald', *Journal of Liberal History,* 41 (2003): 11–14.
195 Walter Forrest, who joined the Conservatives in 1930 was associated with the Liberal Nationals in 1935.
196 Mansel to Lloyd George, n.d., LG/G/33/1/55, Lloyd George Papers.
197 *The Times*, 19 November 1947, p. 2.

5

Liberal defectors to minor parties

They, at any rate, did not leave behind them the slime of hypocrisy in passing from one side to another.'[1]

Liberal Nationals

The majority of the Liberal MPs and former MPs who joined the Liberal Nationals did not do so deliberately to defect from the Liberal Party. From the date of the formation of the National Government in August 1931 to the departure of the Samuelites from the government benches in November 1933, the Liberals and Liberal Nationals were in many respects two branches of one party, both on the government side of the Commons and both listed in the Liberal Yearbook as part of the same party. However, the actions of John Simon, Robert Hutchison and Ernest Brown in advance of the formation of the National Government were a clear and deliberate defection from the Liberal Party. They were, effectively, 'Proto-Liberal Nationals'. Likewise, those who changed allegiance between the Liberals and Liberal Nationals after November 1933 had to cross the floor of the House to do so. Therefore Simon, Brown and Hutchison and the post-November 1933 allegiance-changers could reasonably be considered to be defectors, along with the Lloyd George family group of Liberal MPs who deliberately dissociated themselves from the rest of the party on the formation of the National Government and who sat on the opposite side of the House.

At the time of Simon, Hutchison and Brown's defection in June 1931, no one could realistically have foreseen that a National Government was to be formed within two months. National politics was in turmoil over the rising level of unemployment and the resulting escalation in government spending. The Labour cabinet was failing to agree on a common policy, but its demise was by no means inevitable. The Liberal Party was split, primarily over the attitude to be adopted towards the Labour Government. Within the Liberal Party, opinions on Lloyd

George's leadership were polarised. The events between June 1931 and the transformation of the Liberal Nationals into a separate party were not part of a planned or predictable course of action, with any form of desired result in view. Simon may well have been satisfied to end up as the leader of a new small party, holding a pivotal role in a multi-party government, but this does not appear to have been his specific aim.

John Simon's key ambition was to be in the House of Commons, at the centre of political decision-making. His lucrative career in the law was never an adequate alternative for him. Nor was the role of a political organiser and party manager one which he craved. Simon, by all accounts (including his own), a cool and remote character, ascribed his 'frigid' nature to 'loneliness and dejection' after the death of his first wife in 1902. His was certainly not the typical character profile of an aspiring party leader. Simon had turned down the Lord Chancellorship in 1915 in favour of remaining in the Commons as Home Secretary, from where he hoped to advance his political career. He resigned as Home Secretary over the introduction of conscription in 1916 and later regretted this decision, which removed him from the centre of politics for fifteen years:

> It was a bitter decision which I had to take [but] I greatly feared that the transfer from voluntary enlistment ... would disunite the country and not add to our real power to win ... where I was wrong was in failing to appreciate the psychological effect ... of this demonstration that we would stick at nothing ... But it was a mistake ... it meant the abandonment of Cabinet office and Ministerial opportunity and a long setback in my political career.[2]

Lloyd George, by nature the antithesis of Simon, became the stumbling block in the way of Simon's return to front-line politics. Lloyd George's career had prospered during the Great War despite his early equivocation over the conflict, while Simon's career had been derailed by his principled resignation. Simon lost his Commons seat at the coupon election of 1918 and was thwarted in his attempt to return the following year at the Spen Valley by-election, by the intervention of a Coalition Liberal candidate (see Chapter 4). Lloyd George, motivated by personal animosity, had commented: 'I don't care who wins if that blighter [Simon] is last'.[3] In the event, it was Lloyd George's candidate who came last, with Simon second and the Labour candidate victorious – marking a negative watershed in the fortunes of the Coalition Liberals and a positive one for the Labour Party. For Simon, it was neither: he won the seat at his second attempt, in 1922. For a brief interlude, Simon's path, taking him to the right, intersected with that of Lloyd

George, veering to the left. When defending Spen Valley in 1923, after Liberal reunion, Simon received a telegram of support from Lloyd George. Simon was not convinced that Lloyd George's alignment was of any value to him, commenting caustically: 'Contrast Lloyd George's telegram trying to defeat me in the By-election of 1919 . . . Liberal Unity only disgusted some of my keenest supporters and would not gain me a single vote.'[4]

It was Lloyd George, rather than Simon, who emerged as Liberal leader following Asquith's retirement in 1926. Simon was no match for Lloyd George in party meetings. In a courtroom or formal political setting, where he had a designated opportunity to speak, Simon excelled in making a case. His skill was in gaining the majority support of a jury, or an audience, by logical argument, but without individual personal interaction. In an informal gathering, even with close colleagues, he rarely succeeded in empathising with his listeners or, in some cases, even remembering their names. During the 1920s, Simon's views increasingly diverged from those of Lloyd George, with their respective attitudes to the General Strike making this abundantly clear: Simon took a legalistic and very hostile stance against the strikers, while Lloyd George stretched the boundaries of Liberal policy in the opposite direction. In 1927, Simon accepted the chair of the Indian Statutory Commission, which temporarily drew his focus away from domestic politics. However, his long-term domestic political ambitions still burned. He was re-elected at Spen Valley in the 1929 general election. As had been the case in 1924, he was again without a Conservative opponent, and therefore saw local Conservatives as his allies and Labour as his political enemy.

Despite some by-election victories in the preceding couple of years and Lloyd George's library of policies, the 1929 election result dashed almost all the Liberals' hopes of forming a future government. After the election, Lloyd George led the party on a seemingly erratic – but generally leftward – path, primarily governed by the state of his secret (and ultimately futile) negotiations with the Labour Party, over pacts and the introduction of the Alternative Vote. Meanwhile, Simon conducted a convoluted set of manoeuvres, including his public abandonment of free trade, which made him increasingly acceptable to the Conservatives. However, Simon did not capitalise on his potential value as a defector by gathering and brandishing a group of followers willing to move with him. Instead, he essentially only sought a prominent role for himself, confiding to the Conservative Amery that he wanted the role of Foreign Secretary. Simon's name was publicly linked to a fluctuating pool of supposed followers, who might have defected from the Liberal Party with him, but he did almost nothing to ensure their loyalty. This was in sharp contrast to the emphasis which Churchill had put on the number of his supposed disciples when he was negotiating with the Tories. Simon's focus on his own situation and neglect of his colleagues was to be a source of frustration to fellow politicians on many occasions. The Conservatives considered that Simon was not a significant catch on his own, but that he would be valuable, if he could bring them the support of a score or so of supporters: Chamberlain felt that 'twenty-two would be worth talking about'.[5] Simon's disengagement from the Liberal Party was no secret. On 25 October 1930, he authorised the publication of a letter to Lloyd George in which he declared that he had 'no confidence in the Government and that the Liberals are in danger of carrying offers of assistance to the point of subservience'. In the events of June 1931, Simon coordinated his actions with only two colleagues – Brown and Hutchison; the latter having resigned as Liberal chief whip the previous year. On 26 June 1931 Simon wrote to the new Liberal chief whip, Sinclair, saying:

> [T]he official Liberal Party in the House of Commons reached a lower depth of humiliation than any into which it has yet been led. To the distrust of the electors, the disapproval of Liberals in the country and the jeers of the Conservatives has now been added the outspoken contempt of [Labour Chancellor] Snowden ... Every man is the guardian of his own self-respect, but whatever others may do I must formally dissociate myself from a course which has led to this pitiful exhibition, so I write to say that I do not desire further to receive your official Whip.[6]

Simon's departure drew from Lloyd George his molluscous analogy that Simon had left behind him 'the slime of hypocrisy'.

Robert Hutchison had revealed some of his equivocation about the Liberal Party as early as the 1924 election. He was then the Liberal candidate for the Montrose Burghs, having been defeated at the previous election after one term as National Liberal MP for Kirkcaldy. His predecessor as Liberal MP for Montrose, Sturrock, had moved south to stand as a Constitutionalist, and a constituent had asked Hutchison: 'Seeing that Mr. Leng Sturrock has turned Conservative within a week, would you guarantee, if returned, that you would not do the same?' Hutchison had replied: 'I see no likelihood in the near future of me leaving the Liberal party', which, of course, begged the question about the longer term.[7] Hutchison was returned and in 1926 he was appointed chief whip. His previous military experience as a major-general hardly prepared him for the unwillingness of the Liberal MPs to follow instructions. Ironically, however, he had to resign as chief whip in 1930, after he failed to follow his own orders, when he voted in opposition to the Labour Government, against his own party line. By June 1931, Hutchison had decided to dissociate himself from the Liberal Party, following its support for the Labour Government. The timing and content of Hutchison's and Brown's letters reveal a high degree of coordination with Simon. In his letter to the chairman of Montrose Burghs Liberal Association, also dated 26 June 1931, Hutchison wrote:

> [S]ince I resigned my position of Chief Whip ... I have found myself increasingly out of sympathy politically with the majority of the Parliamentary party. The policy of cooperating with, and of keeping in office at all costs, the Socialist Government is one which I have been unable to support ... the Liberal Parliamentary Party has been driven into a position which compels it to support the Government on any question which may endanger its life. For this support the Socialist Party is not even grateful ... The reward for such continuous support and help at any price was the most humiliating speech of the Chancellor of the Exchequer ... To anyone with a spark of self-respect this treatment is intolerable, and I decline to act along with a Parliamentary party which continues such servility to Socialism.[8]

The third co-conspirator, **Ernest Brown**, had served one term as Liberal MP for Rugby from 1923 to his defeat in 1924. He had then returned to the House of Commons as Liberal MP for Leith at the by-election in March 1927, caused by Wedgwood Benn's resignation on his defection from the Liberal Party. Simon, Hutchison and Brown had all won their seats in 1929 against a strong Labour showing, but without a Conservative opponent. Many potential Conservative voters had supported them and they were anxious not to alienate this support by being seen to be sympathetic to Labour. Angry at the support given by the Liberals to the Labour Government after 1929, from which he believed they should 'stand entirely aloof',[9] Brown resigned the Liberal whip at the same time as, and using similar language to, Simon and Hutchison:

> After the deplorable humiliations to which the Liberal Party has been subjected in recent weeks, terminating in the disgusting scene in the House of Commons last night, when Mr. Snowden rubbed the noses of those who are cooperating with him in the mud ... members of the present Government are to be allowed to treat Liberal members in any manner they think fit and that, notwithstanding this, a certain section of our party is prepared to aid and abet them ... I can no longer be associated with such a policy, and ... must act as an Independent Liberal for the rest of this Parliament ... Please accept my resignation from the Shadow Cabinet and remove my name from the list of those receiving the party whips.[10]

The Times noted on 29 June that Simon, Hutchison and Brown, while resigning from the party, 'still regard themselves as Liberals', but it painted a dire picture of the consequences of their defections, declaring that 'another stage in the disintegration of the Liberal Party' had been reached and that 'other resignations, including those of Sir Murdoch Macdonald and Mr. Hore-Belisha, may follow'. In fact, no other MPs immediately joined Simon, Hutchison and Brown in resigning the Liberal whip. Before the detached trio had time to establish their new political positioning, the events leading to the formation of the National Government overwhelmed any smaller-scale realignments.

Not for the first time, political events pivoted on the weakness of part of the anatomy of one key player: Churchill's appendix in 1922, Bonar Law's throat in 1923 and Eden's gall bladder in 1956 all played a crucial part in political history. In 1931 it was David Lloyd George's prostate which helped to determine the course of events. The formation of the National Government in August 1931 was initially welcomed by all sections of the Liberal Party. Samuel, Reading, Sinclair and Maclean joined Ramsay MacDonald's administration and even Lloyd George's son Gwilym took up a junior post. Simon, Hutchison and Brown were not, at that stage, given posts. David Lloyd George himself was out of action, having undergone an emergency prostate operation at his home on 29 July. Nonetheless he wrote to MacDonald on 30 August tentatively offering his services to the government, saying 'if the promise of the doctors is redeemed I may be of some use later on'. But, crucially he went on to warn: 'I sincerely hope there is nothing in this talk of an early dissolution'. It was on the understanding that there was not to be an election that Lloyd George had given his blessing to Liberal participation in the National Government. On 20 September MacDonald had reassured Samuel, who had taken over the leadership from Lloyd George, that there was not to be an election, but five days later, under irresistible Tory pressure, MacDonald was 'on the point of surrender'.[11] Lloyd George put pressure on Samuel to resist the demand, but Samuel was unable to prevent a dissolution. Lloyd George 'was beside himself with rage' and never again trusted Samuel. Lloyd George then dissociated himself from the party, of which he had so recently been leader. Gwilym resigned from the government. David Lloyd George was loyally followed into self-imposed political exile by those who became known as his 'Family Group' – although they were not all related. The group comprised his children, Megan and Gwilym, Goronwy Owen (whose wife was the sister of Gwilym's wife) and Frank Owen – no relation, but a follower, admirer and later biographer of Lloyd George.

In the election of 1931 the Lloyd George Family Group was reduced to four members. **Frank Owen**, son of a Hereford publican and coyly described by his biographer (Michael Foot) as never ceasing to 'honour his father's trade', who had won his native city by a slim margin in 1929, lost his seat. He withdrew from politics to concentrate on his journalistic career and drinking, although he made two further unsuccessful attempts to regain Hereford for the Liberals in the 1950s. The other four members of the Family Group survived the 1931 election. **Goronwy Owen** narrowly held his seat of Caernarvonshire, which he had first won in 1923. Owen was briefly appointed Comptroller of His Majesty's Household in September 1931, but, like Gwilym Lloyd George, he had resigned his post in the National Government within two months. Owen retained his seat until defeated by Labour in 1945, but made little further impact on Liberal, let alone national, politics. Towards the end of his career he even appeared to think that Lloyd George had forgotten him, pleading: 'I am writing ... to remind you of your kind promise to speak to the Prime Minister about an honour for me ... I need not add that my loyalty to you and my admiration and respect for you will remain undiminished.' His loyalty was rewarded with a knighthood in 1944. Lloyd George later recalled: 'you, Gwilym, Megan and I were about the only four who stood by' Free Trade.[12] Eventually, as Lloyd George predicted, Megan went to the left (see Chapter 3) and Gwilym went to the right (see Chapter 4). David Lloyd George himself, having been the dominant political figure from 1916 to 1922, and a significant player for years before and after, lost his way after the 1931 debacle: his only significant intervention in politics in the last ten years of his life was to be his cameo role in the Norway Debate.

The Liberals' attitude to the National Government caused the defection of another former Liberal MP, who did not join another party. **George Rennie Thorne** had held Wolverhampton East from 1908 to his retirement in 1929. It was later held by Geoffrey Mander until 1945: one of the last Midlands seats to be retained by the Liberals. A devout follower of Asquith, Thorne served as Asquith's joint whip with Hogge from 1919, until he resigned on health grounds in 1923. In November 1924 Thorne had supported Wedgwood Benn's letter to the press claiming that the 'people have no confidence, and rightly so, in Mr. Lloyd George'.[13] However, in the events which precipitated his departure from the Liberal Party, Thorne was in accord with Lloyd George. After the formation of the National Government, Thorne, already retired from the Commons, left the party, 'protesting about Liberalism's association with a protectionist government'.[14] By then aged seventy-eight, he retired from politics completely.

Table 5.1 *Paths of Liberal MPs elected in 1929 at the 1931 election*

Liberal National	24
Liberal*	26
Lloyd George Family Group	5
Labour	1
New Party	1
Retired	2
Total Liberal MPs in 1929 Parliament	**59**

* Includes Runciman, Millar and Granville.

At the 1931 election, called for 27 October, the fifty-nine Liberal MPs elected in 1929 were all still in the Commons. Their paths diverged as shown in Table 5.1.

At the 1931 general election there were no constituencies where Liberals and Liberal National candidates opposed each other. The divisions between the two groups were not totally clear. Runciman, Millar and Granville's names appeared on official lists of both Liberals and Liberal Nationals. Simon was certainly not the undisputed leader of a distinct party at this stage. Clement Davies, one of the Liberal MPs first elected in 1929, considered himself to be adhering to Hutchison, rather than Simon, as the leader of the group of Liberals supporting the National Government. After the 1931 election, but before November 1933, when the Samuelites crossed the floor, the membership of the groups was quite fluid, with both factions on the government side of the House of Commons. Eleven of the MPs elected from 1929 onward changed their affiliations. However, all the MPs who had first been elected before 1929 stayed with the faction which they had first chosen, at least in part due to their stronger personal affiliations. The Liberal MPs who restyled themselves Liberal Nationals between August 1931 and November 1933 did not see themselves as defectors from the Liberal Party, and cannot reasonably be labelled as such, in terms of their motivation. However, the consequences of the Liberal National/Liberal cleft were clear for all to see, when looking back on the split after 1933. The Liberal Party had suffered its third major rift in less than fifty years, following the Liberal Unionists' departures and the Asquith/Lloyd George split. The Liberal Nationals drew away a significant number of MPs from the already shrunken party, some of them high-profile, wealthy and able, and in most cases never to return. A separate Liberal National Organisation was set up in 1933, with Ivor Guest (by then Lord Wimborne) as chairman, and a national convention was held from 1936. After November 1933 a change of allegiance between Liberal and Liberal National parties by a sitting MP required a symbolic crossing of the floor – a move that can reasonably be regarded as a defection. Several MPs were motivated to make the move to the Liberal Nationals, including a disproportionate number of MPs and former MPs from Scotland, where there had been a history of cooperation between Liberals and Conservatives to present a single opponent to socialist candidates.

Joseph Hunter, a doctor by profession, took Dumfriesshire from the Conservatives for the Liberals in 1929. In 1931 he was re-elected as a Liberal, but without Conservative opposition. He remained on the government benches in November 1933, but waited until June 1934 before joining the Liberal Nationals, where he became National Organiser. He died suddenly, aged fifty-nine, shortly before the 1935 election. A Liberal National candidate, Henry Fildes, succeeded Hunter at the ensuing by-election.

Joseph Maclay had re-captured Asquith's old seat of Paisley from Labour for the Liberals in 1931, in the absence of a Conservative opponent. He also remained on the government benches after November 1933, but he did not formally join the Liberal National Group, although he had close family and political connections to it. His deliberate decision not to follow his nominal leader, Samuel, in crossing the floor could be considered to bring his actions within the definition of a defection as a 'falling away from allegiance to a leader [or] party'. Maclay was re-elected, again without Conservative opposition, in 1935. His election address stated that he offered himself as 'Liberal candidate, prepared to support the Government'. He sat until his retirement in 1945, inheriting his father's peerage in 1951. Maclay's father had been a friend of Bonar Law and had served as Lloyd George's Controller of Shipping. Maclay's brother (John) Jack was elected unopposed as a Liberal National MP in 1940 and sat until 1964, serving as chairman of the Parliamentary Liberal National Party from 1947 to 1956, president of the National Liberal Council from 1957 to 1967 and Secretary of State for Scotland in Macmillan's government from 1957 to 1962.

William McKeag was elected for Durham in 1931 as a Liberal, but remained on the government side of the House in November 1933 and joined the Liberal Nationals in June 1934. He was defeated, standing as a Liberal National in 1935. In 1940 he was talked of as a possible Independent Liberal candidate for the Newcastle North by-election, but in the event, he did not stand.[15] However, he did stand again as the Liberal candidate in Newcastle North in 1945 and in 1950 at Newcastle East. McKeag served on Newcastle City Council for 25 years, being first elected in 1936, but by the mid-1950s his political affiliation had shifted. McKeag was nominated by the old disaffiliated Newcastle North Conservative Association as a candidate in the by-election in 1957, caused by the elevation to the peerage of Gwilym Lloyd-George (see Chapter 4), in opposition to the official Conservative. McKeag agreed to accept the nomination, but in the end did not enter the contest.

George Morrison, although a supporter of the National Government, was elected as a Liberal for the Combined Scottish Universities at a by-election in March 1934, occasioned by the death of the Liberal Dugald Cowan. However, Morrison resigned the Liberal whip in July 1935 to join the Liberal Nationals. He retained his seat at the 1935 general election and sat until he resigned, triggering a by-election in April 1945, which was won by the Independent John Boyd Orr, thus ending any form of Liberal representation for the seat.

Electoral considerations influenced many of the changes of allegiance between the Liberals and Liberal Nationals. Although no official pact existed between them, at the 1935 general election only two Liberal National candidates opposed Liberals, so there was virtually no electoral conflict between them, unlike the situation between the Asquithian and Lloyd George Liberals in 1918 and 1922. However, the Liberal National label also offered protection from Conservative opposition, as no Tory opposed a Liberal National candidate. There were other career advantages to be gained from the Liberal National label as well. The case of **Robert Bernays** illustrates the attraction of the Liberal Nationals for ambitious politicians seeking office, which the Liberals could not offer. Bernays was a self-confessed 'carpet bagger' politician. He had no connection with his Bristol North constituency when he first applied for adoption as its Liberal candidate shortly before the 1931 general election. The seat had been won by Labour in 1929, when the Liberal vote had been split between Freddie Guest and Skelton (see Chapter 4). Bernays faced only Labour opposition in 1931 and won the seat. He then cultivated the right local contacts to ensure that no Conservative candidate stood against him at the following election. He chose to position himself politically to maximise his chances of ministerial office. Bernays remained on the government benches when the Samuelites went into opposition in November 1933. This cost him his job at the *News Chronicle*, but opened the way for him to develop contacts with the Conservatives. Having retained his seat in the 1935 election, in the new parliament Bernays was in close contact with leading Conservatives, although for tactical reasons he did not wish to join the Conservative Party: the Conservative queue for office was very long, whereas for non-Conservative supporters of the National Government it could be very short. Bernays was 'neither friend nor admirer' of Simon but, from MacDonald's departure in 1935, Simon was the obvious non-Conservative Government figure to cultivate in the quest for office.[16] In September 1936 Bernays took the plunge and wrote to Simon, to request that 'when Parliament reassembles . . . I may be sent the Liberal National Whip. For many months now I have found myself in agreement with the Government on all main issues of policy and I feel that I have no justification any longer in maintaining my isolation'. Simon replied: 'I am glad to hear that you have decided to count yourself among the Liberal National forces which steadily support the Government . . . The party which I lead welcomes you as a comrade'.[17] Bernays's strategy worked, and in May 1937, when Chamberlain formed his ministry, he was appointed parliamentary secretary to the Ministry of Health and later to the Ministry of Transport. But this was as far as he got, as he was dropped when Churchill took over in 1940. Bernays then joined the army. He was killed in an air crash in January 1945, leaving behind a set of diaries which he did not have the opportunity to edit for publication, due to his untimely demise.

Foreign affairs were the motivation for most of the later defections of former Liberals to the Liberal Nationals. Sinclair, Liberal Party leader from 1935, was a staunch opponent of appeasement and most of his party followed his lead. In this respect the policies of the Liberals and Liberal Nationals were by then distinctly different. **Arthur Murray**'s primary political interest was foreign affairs. First elected in 1908 as Liberal MP for Kincardineshire, Murray had served as PPS to Grey as Foreign Secretary between 1910 and 1914. His elder brother was the Master of Elibank, Liberal Chief Whip from 1910 to 1912, who believed that he had 'been present at the obsequies of the Liberal Party' in late September 1918, when he was involved in a failed attempt to reconstruct the government to include Asquith. A year after his brother's abortive attempt to reunite the party, Murray addressed his constituents, calling for Asquith and Lloyd George to retire, to allow the appointment of an alternative leader who could unite the party – probably hoping that Grey would be that leader. In 1919 Murray went to Washington with Grey on a special ambassadorial mission, and came back to what he later called 'the Lloyd George Dictatorship'.[18] In 1922 Murray had held his seat against his only opponent – a Lloyd George Liberal candidate, but he lost it in 1923 to the Conservatives and was never to return to the Commons. Another brother of Murray's, Gideon, sat as a Conservative MP from 1918 to 1922. In 1931 Murray wrote to *The Times*, claiming still to be an 'active supporter' of the Liberal Party. Murray was no admirer of Simon and felt that 'the drift of policy' had 'passed redemption' when Simon succeeded Reading at the Foreign Office in 1931.[19] Murray had remained a Liberal when the National Government was formed, but eventually joined the National Liberals in the spring of 1936 with a 'scathing public rebuke' to his former colleagues. By then the Foreign Office was in the hands of Eden, and Simon was sidelined from foreign affairs, at the Home Office. Murray supported British policy on Abyssinia in the spring of 1938, but became disillusioned with Chamberlain for his 'little knowledge or understanding of international problems' by the time of the Munich Agreement in September.[20] When Murray eventually returned to parliament after a twenty-eight year gap, on inheriting the viscountcy of Elibank from Gideon in 1951, he was listed in Dod as one of the Liberal peers.

Herbert Holdsworth, who listed his profession as a rag merchant, was elected as Liberal MP for Bradford South in 1931 and was re-elected in 1935, again as a Liberal, but in a straight fight with Labour. However, in October 1938 he joined the Liberal Nationals; defending his change of allegiance at a meeting of his local Liberal association on 4 November 1938, which resulted in his de-selection by 43 votes to 16. Holdsworth had voted for the Munich Agreement, and explained to the meeting that he 'had been on my knees praying for peace . . . I do not regret the vote I gave: I would repeat it'. He believed that the country had faced the choice – 'War or the Munich Agreement'.[21] He held his seat as a Liberal National until he retired from politics in 1945, having served as Liberal National chief whip from 1940 to 1942.

Aled Roberts was another former Liberal MP with a long record of local government service who changed allegiance during his term of office. Roberts was elected for Wrexham as a Liberal in 1931. Initially he supported the National Government and received the backing of the local Conservatives, who did not oppose him even though he was not styled as a Liberal National. However, he crossed the floor with the Samuelites in 1933 and this compromised his support from the Tories. At the 1935 election Roberts again did not face a Conservative opponent, but the chairman of the local Conservative association urged his supporters to abstain rather than voting for Roberts, who lost the seat to Labour. The following year, Roberts, who was a leader of the Welsh community in Liverpool, was elected to Liverpool City Council. Although he had not joined the Liberal Nationals when it could have helped his election prospects in Wrexham, he did become a member and tried unsuccessfully for the Liberal National nomination for the Eddisbury by-election in 1943. In 1945, while he was still deputy leader of the Liberal group on Liverpool City Council, he severed connections with the Liberal Party, 'disputing the practicability of the Liberals' Beveridge scheme'.[22] He joined the Conservatives, and unsuccessfully contested the Kirkdale Division of Liverpool at the 1945 election only a few weeks later. This was his last parliamentary contest.

David Mason was elected as Liberal MP for Coventry in December 1910, retaining the seat until 1918, although he was at odds with the Coventry Liberal Party from 1913 onward for proposing a reduction in the naval estimates and for opposing other government policies. Mason resigned the Liberal whip in January 1914 and sat as an independent anti-war Liberal. He unsuccessfully defended his seat in 1918 as an Independent Liberal against Coalition Conservative, Labour, Liberal (Mansel) and Independent opposition, coming fifth out of five. However, he was reintegrated into the Liberal Party after the war and fought Chislehurst in 1922, Romford in 1923 and 1924 and Barnstaple in 1929 – in all cases as a Liberal and in all cases coming bottom of the poll. He was re-elected, for Edinburgh East, in 1931 as a Liberal supporting the National Government, but then antagonised his Conservative supporters by opposing the National Government's tariff policies. He lost the seat in the 1935 general election, again as a Liberal and again coming bottom of the poll. He then began to agitate for a pact with Labour. History proved Mason wrong when, after being one of the Führer's guests at the Nuremberg Nazi Congress, he concluded that: 'Hitler impressed me as a simple, unaffected, sincere man; quiet, dignified, and capable.'[23] 'My belief is that Germany wants peace above all things'.[24] In 1938 Mason joined the Liberal National Party, after arguing that 'political appeasement and economic appeasement were . . . necessary to enable us to secure peace and prosperity'.[25] In his letter resigning from the Liberal Party Mason explained: 'Peace, to my mind, is the supreme question of the day.'[26] The *Star* on 22 November 1938 commented that Mason 'has resigned once again. His rugged independence, even when he has reached 72, has impelled him to renounce the Liberal Party'.

Ellis Davies had already left the Liberal Party and joined Labour in 1934 (see Chapter 3). In 1939 he made a further defection, this time to the Liberal Nationals, arguing that 'like a policy of entanglements . . . the League of Nations will lead to War . . . I refused to support the Treaty of Locarno . . . the policy of the League, Locarno, and the Commonwealth, may lead us in a War which I wish to avoid'.[27] He was quoted in the national press in February 1939 as saying: 'I support Mr. Chamberlain's foreign policy because I think it will help to keep this generation from war.' Davies died in April 1939, just weeks after his last conversion.

The year 1939 was to mark the turn of the tide in defections from the Liberals to the Liberal Nationals. Generally, the earlier defectors had been motivated by career aspirations – either electoral advantage or promotion opportunities. The later defectors were typically motivated by foreign affairs. The attraction of the Liberal Nationals for potential inward defectors seriously diminished once war was declared, appeasement had failed and all the main parties were represented in the government. After the outbreak of the Second World War, no more sitting or former Liberal MPs defected to the Liberal Nationals, and some earlier converts returned. Clement Davies left the Liberal Nationals in 1939 and in 1942 he rejoined the Liberals. He was followed by Edgar Granville, who left the Liberal Nationals in 1942 and rejoined the Liberals on the eve of the 1945 election. The Liberal Nationals, from 1940 under the leadership of Ernest Brown, suffered not only these defections back to the Liberals, but also the loss of the seat of Eddisbury to the Common Wealth candidate in a 1943 by-election. In addition Hore-Belisha, Murdoch Macdonald and Henry Morris-Jones (temporarily) relinquished the Liberal National whip, so undermining the party's representation in the Commons. Intermittent attempts at reunification between the Liberals and the Liberal Nationals were made during and immediately after the Second World War, with some localised success: the London Liberal Nationals, against their leadership's advice, agreed a reunification with the Liberals in July 1946, although the merger involved no sitting Liberal National MPs. The 1947 Woolton-Teviot Agreement effectively marked the absorption of the Liberal Nationals into the Conservative Party, so ending any separate attraction of the Liberal Nationals as a potential destination for defectors, although it was not until 1968 that the Liberal Nationals were officially disbanded.

While Chapter 4 revealed that there was little difficulty for former Liberals to feel at home in the Conservative Party, there was still less so for those who found a new home among the Liberal Nationals, who largely shared the same roots. However, the Liberal Nationals did more than simply attract later rightward defectors from the Liberals. While some of the converts to the Liberal Nationals such as Roberts and McKeag would almost definitely have gone straight to the Conservatives, had the Liberal Nationals not existed, others such as Mason, Ellis Davies and Murray would almost certainly not have joined the Conservatives. Therefore, the Liberal Nationals acted as more than just a bridge from the Liberals to the Conservatives.

Radical Populists

The defections considered so far to Labour, the Conservatives and the Liberal Nationals did not require those defectors to make radical changes in their policy positions. Probably the most significant modification of views was by those who abandoned free trade, in particular the Protection Convert Industrialists. However, as the title implies, these figures were primarily taking an industrialist's rather than a politician's point of view. Perhaps much more surprising was that the Liberal Party also lost defectors to the Bottomley Party, to the New Party, to the National Party of Scotland and to the right-wing National Party.

Despite having sixty-seven bankruptcy proceedings and writs against him, **Horatio Bottomley** used his wit and publicity skills to escape from his creditors with a personal fortune of £3 million.[28] In 1906 he founded the journal *John Bull*, which was to cause Ramsay MacDonald much pain and embarrassment during the First World War by publishing the birth certificate, revealing his illegitimacy. In the landslide of 1906, Bottomley became Liberal MP for South Hackney, only to file for bankruptcy in 1911 and have the Liberal whip withdrawn. He left the Commons the following year. Although Bottomley was not a Liberal defector at that stage, as the party took the decision to part company with him, in 1918 Bottomley was re-elected to the Commons for the same constituency as an independent. Bottomley gathered around him a parliamentary group which included Christopher Lowther and his distant relative Claude Lowther, Charles Palmer, elected in February 1920, but who died later the same year and his replacement MP for the Wrekin, Charles Townshend. They were joined by Murray Sueter, who was the successful Anti-Waste League candidate in the Hertford by-election in June 1921, sponsored by Lord Rothermere and supported by Bottomley. They were to be joined by a lone Liberal convert, **Cecil Beck**. Beck entered parliament in 1906 as a Liberal. Couponed and victorious in 1918, by July 1921 he had come within the orbit of Bottomley and was persuaded to seek a political future under his populist right-wing banner. Beck did not initially share his decision with his constituents, and only under questioning from a local journalist did he reveal his change of allegiance. The local press reported: 'Beck Leaves Coalition and Joins Mr Bottomley's Group'. When pressed, Beck confirmed his defection: 'I have severed my connection with the Coalition party. I wish to be independent. I have been asked to fight a London seat at the General Election, and I can only do so on independent lines. I am out and out for anti-waste, and want to be entirely independent.'[29] Bottomley himself remained in the Commons until he was expelled on 29 May 1922, after his conviction and sentencing to seven years imprisonment for fraudulent conversion. He never returned. The 1922 general election also marked the end of the parliamentary careers of Townshend, Christopher and Claude Lowther and for Beck, who, in the event, did not contest a London, or any other, seat ever again. Only Sueter was re-elected, under Conservative colours, at the following six general elections.

Horatio Bottomley was not the last radical populist leader to tempt defectors from the Liberal Party: Oswald Mosley, who was at one stage an admirer of Bottomley, managed the same feat in 1931. One sitting and one former Liberal MP joined Oswald Mosley's New Party and contested the 1931 election under its banner. Hore-Belisha was also rumoured to have thought of joining. Five Labour MPs and one Ulster Unionist member also joined. Mosley hoped that other young Conservatives such as Oliver Stanley, Robert Boothby and Harold Macmillan might also join. Others who were tempted by the attractions of the New Party ranged from Harold Nicolson to Nye Bevan. Their opinions should be considered in the light of what was then known about Oswald Mosley and his party. The nature of the New Party was unclear and evolving. Mosley's days as an overt fascist were still in the future. In 1931, he carried a certain amount of prestige as a former minister who had made a principled resignation over the failure of his Labour colleagues to adopt his practical policies for reviving the economy. In May 1930 he and Strachey had resigned from the government when Mosley's expansionist programme was rejected in favour of economic orthodoxy.

Cecil Dudgeon was first elected to parliament as Liberal MP for Galloway in 1922. He lost the seat in 1924, but regained it in 1929. He resigned from the Liberal Party and joined the New Party immediately following the announcement of the dissolution on 8 October 1931. Dudgeon claimed that he had resigned from the Liberal Party because he believed that it had ceased to be 'an effective force in British politics' and he had come to the view that tariffs had become necessary.[30] Dudgeon came fourth out of four candidates with 986 votes, behind the Unionist with 18,993, the Liberal with 9,176 and the Socialist with 3,418. The figures suggest that, had Dudgeon remained in the Liberal party and stood as their candidate, he would almost certainly still have lost. This was to be the end of Dudgeon's political career. In the event, the New Party turned out to be less a rearrangement at the centre of British politics and more a meeting of the 'marginalised and disaffected'.[31] Dudgeon never contested another election and his *Who's Who* entry made no mention of his candidacy for the New Party. He later worked in public administration, reaching the position of Chief Food Officer for Scotland in 1950; receiving a CBE the following year.

The other former Liberal MP who joined the New Party and contested the 1931 election alongside Dudgeon was **John Pratt**. Pratt had been a Liberal MP from 1913 to 1922, retiring as a Coalition Liberal in 1922. He expected a realignment of political forces, believing that:

> [T]he two parties of the future will not be the two parties of the past ... the Coalition will pass, but ... the security of the British Commonwealth ... will remain. Whatever its name, men and women will in days not far distant range themselves together in what will be in fact the *British Commonwealth Party*.[32]

When the changes Pratt expected did not materialise, he made three attempts to re-enter parliament as a Liberal, at each of the successive general elections. After his 1929 failure at Sunderland, his politics moved to the right and he was in financial difficulty. These two factors drew him towards Beaverbrook, whom Pratt believed could be a solution to his financial problems and a new political sponsor. If there was any doubt about Pratt's motives for wanting to return to parliament, that money was among them is made very clear from his desperate pleas to Beaverbrook during December 1930:

> After seven years of desperate struggle I am facing absolute disaster ... every other possible effort having failed I am writing this to implore your help. I beg of you to make me a personal loan of £600 ... I would give my services to platform work on your behalf throughout the whole of next year. I am willing to go through the industrial areas of Great Britain ... if you will do this for me. Otherwise it means Bankruptcy & it will kill my wife who has been an invalid for seven years.[33]

Pratt had already been bailed out by another benefactor three years earlier, but had sunk back into financial chaos, admitting: 'My debts ... are the results of riotous living ... I have lied and lied and lied.'[34] Despite a less than encouraging response from Beaverbrook, Pratt was not deterred from one more attempt to relieve the millionaire press baron of some of his small change.[35] 'After another terrible week I am appealing to you again. I have a purchaser for my wife's grand piano ... but I still need £270'.[36] Beaverbrook was again not prepared to help. The 'industrial areas of Great Britain' were spared the 'going through' that Pratt had volunteered in return for Beaverbrook's patronage. Reports of his wife's impending demise happily proved to be premature – she survived until 1945. However, Pratt's attempt to solve his financial problems by a return to politics was less than happy or profitable. His political ambitions (together with £150) were finally sunk when he lost his deposit standing as the New Party candidate in Manchester Hulme in 1931. He achieved the third-highest share of the vote among the 24 New Party candidates – but that was a meagre 4.4%.

The verdict on the inter-war Scottish nationalist movement that its 'most ... striking feature ... was its divisiveness and the difficulty it had in maintaining a united and cohesive front' might have sounded all too familiar to Liberals at the time. However, one former Liberal MP was tempted to swap the discord of the Liberals for the discord of the Scottish nationalists – **Henry Dalziel**, first Baron Dalziel of Kirkcaldy. The National Party of Scotland (NPS) had been formed in 1928 'on a foundation of uneasy compromise' through the merger of the pro-independence Scots National League and the devolutionist Scottish Home Rule Association. Goals and means were a source of contention. In the early 1930s, the party's chief strategist John MacCormick oversaw the expulsion of extremists and an attempt to make the party more attractive to moderate potential supporters: such was Dalziel. The poet Hugh MacDiarmid was a member, but was expelled on account of his communist beliefs; although, ironically, he was later expelled from the Communist Party for his Scottish nationalist beliefs.[37] Dalziel entered parliament as an 'advanced Radical and Home Ruler' at a by-election in 1892 and sat in the Commons as a Liberal, and subsequently Coalition Liberal, until his elevation to the peerage in 1921. In 1894 he had introduced a bill designed to give home rule to Scotland. This brought him into alliance with Lloyd George, who wanted to see equivalent measures for Wales. The partnership between Lloyd George and Dalziel – both from shoemaking families – was to be long-lasting and mutually beneficial. It was in his links to the press that Dalziel was to be of most value to Lloyd George. In 1909 he brought Lloyd George together with Northcliffe. In 1914 Dalziel became sole owner of *Reynolds's News*, and during the Liberal split in 1916 the paper became a mouthpiece for Lloyd George. In 1918 Dalziel was the organizer of Lloyd George's purchase of the *Daily Chronicle*. Dalziel acted as Lloyd George's agent at the paper, in an attempt to give Lloyd George editorial control. The arrangement did not work out to Lloyd George's satisfaction and in 1921 Dalziel was replaced, but consoled with a peerage: the arrangements for which were organised with rather unseemly haste.[38] After the situation in Ireland had been addressed, but without any commensurate (or even any) legislation for Scottish home rule, Dalziel sold all his newspaper interests the following year and retired – temporarily as it turned out – from politics, until he was tempted into the National Party of Scotland by MacCormick in September 1932. The latter, struggling to attract attention for his party, was eager to reel in his catch, commenting that in view of his 'political connections and great wealth it seemed to me that he could render great service to the National Party [of Scotland, but] I ... was not ... very sure that he fully understood what our aims were'.[39] Dalziel, on his way from the Liberals to the NPS, crossed paths with the Duke of Montrose, a former Conservative, who briefly associated himself with the NPS, before joining the Liberals. Dalziel's membership of the NPS was to be brief and relatively unproductive; he died without heirs in 1935 and left most of his £407,886 estate to the fund for the repayment of the national debt – then standing at a figure of £7,800,436,867. His legacy could have had a much greater political impact, had he left the money to the National Party for Scotland, or to the Liberals. The case of Dalziel is one of only two, from the 116 defectors studied, where support for nationalist policies was a major factor in the defection; the other being Edward John who went to Labour in the vain hope of achieving Welsh home rule. Considering the strength of feeling and the political consequences of the Irish home rule issue, it is, perhaps, surprising that Scottish and Welsh nationalism played such a minor role in the fortunes of the Liberal Party.

A total of six by-elections occurred in Liberal-held seats during the Second World War. The party truce ensured that in these cases the Liberal candidate was guaranteed a by-election without competition from Labour or the Conservatives. William Gruffydd, himself a former vice-president of Plaid Cymru, but by then standing as a Liberal, beat off the challenger from his former party to win the University of Wales by-election, caused by the appointment of sitting Liberal MP Ernest Evans as a county court judge in 1943. Gruffydd was the only one of the Liberal wartime by-election victors to be re-elected in the 1945 general election. David Seaborne Davies fought off a Plaid Cymru challenger to replace David Lloyd George in the April 1945 by-election in Caernarvon Boroughs, only to lose the seat just over two months later: Lloyd George believed that even he himself would not have held the seat had he contested it at the next election, and this was a factor in his accepting the earldom. In the event, Lloyd George had died before the election. Berwick-upon-Tweed saw two wartime by-elections. The sitting Liberal, Hugh Seely was raised to the peerage in 1941, allowing George Grey to take the seat unopposed. Grey was widely believed to have been a possible future party leader, but the party was deprived of his talents when he was killed in action in 1944 as a tank commander in France. His replacement was also a very high-calibre choice – William Beveridge. Wilfrid Roberts, chairman of the Organising Committee for the latter half of the war, had deliberately recruited distinguished people to stand for the Liberals. Some, like Beveridge, had been ideologically sympathetic; others, like Air Vice-Marshal Bennett, had not.

Donald Bennett, Australian by birth, was a controversial character. He was elected unopposed in May 1945 in the Middlesbrough West by-election caused by the death of sitting Liberal MP Harcourt Johnstone; the second wartime by-election in this constituency too. Johnstone himself had been the beneficiary of an unopposed election, when he took over the seat from fellow Liberal Kingsley Griffith on the latter's appointment as a County Court judge in 1940. Johnstone had been a popular and munificent figure within the Liberal Party, with a large girth and a large wallet. He was said to have 'dug his grave with his teeth'.[40] However, he had been less assiduous with his visits to his constituency than to his favourite restaurants. Johnstone once met a parliamentary colleague at a London station and bemoaned that fact that he had to visit his constituency, saying that 'what makes it worse is that I may have to go again next year'.[41] After his unopposed election as Johnstone's replacement, Bennett served as a Liberal MP for a grand total of seventy-three days, before losing the seat to Labour at the 1945 election. Long after this cameo appearance at Westminster, Bennett was to defect from the Liberal Party, but this was only one of a series of ruptures in a tumultuous career. Bennett was courageous, perhaps to the point of recklessness. He held a pre-war seaplane long-distance record, was shot down in his bomber during the war, escaping on foot to Sweden, and later he personally flew 250 sorties to Berlin as part of the airlift. As an air vice-marshal during the war and leader of the Pathfinder force, Bennett had fallen out with senior personnel in the RAF. After the war, as chief executive of British South American Airways, he fell out with Lord Nathan (himself a former Liberal defector), who was by then Minister for Civil Aviation. Bennett had insisted that his aircraft were safe, despite several accidents; but Nathan had grounded the rest of the aircraft. Bennett denounced the minister to the national press and was sacked. Bennett was involved in several court cases, including commercial litigation and a tax case, and he also defended a libel action by another former air vice-marshal who objected to Bennett's revealing in a book that he had worn short trousers to a meeting. Bennett's colourful character did not ensure his popularity at the polls. He fought two further unsuccessful elections as a Liberal: in 1948 he lost his deposit in the Croydon North by-election and in the 1950 general election he held on to his £150 in Norwich North, but still came bottom of the poll. It was not the cost or the popular rejection, but the Liberal Party's enthusiasm for the European Economic Community and its defence policies which were to alienate Bennett from the party.

Bennett left the Liberal Party in 1962, and rambled into the right-wing political undergrowth, in the company of a few other former Liberals. In 1967 he polled 517 votes as a National Party candidate at a by-election in Nuneaton. The National Party was founded by a former Liberal parliamentary candidate and party organiser, Edward Martell, who had been one of the architects of the party's failed 1950 Broad Front strategy. He had also been a Liberal member of the LCC, elected in 1946 along with Percy Harris, when they had captured the first Liberal seats since 1931. However, in the 1950s Martell had drifted away from the Liberal Party and became an anti-trade union newspaper owner and business partner to former Liberal MP Horace Craufurd. Together they formed the People's League for the Defence of Freedom in 1956. It lasted little more than a year, but in 1958 Martell was involved with the launch of a new right-wing group, the Anti-Socialist Front. This organisation was also short-lived, but Martell was not deterred. In the early 1960s he founded The Freedom Group, which eventually became the National Party in 1966. It had aimed to recruit a million members and to put up parliamentary candidates. The membership total was never reached and Bennett was to be the party's only election candidate. Martell's enterprises collapsed in debt in 1967. Although Bennett was never a member of the National Front, he supported some of its policies, such as the voluntary repatriation of immigrants. The case of Bennett illustrates one of the consequences of the wartime electoral truce – that of not being vetted by the normal political process of a contested by-election.

The defections to the radical populist parties probably say more about the individuals concerned than they do about the Liberal Party, except that they illustrate that the party was a very broad church in terms of the personalities it attracted. There are, however, some common threads. The cases of Bottomley, Pratt and Dalziel, in different ways, illustrate money's distorting effect on political motives, the Lloyd George Fund having been the prime example of the perversion of political principle by the influence of money.

Independent Liberals

It is debatable whether **Austin Hopkinson** was ever a Liberal MP, but if he was, he had defected from the party by February 1922. However, his name was sometimes included in lists of Liberal MPs. Hopkinson was first elected under the First World War electoral truce for Prestwich to replace the Liberal MP Oswald Cawley, who had been killed in action – the second of Chancellor of the Duchy of Lancaster Frederick Cawley's

Liberal MP sons to suffer that fate. Hopkinson was elected unopposed at the by-election in October 1918 with the Liberal label attached to his name, but without the need for a contest at which to parade his credentials and thus have them challenged. During his successful general election campaign less than two months later, in the newly created constituency of Mossley, Hopkinson was quoted as saying that although he allowed himself to be called the coalition candidate this 'did not bind him to support the Coalition Government'. He went on to declare that he might vote against anything the government did and he had simply taken their 'badge' because he felt it would be 'for the good of the country to do so'. He claimed that he was not a member of any party and that he had been adopted by both local Conservative and Liberal associations. In 1922 Hopkinson defeated an Asquithian opponent, and by 1923 the re-united Liberal Party clearly did not count him as one of their own, as he was opposed in that election, and the following two, by a Liberal candidate. Hopkinson sat under various (non-Liberal) party labels until his defeat as a National Independent in 1945, apart from a gap of two years from 1929 to 1931 when Labour held the seat. His failure in 1929 owed something to the outspoken opinions set out in his election address, which managed to alienate many of his erstwhile supporters. He dismissed some of the local Liberals as the 'impertinence of a little clique', condemned Lloyd George's 'wild-cat schemes' and told the Conservatives that he disagreed with some of their policies. If he ever had any party allegiance, it was most likely to have been to the Conservative Party, for which his father Alfred was elected as an MP for the Combined English Universities. In divining Hopkinson's obscure party allegiance, it is instructive to consider his parliamentary associates. Writing jointly with two then Conservative MPs – Murray Sueter (originally elected as the Hertford Anti-Waste candidate) and Esmond Harmsworth (son of Lord Rothermere) – to Baldwin, the Conservative prime minister, on 7 March 1924, Austin Hopkinson placed himself clearly on their side of the fence: 'The undersigned members of your party ... feel that it would be an advantage ... if we could gain the adherence of a body of Liberals ... who while preserving their own identity would work ... with us.'[42]

With all the splits and dissent in the Liberal Party, it is, perhaps, surprising that there was not a greater number of former Liberal MPs who stood as Independent Liberals after being defeated or de-selected. In fact between December 1910 and May 2010 only six former Liberal MPs attempted to re-enter parliament as Independent Liberals after being rejected by the voters, or by their own party.[43] Three had found themselves in this position as a result of their opposition to the Great

War – Outhwaite, Mason and Whitehouse (see Chapter 3) and the fourth was Freddie Guest in 1929 (see Chapter 4). The other two former Liberal MPs who stood as Independent Liberals – John Hope and Charles Royle – emerged as a result of controversial local selection contests.

John Deans Hope was first elected in 1900 and sat as Liberal MP for West Fife until defeated in December 1910. He had only been out of parliament for four months when he replaced the recently ennobled Haldane at the Haddingtonshire by-election in April 1911, defeating his only challenger, a Conservative, by 468 votes. In 1918 Hope was couponed and held his seat against Labour and Liberal opposition, in the absence of a Conservative candidate. However, by 1922, after twenty-two years in parliament, Hope had never made a speech in the Commons and was criticised for not taking 'any interest in county matters'. The local Unionists made unavailing efforts to 'induce' the National Liberal Party to secure the withdrawal of Hope, and to substitute a candidate who 'would be more acceptable to the electorate'. A motion in support of Hope was defeated by an 'overwhelming majority'. Lloyd George made a visit to the constituency and, after hearing from Hope's own agent, but not from Hope himself, had Hope, as he saw it, 'thrown overboard as a sop to the Conservative voters'. Hope was resentful at the way he had been treated and decided to stand as an Independent Liberal. The upshot of the debacle was that the voters were treated to a choice of one Labour and three varieties of Liberal candidate in the constituency at the 1922 election. Walter Waring emerged as the successful National Liberal candidate, the Labour candidate came second, Pringle, the Liberal, was third and Hope trailed in last. Hope's quiet parliamentary career was finished.[44]

The other dispute occurred in 1929 at Stockport, a two-member borough, where the Liberals had only put forward one candidate at each election from 1900 to 1925: the only exception had been the 1923 election, when **Charles Royle** and Henry Fildes had both fought as Liberals. At different times each man had served a brief term as Liberal MP for the borough – Fildes from 1920 to 1923 and Royle from 1923 to 1924. As the 1929 election approached, the local Liberals again adopted Fildes as their sole candidate. The issue was raised as to having two candidates, but the executive committee decided almost unanimously on one candidate. Royle's supporters formed their own 'Radical Association', arguing that fielding only one candidate was a 'nerveless policy' and that Royle should be allowed to stand in harness with Fildes. An official of the Liberal association was quoted as saying that if Royle stands 'it will be under his own colours and not ours'. The dispute caused ructions in the town council, where Royle was leader of the Liberal group. He vacated his usual seat on the Liberal benches and changed over to the Independent seats. He explained that 'in view of the attitude which had been adopted' towards him by some of his Liberal colleagues, he felt that he and they would be 'more comfortable if he were not sitting among them'. Fildes was reported as 'falling between two stools' and being unclear 'whether to appeal to the Right or to the Left', although he was definitely anti-Socialist.[45] He had been supported by Lloyd George to fight the 1925 Stockport by-election, but had come third.[46] Royle stood as Independent Liberal on a platform of Free Trade, support for the League of Nations and Liberal programme for reduction of unemployment. In the event, the Conservatives put up two candidates, once Royle decided to stand in addition to Fildes. Labour had threatened to field two, but only produced one candidate. Royle came fifth out of five candidates and lost his deposit, while Fildes was also defeated, coming third. The Labour candidate topped the poll and was elected along with one of the Conservatives. Fildes returned to parliament as a Liberal National at the Dumfriesshire by-election caused by the death of Joseph Hunter in 1935. However, Royle's unofficial intervention was to be his last parliamentary contest, although he went on to clock up forty-four years' service on the town council.

The university seats were in existence until 1950. These seats were unusual in that their constituencies were not geographical, but comprised the graduates of the universities. These electors normally would also have qualified for a vote in their home constituency. Many university constituencies were multi-member seats – up to three in the case of the Combined Scottish Universities. Voting was carried out on the basis of a single transferable vote. Most of the candidates for the university seats fought under party labels, although a higher proportion stood as independents compared to the rest of the country's geographical constituencies. Seven Liberal MPs represented university seats between 1918 and 1950. (No Liberals had represented university seats between 1910 and 1918.)

The University of Wales was the Liberals' only university stronghold; the single-member seat being represented by four successive Liberals from 1918 to its abolition in 1950, with just one break between 1923 and 1924. The lacuna in Liberal representation was the result of the intervention of an Independent Liberal candidate. The Independent Liberal was **John Edwards**, who had previously sat as Coalition Liberal MP for Aberavon from 1918, until he had lost the seat to Ramsay MacDonald in 1922. That election campaign had opened with a 'maladroit attempt' by the local Conservatives to persuade Edwards to withdraw, on the grounds that the only way to keep MacDonald out was to form an anti-Labour alliance. Edwards was said to have been 'lax in his attendance' at Westminster and 'a poor constituency member', so the Conservatives decided to run a candidate of their own.[47] Edwards had come third in that poll. The following year, 1923, Edwards, a graduate of the university, contested the University of Wales as an Independent Liberal, standing against the official Liberal candidate, Rev. J. Jones. The result was that Edwards split the Liberal vote and allowed George Davies, standing as a Christian Pacifist, to win the seat by ten votes. The Liberals won the seat back from Davies (this time standing for Labour) in 1924. The Liberal victor was Ernest Evans, who served until his appointment as a county court judge in 1943. He was then succeeded by the last of the Liberal MPs for the University of Wales, Professor William Gruffydd. John Edwards did not contest any further elections.

One of the three seats for the Combined Scottish Universities was also held in succession by two Liberals from 1918 to 1945. Dugald Cowan was the incumbent from 1918 until his death in December 1933. He was succeeded by the Liberal, then Liberal National, George Morrison, who held the seat until his resignation in 1945.

The Combined English Universities, a two-member constituency, had Herbert Fisher as one of its MPs from 1918 until his resignation in 1926. Fisher had an easy passage in parliament as far as his constituency duties were concerned. Fisher's is virtually the only case where it is difficult to determine whether he should be classified as a defector, or not. Fisher served as President of the Board of Education from 1916 to 1922 and he was only in parliament from 1916 to 1926. His role has similarities to that of Reginald McKenna, who thought of himself as a technical expert there to do a particular job, or perhaps, later, Nigel Lawson, who went into politics to be Chancellor of the Exchequer. Fisher was not a convinced party politician and certainly not a hands-on constituency MP, as he readily admitted. His first constituency, Hallamshire, which he represented from an unopposed by-election in 1916 until 1918 'was willing in the exceptional circumstances of the War to be represented by a Liberal on condition that the seat should be regarded as being again at the disposal of the Tory party at the next election'. For two years Fisher represented a constituency which 'I was not expected either to canvass or to address, from which I received not a single letter, to which I contributed not a single subscription'. His next constituency, the Combined English Universities, where he sat from 1918 to 1926 was 'almost as indulgent', as the member for this new academic constituency was not expected to canvass for support or to address meetings.[48] Opinions differ as to whether Fisher remained a

Liberal after he resigned his seat in 1926 to resume his academic career. His biographer's view was that although of 'Anglican and Conservative ancestry' Fisher became at an early age 'an enthusiastic devotee of Mr. Gladstone, and throughout his life he remained a staunch Liberal and Free Trader'.[49] However, Hart describes Fisher as being among those who left the Liberal Party in the mid-1920s. He believed that for Grigg, Mond, Hilton Young and Fisher, 'their only reason for being Liberal after 1922 was Lloyd George. When his ideas veered towards planning, spending and state enterprise, they quit the party'.[50] Fisher's own view does not exactly settle the matter, but gives the impression that he felt that he was left without a party at all: 'Poor Liberal Party! It looks, as if it were indeed breaking up . . . As for my own position no party exactly represents me. In matters educational the Labour people generally seem to me . . . better . . . in matters fiscal the Liberals, in matters imperial the Conservatives'.[51] Rather than simply deserting the Liberal Party, Fisher left politics completely. He could perhaps fairly be described as a political deserter, but not a defector.

The victor of the by-election resulting from Fisher's resignation was Sir Arthur Hopkinson, father of Austin (see pp. 169–70), who had been a Liberal candidate, then a Liberal Unionist MP in the previous century, and who was elected to the university seat as a Conservative at the age of seventy-four. The last candidate for the Combined English Universities to adopt the unambiguous label 'Liberal' was Professor R.S. Conway, who stood unsuccessfully in 1929. However, a former Liberal MP, **Thomas Edmund (Ted) Harvey**, was elected to represent one of the seats in 1937, standing as an Independent Progressive. Harvey had been an outspoken War Policy Objector in the Great War when he had been Liberal MP for Leeds West (see Chapter 3), but he had remained within the Liberal Party and had served as Liberal MP for Dewsbury from 1923 to 1924 and had unsuccessfully contested Leeds North for the party in 1929. Harvey was the brother-in-law of Arnold Rowntree.[52] In his successful 1937 university by-election campaign Harvey distanced himself from all the political parties, saying in a comprehensive note on policy that he would, if elected, 'accept no party Whip'. After the declaration of the poll he said that the result was evidence that there was a 'widespread conviction the representatives of the Universities elected on an additional franchise ought not to be chosen on the ordinary party grounds'. However, it was significant that Liberal leader Sinclair, Ramsay Muir and the Liberal Party Organisation, sent messages of congratulation to Harvey.[53] Harvey retired in 1945.

Another MP for the Combined English Universities who had Liberal origins, but who sat as an Independent, was Eleanor Rathbone, who represented one of the seats from 1929 until her death in 1946. Rathbone's father had been a Liberal MP, but she had sat as an Independent, and the only female, member of the Liverpool City Council since 1909. In 1922 she had stood unsuccessfully for parliament as an independent candidate for East Toxteth, but with the support of the local Liberal Party. In parliament, as an independent university MP, she frequently allied herself with the Liberals, but never took the party whip. She was a close confidante of Clement Davies during the Second World War and early stages of his party leadership, when the Liberals managed to augment their strength by associating with like-minded independents. When Rathbone died in 1946, Samuel, then Liberal leader in the Lords, and Davies approached William Beveridge to stand in the by-election. Beveridge had served as Liberal MP for Berwick-upon-Tweed from his unopposed election in 1944 to the loss of his seat in the Liberals' decapitation in the general election the following year. He had earlier held tentative discussions with Samuel over the possibility of a seat in the Lords, but before they had reached a conclusion, the Combined English Universities by-election arose. Beveridge believed that he could win the universities seat if he fought as an independent, as he might well have been unopposed, but he was concerned that this could make it appear that he had turned his back on the Liberal Party. Alternatively he could have contested the seat as a Liberal, but this choice would have been more likely to bring other opponents into the field. Davies and Samuel agreed that Beveridge should feel free to fight the seat as an independent if he wished. In the event, Beveridge opted for the seat in the Lords instead of the university contest. Ernest Simon, former Liberal MP and soon-to-be Labour Party member and later peer (see Chapter 3), unsuccessfully contested the seat under an Independent banner.

Cambridge University was also represented for one year by an Independent Liberal, James Ramsay Montagu Butler, who served from 1922 to 1923. He had never stood as an official Liberal candidate, but was allied in policy to the Liberal Party. A.P. Herbert, the Independent member for Oxford University from 1935 to 1950, although slightly more Conservatively-inclined, also allied himself on some issues with Clement Davies and the Liberals. The preponderance of independent candidates for the university seats was a phenomenon not restricted to the Liberal Party and its associates. Party labels tended to be worn more loosely by candidates of all political persuasions. The university seats were abolished in 1950 and with them disappeared most of the independents in the House of Commons.

The tide of outward Liberal defectors had been stemmed in the

1950s, but two much later defectors separately left the party because of their disagreement with specific party policies – Michael Meadowcroft and David Alton. **Michael Meadowcroft** was Liberal MP for Leeds West from 1983 to 1987, having served as a local councillor and on the Liberal Party's full-time staff. He was 'profoundly suspicious' of the proposed alliance with the SDP. Writing in a sceptical pamphlet, *Social Democracy: Barrier or Bridge*? that the SDP was 'at one and the same time the greatest opportunity and the greatest danger to Liberalism for thirty years'. Meadowcroft was a member of the Liberal/SDP merger negotiating team, but was one of the Liberal negotiators who walked out in January 1988 and afterward led a last-ditch 'no' campaign. He did not leave immediately and helped Alan Beith in his campaign for the leadership of the merged party, which was instead won by Paddy Ashdown. However, in the early spring of 1989, Meadowcroft launched the 'continuing Liberal Party'. It attracted few members, and no high-profile figures, but in some areas of the country it did win seats on local councils.[54] Meadowcroft's brother and son both remained in the Liberal Democrats and Meadowcroft himself re-joined in 2007, in part because he wanted a higher-profile platform from which to promote his policies for a 'civil society'.[55]

David Alton was an example of an MP from a minority religion within the party, whose Catholic faith collided with Liberal Democrat Party policy over the issue of abortion. Alton won Liverpool Edge Hill for the Liberals at a by-election in March 1979, at the tail end of the Callaghan Government, after having stood twice in the seat in 1974. Alton, although not enjoying a smooth relationship with party leader David Steel, was appointed chief whip in 1985. Despite boundary changes, Alton held on to his seat. However, after the 1992 contest he announced that he would not stand again as a Liberal Democrat, after the party made abortion a party policy for the first time. He was incensed that the same conference had passed an animal welfare motion which included protection for goldfish on sale in amusement arcades and funfairs. His seat was effectively abolished in 1997 and Alton left the Commons and the Liberal Democrats and became a life peer. He considered establishing his own 'Christian Democrat Party', but instead decided to sit as a crossbencher.[56]

Meadowcroft and Alton correctly indentified the inertia in the system and the barriers which stand in the way of forming and sustaining new political parties in Britain – old parties refuse to die, despite defections, election defeats and splits; while new parties and unattached individuals find it very difficult to sustain an independent existence, as this chapter has illustrated.

Notes

1. Lloyd George on Simon, House of Commons debate, 3 July 1931, *Hansard.*
2. Simon, John, *Retrospect* (Hutchinson, 1952), pp. 45–6 and 106–8.
3. Dutton, David, *A History of the Liberal Party* (Palgrave, 2004), p. 87.
4. Hart, 'Decline', p. 220.
5. *Neville Chamberlain Diary Letters*, quoted Dutton, David, *Liberals in Schism* (Tauris, 2008), p. 31.
6. *The Times*, 29 June 1931, p. 14, col. a.
7. *Montrose Review*, 24 October 1924, p. 6, col. a.
8. *The Times*, 29 June 1931, p. 14, col. a.
9. Ryan, A.P., 'Brown (Alfred) Ernest (1881–1962)', rev. Brodie, Marc, ODNB.
10. *The Times*, 29 June 1931, p. 14, col. a.
11. Lloyd George to MacDonald, 30 August 1931 and Samuel to Lloyd George, 25 September 1931, quoted in Owen, Frank, *Tempestuous Journey* (Hutchinson, 1954), p. 719.
12. Owen to Lloyd George, 29 October 1942, LG/G/15/16/7 and Lloyd George to Owen, 20 February 1936, LG/G/15/16/2, Lloyd George Papers.
13. *Daily News*, 14 November 1924.
14. Minutes, Midland Liberal Federation, 4 February 1932, quoted Hart, 'Decline', p. 258.
15. Ball, Stuart (ed.), *Parliament and Politics in the Age of Churchill and Attlee: The Headlam Diaries 1935–1951* (Cambridge University Press, 1999), p. 185.
16. Smart, Nick (ed.), *The Diaries and Letters of Robert Bernays, 1932–1939* (Mellen, 1996), pp. xviii–xxv.
17. Bernays to Simon, 10 September 1936, 83/190 and Simon to Bernays, 11 September 1936, 83/191, Simon Papers.
18. Obituary, *The Times*, 6 December 1962, p. 19, col. a.
19. Murray, Arthur, *Master and Brother* (John Murray, 1945), pp. 185–6.
20. Obituary, *The Times*, 6 December 1962, p. 19, col. c.
21. *Telegraph and Argus*, 5 November 1938, p. 5, cols a–b.
22. *Liverpool Daily Post*, 16 June 1945, p. 4, col. d.
23. *Edinburgh Dispatch*, 18 September 1936, MAS/30, Mason Papers.
24. *Morning Advertiser*, 19 September 1936, MAS/30, Mason Papers.
25. *Edinburgh Evening News*, 29 April 1938, MAS/30, Mason Papers.
26. Mason to Meston, 22 November 1938, quoted *The Times*, 23 November 1938, p. 9, col. c.
27. Ellis Davies to Lord Davies of Llandinam, 8 September 1936, 29/21, Ellis Davies Papers.
28. Brack, Duncan, 'Horatio Bottomley', DLB, pp. 48–9.
29. *Saffron Walden Weekly News*, 19 August 1921, p. 9, col. c.
30. *Galloway Gazette*, 10 October 1931, p. 5, col. c and 17 October 1931, p. 4, col. a.
31. Worley, Matthew, 'A Call to Action: New Party Candidates and the 1931 General Election', *Parliamentary History*, 27(2) (2008): 236–55.

32 Pratt, John, article in *Illustrated Sunday Herald*, 4 January 1920, BBK/B/112, Beaverbrook Papers, Parliamentary Archives.
33 Pratt to Beaverbrook, 14 December 1930, BBK/B/171, Beaverbrook Papers.
34 Pratt to Davies, 12 April 1927, B22, A.J. Sylvester Papers, National Library of Wales.
35 Beaverbrook to Pratt, 16 December 1930, BBK/B/171, Beaverbrook Papers.
36 Pratt to Beaverbrook, 21 December 1930, BBK/B/171, Beaverbrook Papers.
37 Finlay, Richard, *Independent and Free* (John Donald, 1994), pp. 129 and 251.
38 Guest to Lloyd George, 10 September 1920, LG/F/22/2/12, Lloyd George Papers.
39 MacCormick, John, *The Flag in the Wind* (Birlinn, 2008), 68–9.
40 Reynolds, Jaime, and Hunter, Ian, '"Crinks" Johnstone', *Journal of Liberal Democrat History*, 26 (2000): 18.
41 Coote, Colin, *The Other Club* (Sidgwick & Jackson, 1971), pp. 128–9.
42 Hopkinson, Harmsworth and Sueter to Baldwin, 7 March 1924, quoted Gilbert, *Churchill, V Companion 1*, p. 118.
43 Excluding two candidates for University seats and excluding Rhys Hopkin Morris, whose case is discussed in Chapter 3.
44 *Berwickshire News*, 14 November 1922, p. 5, col. a; 31 October 1922, p. 7, col. f; 7 November 1922, p. 5, col. d; and 10 May 1929, p. 11, col. b.
45 *Stockport Advertiser*, 26 April 1929, p. 13, col. e; 3 May 1929, p. 7, col. b; and 17 May 1929, p. 13, col. b.
46 Phillipps to Lloyd George, 24 August 1925, LG/G/16/5/6, Lloyd George Papers.
47 Marquand, David, *Ramsay MacDonald* (Cape, 1977), p. 282.
48 Fisher, H., *An Unfinished Autobiography* (Oxford University Press, 1940), pp. 117–18.
49 Ogg, David, *Herbert Fisher 1865–1940: A Short Biography* (Arnold, 1947), p. 196.
50 Hart, 'Decline', p. 272.
51 Fisher to Young, 22 February 1926, quoted Hart, 'Decline', p. 272.
52 Vipont, Elfrida, *Arnold Rowntree: A Life* (Bannisdale, 1955), p. 55.
53 *The Times*, 3 March 1937, p. 7, col. g and 23 March 1937, p. 16, col. f.
54 Smulian, Mark, 'Michael Meadowcroft', DLB, pp. 255–6.
55 Nowosielski, Noel, UK Polling Report, www.ukpollingreport.co.uk (accessed 15 January 2010).
56 Rennard, Chris, 'David Alton', DLB, pp. 12–15.

6
Inward defectors

> What a third party struggling for attention hopes for most after a by-election victory – a defector.[1]

For contrast and completeness, the scale and timing of inward defections to the Liberal/Liberal Democrats between 1910 and 2010 can be compared to the loss of outward defectors considered in the previous chapters. In this research an inward defector has been defined as someone who sat as an MP for another party, or as an independent, before becoming a Liberal or Liberal Democrat MP. Both outward and inward defectors must have served as an MP before the defection and in both cases they must have served at some stage as a Liberal or Liberal Democrat MP. However, this inevitably means that the criterion for qualifying as an inward defector is more stringent. A person who was simply a member of another party who then became a Liberal or Liberal Democrat MP would not be included, as a person's allegiance before he or she enters parliament is of less significance than it is after he or she has been elected. By this definition, six MPs defected into the party between December 1910 and May 2010.[2] Also, during this time eighteen former Liberal MPs, who had earlier defected from the party, returned to it.[3]

The SDP and its antecedents

Compared to the Liberals with their on-going problems, the Labour Party recovered relatively quickly from its 1931 debacle and its reduction to only fifty-two seats in the election that year. Ramsay MacDonald's secession to lead the National Labour group only deprived the Labour Party of a handful of, mainly older, MPs: only thirteen National Labour MPs were elected at the 1931 election. By 1935, National Labour had virtually disintegrated and the Labour Party had recovered to 154 seats. For Labour this was not a false dawn, as 1923 had been for the Liberals;

when they achieved 159 seats, only to be crushed down to forty a year later. The Labour Party, under Clement Attlee's leadership, played a significant part in the Second World War coalition and went on to win a landslide in 1945 and a narrower victory in 1950, before going down to defeat the following year. However, once in opposition again, the Labour Party was dogged by internal tensions during the 1950s – largely centred on the personalities of Attlee and Morrison, Bevan and Gaitskell.

Despite the problems of the Labour Party, no sitting Labour MPs defected to the Liberals before the end of the 1960s and just two of the earlier Liberal defectors to Labour had returned – Percy Alden had returned in 1927, during Lloyd George's leadership and George Garro-Jones returned in 1958, under the leadership of Jo Grimond.[4] With their return to power in 1964, the Labour Party initially became more united, but policy differences began to split the party – divisions over Europe being the most serious. The boldest of the Labour dissenters was Dick Taverne. His path out of the Labour Party blazed a trail which was to be followed, first by Christopher Mayhew and then by the breakaway Social Democratic Party (SDP). Taverne had been elected as Labour MP for Lincoln in 1962, but despite a flourishing parliamentary career, relations with his increasingly left-wing local party had deteriorated. There was resentment at his public school and London barrister background, but it was Europe that provided the flashpoint.[5] Taverne forced the issue to a head by resigning his seat, causing a by-election, which he won as an independent 'Democratic Labour' candidate in March 1973. He held the seat again in February 1974, but lost in October. While still in the House of Commons he had launched his Campaign for Social Democracy, and in 1981 he went on to play a prominent role in the foundation of the SDP. While Taverne had taken a bold stance and put his views to the test in a successful by-election, he never went on to sit as a Liberal or Liberal Democrat MP, having lost his seat in the Commons before the formation of the SDP and having failed to be re-elected under the party's auspices. He did, however, eventually become a Liberal Democrat peer and his path out of the Labour Party was followed by **Christopher Mayhew**, who became the first sitting MP to defect into the Liberal Party for over sixty years.[6]

Mayhew was first elected as Labour MP for South Norfolk in 1945, transferring to Woolwich East in 1951, after having lost his seat in 1950. He reached the level of Navy Minister in the 1964 Wilson Government, but became increasingly mistrustful of Wilson and at odds with the Labour Party over naval policy and Europe.[7] He resigned his ministerial post in 1966, feeling that the Labour Party was falling into the hands of 'leftists whose views are wildly unrepresentative' and that the extremists tended to 'dominate or scare away the rest'.[8] In 1967 he founded the pro-EEC Campaign for Europe. He was in close contact with Roy Jenkins and with other right-wing Labour MPs opposed to Wilson, many of them former Gaitskell admirers, including future SDP defectors Bill Rodgers and Dickson Mabon. Despite trying to change the Labour Party from the inside, and then trying to organise a breakaway of Labour moderates, Mayhew felt he had achieved nothing. Mayhew discussed his plan to defect with Roy Jenkins, who tried to rein him back, saying: 'Don't go yet. Wait for the rest of us'.[9] However, in July 1974 Mayhew made the break alone and joined the Liberal Party in the House of Commons. He was the first sitting MP to defect into the Liberal Party since Archibald Corbett, a former Liberal Unionist, in 1910. Mayhew stood as the Liberal candidate for Bath at the October 1974 general election, but came 2,122 votes short of taking the seat. He was elevated to the Lords as a Liberal peer in 1981. Mayhew's former agent, John Cartwright, succeeded him at Woolwich East, as a Labour and later SDP MP.

As a result of the creation of the SDP, the Labour Party suffered the largest mass defection of MPs from any party since the Liberal Unionists split from the Liberals in 1886. Twenty-eight sitting Labour MPs (along with one Conservative), joined the SDP. However, despite the alliance of the SDP with the Liberal Party and the subsequent merger in 1988, **Robert Maclennan** was the only one of the defecting MPs who went on to serve as a Liberal Democrat member in the House of Commons.[10] All the others had been defeated or retired by the time of the merger.

After initially ruling out the Liberal Party as a viable vehicle for a political career, Maclennan had been elected as Labour MP for Caithness and Sutherland in 1966.[11] Ironically, Maclennan won the seat by ousting the Liberal incumbent, George Mackie, who had two years earlier regained the seat for the Liberals for the first time since the defeat of Sinclair in 1945. Maclennan's career initially prospered in the Labour Party, but he felt very angered about Labour's U-turn over Europe and he resigned his opposition front-bench position in 1972. Despite this, he was appointed under-secretary at the Department of Prices and Consumer Protection, under Shirley Williams, in the Labour Government after the February 1974 election – a post he held until Labour's defeat in 1979. Maclennan had become concerned about the 'bullying tactics' of the trades unions and disenchanted with the class politics of the Labour Party.[12] He reached a break point in the autumn of 1980, after there had been moves to de-select some of the Labour Party's right-wing MPs. Maclennan announced his departure from

Labour shortly after the Limehouse Declaration of January 1981, before the SDP was formally in being. He had talked with Jenkins and some sitting Labour MPs before the announcement of the formation of the new party, but there was no coordinated action within the Labour Party.

Twelve Labour MPs joined the SDP on the first day and others followed sporadically. Around a third of Maclennan's local party's management went with him immediately and another third followed later. Maclennan believed that he retained sufficient support to have won a by-election on his change of party allegiance, but that other former-Labour converts to the SDP were in more vulnerable positions in their constituencies, where support for Labour was 'instinctual and almost hereditary'.[13] In Caithness and Sutherland the Liberal tradition was still strong, but the local party, despite having held the seat between 1964 and 1966, had not fielded a candidate against Maclennan in 1979.

Two years after her defeat as a Labour MP in 1979, Shirley Williams won Crosby for the SDP in a by-election. After a narrow defeat in Warrington in 1981, Roy Jenkins captured Glasgow Hillhead in a by-election in March 1982, thus returning to parliament after having resigned his seat as a Labour MP in 1976 to take up the post of President of the European Commission. Thus all the 'Gang of Four' who founded the SDP were back in the House of Commons.[14] However, none was to go on to serve as a Liberal Democrat MP. A cautionary note was sounded when one of the Labour defectors to the SDP, Bruce Douglas-Mann, resigned his seat in 1982, precipitating a by-election, which he lost to the Conservatives. The Conservative Party's fortunes continued to recover after the Falklands War and the prospects for the SDP correspondingly began to ebb. The Labour Party, under the leadership of Michael Foot, however, remained in the doldrums.

In general the SDP was stronger in areas where the Liberals were weaker, and this eased many, but not all, of the potential conflicts in allocating seats between the parties when they fought elections in alliance.[15] Despite their high hopes, and partly because of their differing geographical strengths, the 1983 election result was a severe disappointment for the alliance: Maclennan's later reflection that they 'had not learned about targeting seats', was something of an understatement.[16] It was almost a perverse achievement to have won 25.4% of the vote between the alliance parties, but to have ended up with just seventeen Liberal MPs and only six for the SDP.[17] Of these six, four were surviving former-Labour MPs – Robert Maclennan, Ian Wrigglesworth, John Cartwright and David Owen. The only newly-elected SDP MP at the 1983 general election was Charles Kennedy, later to become leader

Table 6.1 *Fate of SDP defectors at 1983 general election and after*

	1983 election	Post-1983 political career
Roy Jenkins*	won	SDP MP, Lib Dem peer
Bill Rodgers	lost 3rd	Lib Dem peer
Shirley Williams*	lost 2nd	Lib Dem peer
David Owen	won	SDP/Ind SDP MP, crossb peer
John Cartwright	won	SDP/Ind SDP MP
Robert Maclennan	won	SDP/Lib Dem MP, Lib Dem peer
Ron Brown	lost 3rd	
Tom Bradley	lost 3rd	
Richard Crawshaw	lost 4th	life peer 1985
George Cunningham	lost 2nd	
Ednyfed Hudson Davies	lost 2nd	
Bruce Douglas-Mann+	lost 3rd	
James Dunn	did not stand	
Tom Ellis	lost 2nd	
David Ginsburg	lost 3rd	
John Grant	lost 3rd	rejoined Labour
John Horam	lost 3rd	Conservative MP
Edward Lyons	lost 3rd	
Tom McNally	lost 3rd	Lib Dem peer
Dickson Mabon	lost 2nd	rejoined Labour 1991
Bryan Magee	lost 3rd	
Richard Mitchell	lost 2nd	
Eric Ogden	lost 3rd	
Michael O'Halloran	lost 4th	tried to rejoin Lab, Ind Lab cand
John Roper	lost 3rd	Lib Dem peer
Neville Sandelson	lost 3rd	rejoined Labour Party 1996
Jeffrey Thomas	lost 3rd	rejoined Labour Party
Mike Thomas	lost 3rd	
James Wellbeloved	lost 2nd	rejoined Labour Party
Ian Wrigglesworth	won	SDP MP
Chris Brocklebank-Fowler	lost 2nd	joined Labour Party 1996

* By-election victors after 1981.
+ Douglas-Mann had resigned and fought a by-election in June 1982, coming second.

of the Liberal Democrats. Roy Jenkins held Hillhead in 1983, but lost it in 1987. Shirley Williams was defeated in Crosby in 1983.

Table 6.1 charts the electoral fate of the SDP defectors at the 1983 general election and after, showing that several subsequently returned to the Labour Party, while six became Liberal Democrat peers, but only Maclennan became a Liberal Democrat MP.

Vincent Cable and Bob Russell are the only other Liberal or Liberal

Democrat MPs to have stood as candidates for another party since December 1910, before becoming a Liberal or Liberal Democrat MP. Both became Liberal Democrat MPs in 1997, having stood, unsuccessfully, for Labour in the 1970s and having joined the SDP in 1982.

After the 1987 election, when the combined SDP and Liberal tally of MPs was reduced by one, pressure for the alliance parties to merge became intense. The negotiations did not proceed smoothly. John Cartwright and David Owen refused to join the merged party and continued briefly with a separate rump SDP after the Social and Liberal Democrat Party was formed in 1988. Paddy Ashdown took over the leadership of the merged party from Maclennan, who had held the fort during the merger negotiations. The merged party was renamed the Liberal Democrats the following year.

The net long-term result of the SDP venture was undoubtedly positive for the Liberal Democrats, but only temporarily damaging to the Labour Party, which again showed its resilience, returning to power with a landslide victory in 1997. For the Liberal Democrats, the adhesion of respected figures such as Roy Jenkins, Shirley Williams, Bill Rodgers and Tom McNally added credibility, although only the one defector (Maclennan) actually sat as a Labour and then eventually as a Liberal Democrat MP.

While inward defectors can bring attention to a 'third party struggling for attention', the third party does not necessarily choose who the new entrants will be, nor what sort of attention they will bring with them.[18] Two later defectors joined the Liberal Democrats from the Labour Party, but the cases of Marsden and Sedgemore illustrate the mixed blessings of some inward defections.

Paul Marsden was elected Labour MP for Shrewsbury and Atcham in 1997 and re-elected in 2001. But, within a year of his re-election he had complained to Prime Minister Blair and to the Speaker that he had been 'physically and verbally attacked' by MPs from his own party, during voting on anti-terrorism legislation.[19] Marsden was friendly with two neighbouring Liberal Democrat MPs, Lembit Opik and Matthew Green, and on 10 December 2001 he sought refuge within the Liberal Democrat Party, which was initially glad of the publicity. After his defection, the Labour Party announced that they were leaving Marsden to 'make a fool of himself', and that, unfortunately for him and for the Liberal Democrats, is exactly what he did. Lurid stories of extra-marital sexual encounters by Marsden appeared in the press and on-line, together with romantic poems written by the MP. On the eve of the 2005 election Marsden, who had announced that he was not going to contest the election, defected back to Labour. His welcome back into the Labour Party was less than fulsome, a local party official telling Marsden to 'get lost', having 'demonstrated his treachery on more than one occasion'.[20] At the 2005 election the Liberal Democrats' share of the vote in the constituency rose from 12.4% to 22.8% compared to that in 2001, while Labour's vote dropped from 44.6% to 34.1%. However, the real beneficiaries were the Conservatives, who were able to take the seat on a virtually unchanged share of the vote.[21] Marsden's return to Labour on 5 April 2005 coincided with the defection to the Liberal Democrats of the Labour candidate for Ribble Valley. Less than two weeks later, Charles Kennedy's Party was to be the recipient of another defecting Labour MP, Brian Sedgemore.

Brian Sedgemore had served as a Labour MP since February 1974, with a break from 1979 to 1983. In his early parliamentary career he had been opposed to the EEC, against free trade and had been associated with the views of the left-wing Tribune Group.[22] He had served as PPS to Labour Energy Secretary Tony Benn, but was sacked in 1978 for disclosing the content of a cabinet document.[23] His confrontational approach led to his being barred from the House of Commons for five days in 1985, after he accused Conservative Chancellor of the Exchequer Nigel Lawson of perverting the course of justice over the Johnson Matthey Affair and then refused to withdraw the remark. His early career had shown little connection with Liberalism, but Sedgemore was brought into sympathy with the Liberal Democrats, and into opposition to Blair's Government, when he strongly opposed the Iraq War and university tuition fees. On 25 April, less than two weeks before the 2005 election, at which he was due to retire, Sedgemore defected to the Liberal Democrats, making outspoken televised attacks on Blair, and accusing him of 'stomach turning lies' over Iraq and asking voters to give Blair a 'bloody nose'.[24] In the heat of the election campaign, the publicity was, on balance, beneficial to the Liberal Democrats. In Sedgemore's former seat at Hackney South and Shoreditch, the Liberal Democrat share of the vote rose from 14.6% to 21.2%, while Labour's fell from 64.2% to 52.9%, compared to results of the 2001 election. On calmer consideration two years after the election, Sedgemore, a barrister by training, reflected that he 'left Labour in disgust over the erosion of liberty'.[25]

Defectors from the Conservatives

During the one hundred years from December 1910, the Conservatives were the recipients of thirty-four Liberal defectors: and none of these returned to Liberals. However, the tide turned for the Conservatives in the 1990s. John Major's Conservative Government was re-elected in April 1992 with an overall majority of twenty-one seats, and yet by the dissolution before the general election of 1997, this majority had been completely eroded and Major's administration was in a minority by three seats. The Liberal Democrats gained four seats from the Conservatives in by-elections – Newbury (1993), Christchurch (1993), Eastleigh (1994) and Littleborough and Saddleworth (1995). The Conservatives also lost two serving MPs who defected to the Liberal Democrats.

Emma Nicholson, sitting Conservative MP for Devon West and Torridge since 1987, a former vice-chair of the Conservative Party and daughter of a Tory MP, defected to the Liberal Democrats on 29 December 1995. First rumours of her possible defection reached the Liberal Democrats on 5 December 1995, but the party leadership was suspicious that she might be playing a double game. Nicholson was concerned by the slowness of the Liberal Democrats' response, but when asked directly if she would join the party, she responded: 'I might if you asked me.'[26] Nicholson had also been chased by Labour for three months, but said that she 'didn't feel like a socialist'.[27] Nicholson had been unhappy with Conservatives' xenophobic attitudes, especially in relation to asylum seekers.[28] She was also uncomfortable with the party as she felt she knew too much about the supply of arms to Iraq and the extent to which parliament had been 'misled'.[29] When Nicholson gave evidence to the Nolan Committee on Standards in Public Life, set up in 1994, she was told by the Conservative whips that she was 'betraying the party'.[30] They said that she had 'stuck a knife into the heart of the Tory Party' when she voted for public disclosure of MPs' outside financial interests.[31] In the back of her mind she had the experience of her father after he had voted against Chamberlain.[32] On the day of her defection, 29 December 1995, Nicholson faxed a letter to the Prime Minister, saying: 'I am today leaving the Conservative Party and joining the Liberal Democrats ... Rather than become a permanent rebel ... I deem it proper and honest to cast my votes, which will quite often be against the Government, from the Liberal Democrat benches.'[33] The Conservative Party had no advance intelligence of Nicholson's defection.[34] They found out half an hour before the news broke on television.[35] The story dominated all the television news and newspapers for the rest of that day and the following morning. Major subsequently confirmed that he knew nothing of the defection until it was reported on television.[36] The Chairman of the Devon West and Torridge Conservative Association sent a 'round robin' letter to members telling them not to demand a by-election, since they could neither win nor afford one.[37] Nicholson did not want to fight her former Commons seat, which was won by the Liberal Democrats at the 1997 election, but she went on to become an MEP and Liberal Democrat peer.

Liberal Democrat contacts with **Peter Thurnham** had actually begun before those with Nicholson. Thurnham, owner of a successful refrigeration business, had held the marginal constituency of Bolton North East for the Conservatives since 1983. Because of impending boundary changes and the knife-edge electoral conditions, Thurnham wanted to contest Westmorland and Lonsdale, but he was not even shortlisted for the Conservative candidacy. As well as this personal rebuff, Thurnham wanted to leave the Tories because of his disgust at the handling of the Scott and Nolan inquiries. He held back, not wanting to let down his constituency and concerned that, if he left, the Tory Party would be 'absolutely vicious'.[38] Major was aware of Thurnham's likely defection and spent two hours talking to him and his wife in a last-ditch attempt to keep him in the Conservative Party; but within hours Thurnham announced his intention of resigning the Conservative whip.[39] He left the Conservatives on 23 February 1996, saying that he could no longer support a party that had lost touch with 'basic values of decency'. Thurnham's lasting damage was to help bring 'sleaze' back onto the agenda and he raised fears that others would follow.[40] Thurnham wanted to leave the Conservatives and then only later join the Liberal Democrats. This meant that the Liberal Democrat Party would be unable to help and support his defection in the way in which they had handled Nicholson's. Ashdown, aware that there comes a moment for any defector when, all tension gone, his or her morale collapses, wanted Thurnham to join the Liberal Democrats straight away. However, in the event, Thurnham sat as an independent first and only later joined the Liberal Democrats, on 12 October 1996. In Bolton North East, affected by boundary changes in 1997, the Liberal Democrat share of the vote remained around 10%, while the seat was captured by Labour. While the Liberal Democrats did not benefit from a local electoral advantage, the party did gain financially. Thurnham became a significant donor to the party, including a gift of £16,000 in 2001. He died on 10 May 2008, having remarried the day before.

The Liberal Democrats were also the recipients of other former Conservative MPs, who defected to the party after they had left parliament – Hugh Dykes (1997); John Lee (2001); the former Thatcher 'stalking horse' Anthony Meyer (2001); and Harold Elletson (2002).[41] In addition to the Tory MPs who defected to the Liberal

Democrats, an unusual feature of the period from 1995 to 2007 was the number of sitting MPs who defected from the Conservatives straight to Labour – Alan Howarth (1995); Peter Temple-Morris (1997); Shaun Woodward (1999); Robert Jackson (2005) and Quentin Davies (2007).[42]

The inward defectors from Labour and the Conservatives to the Liberal Democrats all brought either a direct local electoral advantage or donations of much needed money. They also brought an indirect electoral advantage at a national level. As Chapters 3 to 5 demonstrated, outward defectors were motivated more by problems with the Liberal Party than by the attractions of another party. Correspondingly, the inward defectors mainly arrived as a result of dissatisfaction with another party, rather than the attraction of the Liberals or Liberal Democrats. This was certainly the case with the SDP. The other four inward defectors – Marsden and Sedgemore also from Labour and Nicholson and Thurnham from the Conservatives – all left their former parties due to their perceived failings, rather than for the attraction of the Liberals/Liberal Democrats. Five of the six inward defectors remained in the Liberal/Liberal Democrat Party.[43] As a proportion this almost exactly equals the eighteen returnees from among the 116 outward defectors.

The year 1956 turned out to be the watershed for the Liberals in terms of defections. After that year more defectors came to the party than those who left. The party went on to reach a new peak of sixty-three Westminster seats in 2006, an almost unimaginable position from the low point of the 1950s, when the party had been reduced to just five seats.[44]

Returning former Liberal defectors

Eighteen of the defectors who left the Liberal Party later returned, as shown in Table 6.2. All the returning defectors have been considered in earlier chapters, according to their destination after they left the Liberals. The majority of the returnees comprised four former Constitutionalists, the five Lloyd George Family Group members and four former Liberal Nationals. Five of the eighteen defected from the Liberal Party again, after having returned. Nine of the eighteen returnees came back during Sinclair's leadership, six returned during Asquith's tenure, only one during Lloyd George's.

Table 6.2 *Returning former defectors*

MP	Date defected from Liberals	Destination	Date returned to Liberals
David Mason	1914	Independent Lib	1922 ^
John Whitehouse	1918	Independent Lib	1922
John Ward	1924	Constitutionalists	1924
Hugh Edwards	1924	Constitutionalists	1924
Thomas Robinson	1924	Constitutionalists	1924
Abraham England	1924	Constitutionalists	1924
Percy Alden	1919	Labour	1927
David Lloyd George	1931	Lloyd George Family	1935
Gwilym Lloyd George	1931	Lloyd George Family	1935*
Megan Lloyd George	1931	Lloyd George Family	1935+
Goronwy Owen	1931	Lloyd George Family	1935
Frank Owen	1931	Lloyd George Family	1935
William McKeag	1934	Liberal Nationals	1936*
Arthur Murray	1936	Liberal Nationals	1938
Clement Davies	1931	Liberal Nationals	1942
Edgar Granville	1931	Liberal Nationals	1945+
George Garro-Jones	1929	Labour	1958
Michael Meadowcroft	1989	Continuing Liberals	2007

* Subsequently defected to the Conservatives.
+ Subsequently defected to Labour.
^ Subsequently defected to Liberal Nationals.

Notes

1. Ashdown, Paddy, *A Fortunate Life* (Aurum, 2009), p. 289.
2. Excludes Rhys Hopkin Morris, first elected as an Independent Liberal. See Chapter 5.
3. Includes Clement Davies and Edgar Granville, who became Liberal Nationals in the 1931 split, but who defected back to the Liberal Party in the 1940s.
4. By the time of his return in 1927, Alden was out of parliament. Garro-Jones sat in the House of Lords as Baron Trefgarne at the time of his return in 1958. David Rees-Williams, former Labour MP for Croydon South from 1945 to 1950, ennobled as Lord Ogmore, defected to the Liberals in the Lords in 1959 and went on to serve as Liberal Party President from 1963 to 1964.
5. Stockley, Neil, 'Dick Taverne', DLB, p. 347.
6. Excluding former defectors who returned to the Liberal Party.
7. Mayhew, Christopher, *Time to Explain* (Hutchinson, 1987), p. 178.
8. Mayhew, Christopher, *Party Games* (Hutchinson, 1969), p. 87.
9. Mayhew, *Time to Explain*, p. 203.

10 The merged party was initially called the Social and Liberal Democrats, renamed the Liberal Democrats in 1989.
11 Tony Little, Interview with Maclennan, *Journal of Liberal Democrat History*, 25 (1999–2000): 40.
12 Ibid., 41.
13 Ibid.
14 Bill Rodgers and David Owen were sitting as MPs.
15 See Chapter 3 for discussion of the case of Bill Pitt.
16 Little, interview: 43.
17 The Liberals' fifty-nine seats with 23.4% of the vote in 1929, or Labour's sixty-three seats from 22.2% in 1918 are the nearest comparable failures to convert votes into seats.
18 Ashdown, *Fortunate Life*, p. 289.
19 *Guardian*, 6 December 2001, p. 2.
20 *Shropshire Star*, quoted *Guardian*, 9 April 2005, p. 24.
21 www.ukpollingreport.co.uk/guide/seat-profiles/shrewsburyandatcham (accessed 7 October 2009).
22 *The Times*, 8 July 1974, p. 15, col. e.
23 *The Times*, 13 November 1978, p. 2, col. f.
24 www.news.bbc.co.uk/1/hi/uk_politics/vote_2005/frontpage/4484043.stm (accessed 7 October 2009).
25 Brian Sedgemore, Liberal Democrat History Group meeting, London, 5 February 2007.
26 Ashdown, *Fortunate Life*, p. 291.
27 Ashdown, Paddy, *Diaries 1988–97*, 21 December 1995 (Penguin, 2000), p. 368.
28 Ashdown, *Diaries*, 23 December 1995, p. 370.
29 Nicholson, Emma, *Secret Society* (Indigo, 1996), p. 190.
30 Ibid., p. 189.
31 Ashdown, *Diaries*, 23 December 1995, p. 369.
32 Ibid., p. 372.
33 Nicholson to Major, 29 December 1995, quoted Ashdown, *Diaries*, p. 598.
34 Seldon, Anthony, *Major: A Political Life* (Phoenix, 1997), p. 627.
35 Ashdown, *Diaries*, 29 December 1995, p. 375.
36 Major, John, *Autobiography* (Harper Collins, 1999), p. 576.
37 *Observer*, 14 April 1996, p. 2.
38 Ashdown, *Diaries*, 29 November 1995, pp. 363–4.
39 Seldon, *Major*, p. 631.
40 *Sunday Times*, 13 October 1996, quoted Seldon, *Major*, p. 677.
41 *Guardian*, 11 December 2001, p. 1.
42 Temple-Morris left the Conservatives in 1997 and took the Labour whip in 1998.
43 Marsden was the one exception.
44 After the death of Rhys Hopkin Morris in November 1956.

7

Conclusions

After almost a century, the Liberal Party's near-demise is still an unresolved case. Many suspected causes have been investigated. Previous researchers have focused their attentions on elections (Cook, Hart), the role of the party leaders (Douglas, Owen), the rise of the Labour Party (McKibbin, Wrigley, Tanner), social changes (Dangerfield, Pelling), the failure of Liberalism to cope with the Great War (Wilson, Tanner, Bentley) and the Liberal Nationals' split (Baines, Dutton). All of their evidence is relevant to the case, but it has not proved conclusive and it is not always corroborative.

This research set out to investigate, not to justify any particular assertion. It has revealed for the first time the full scale and pattern of defections by MPs and former MPs to and from the party since December 1910. In so doing, it has demonstrated the insiders' views of the health of the party at specific points in time. It adds new evidence, drawn from over a hundred expert witnesses – the defectors – who were actually involved in the events. The defectors comprised one-sixth of all those who sat as Liberal MPs after December 1910. About half of the defectors were in parliament at the time of their defection, and most of the others also played a further role in national politics after they defected. While most defectors left individually, there are clear patterns to the reasons for the defections and differences which distinguished the defectors as a whole from those who did not defect.

The argument for a pre-war Liberal decline, propounded by historians such as Dangerfield, McKibbin and Pelling, is contradicted by the evidence from this study. The Liberal Party was not suffering outward defections before the war: in fact the contrary was true. The assertion of Wilson, Tanner and Bentley that the war was the cause of the decline is also not supported by the study of the defectors. From this study it is clear that the Great War was not the cause of significant outward defections. Hart, in putting emphasis on the 1918 election, is closer in date to the critical point identified in this research, but not in his reasoning. His generalisation about the Liberal Party not tolerating war objectors is largely contradicted by the findings of this study. Although thirty-five Liberal MPs objected to the Liberal Government's war policies, for twenty-eight of them this did not prevent their continuing to pursue a career in Liberal politics. For most of the war, the Labour Party was more severely split over policy than the Liberals and it was not actively trying to recruit Liberal defectors. The factors which led to the defections included local Liberal associations' deselecting candidates who wished to stand again, as in the case of Ponsonby, Trevelyan and Outhwaite. This was not party policy, and other War Policy Objectors were re-adopted as Liberal candidates in other constituencies. Some were re-elected. The only former Liberal MPs to stand as Labour candidates in 1918 were Money and John. Money was motivated by a highly individualistic focus on shipping nationalisation and John by Welsh Nationalism. Neither re-entered parliament and both later became dissatisfied with Labour's stance on their chosen topics. The timing of the defections revealed in this research demonstrates that even after the 1918 election, the Liberal Party was believed by those closest to the centre to be in a recoverable state, but that by 1922 many of them felt that the opportunity had been lost. As belief is a foundation for future success, this collapse of confidence had serious consequences for the party's prospects.

At first sight, the opinion of a partisan politician, personally involved in the events, seems unlikely to offer a theory to challenge later detailed objective historical analysis. However, Asquith's claim that the 'disintegration of the Liberal Party began with the Coupon election'[1] is broadly in line with the findings from this study. Asquith himself played a relatively passive role in the Liberal defections. He was criticised for 'waiting and seeing' rather than leading, but virtually no defectors left the Liberal Party blaming Asquith for their departure: a much greater number left feeling very reluctant to sever their relationship with him. Six of the eighteen defectors who returned to the party came back under Asquith's leadership. However, Asquith's complacency – 'off to the Riviera . . . confident, convinced, etc, that the Party would be unimpaired, united, and anything else that begins with a u2' – was not justified by events.[2] Asquith certainly bears some responsibility for the Liberal Party's problems, but the defectors apportion little of the blame to him.

Lloyd George was the leader who presided over the most serious attrition rate of defectors, due both to his personality and to his policies. No fewer than fifteen defectors blamed Lloyd George entirely for their defections and he was severely criticised by many other departing defectors. His decision (although not his first choice) to appoint Freddie Guest as chief whip was a serious error of judgement from the point of view of the revival of the party. The effects of the 1916 split and the coupon election could have been overcome, if they had been remedied before 1921. While Asquith could fairly be criticised for a lack of policy and weak leadership, Lloyd George could be considered to have gone to the opposite extreme and in the process alienated a significant section of his party, including several who actually personally liked him.

Churchill actively tried to keep a group of followers with him when he moved between parties. From his point of view, this strengthened his bargaining power. Some followers were motivated by a strong personal loyalty to him. However, his pet projects of fusion and the Constitutionalists achieved little, although they provided a bridge out of the Liberal Party for a few like-minded defectors. Even so, four of the seven victorious Constitutionalists re-took the Liberal whip after the election. Churchill was the greatest asset acquired from the Liberals by the Conservatives, although he did retain a relatively benign approach towards the Liberal Party for the rest of his life, as demonstrated by his attempted pacts with the Liberals in the 1940s and 1950s and his coalition offer of 1951.

Simon, despite having few skills of people management and little apparent interest in others, actually led a larger number of followers than did Churchill or any other defector. His Liberal Nationals were successful in attracting former Liberals. His adherents were disproportionately (to their numbers and their talents) offered ministerial office, but this was due to the circumstances of the time, not to Simon's leadership abilities.

The, hitherto relatively unexplored, roles of William Wedgwood Benn, Reginald McKenna and Freddie Guest in relation to the whip's office played a crucial part in the party's decline. All of them defected from the party, although it was not their personal defections which were critical. Benn was Lloyd George's first choice as chief whip in 1916, and he could have provided a vital bridge between the Asquithian and Lloyd George wings of the party. He was persuaded by Reginald McKenna not to accept the post. Freddie Guest instead became chief whip (after Primrose's very brief tenure) and was responsible for prising open the rift with the Asquithians over the Maurice Debate, the 1918 election arrangements, party finances and the Spen Valley by-election.

The Labour Party played a relatively passive role in the Liberals' decline – although perhaps its role could be characterised as malevolently passive. It was the recipient of many Liberal defectors, but it was, in fact, more split than the Liberal Party at the crucial times, especially during the Great War and the 1931 crisis. Ramsay MacDonald did little actively to entice Liberal defectors during and immediately after the Great War: he was really in no position to do so. He did, however, lure six former Liberal MPs between 1922 and 1930 with inducements of office and honours, although his motivation was more to bolster his own position than to damage the Liberal Party. He eventually fell out with most of the converts from Liberalism. MacDonald's actions suggest that he was waiting for the Liberal Party to destroy itself, rather than actively seeking to destroy it. Arthur Henderson's administrative arrangements contributed significantly to the Labour Party's overtaking of the Liberals at the polls and hence the attraction of Liberal defectors. However, Henderson was not closely personally involved with many of them. His role in the Liberal decline, although indirect, should not be underestimated.

The outward defections were not a result of the failure of Liberalism, but of a breakdown of the Liberal Party organism. The role of the Liberal leadership, and especially that of the whips, contributed to the disintegration of the party. It was a mechanical, rather than ideological, failure. In almost every case, those who departed to the left went not because Liberalism had failed, nor because they had ceased to believe in Liberalism, but because they no longer believed that the Liberal Party would be capable of putting liberal policies into practical effect. Negative aspects of the Liberal Party overall exerted a much stronger influence on the defectors' decisions, than did the positive attractions of any other party. Many Liberal MPs suffered like the neglected children of divorcing parents during the Liberal split of 1916 to 1923. Party and people management was sacrificed as leaders' energies were put into conflict. The largest group of defectors, the Disillusioned Progressives, found a foster home in the Labour Party as a refuge from their collapsing former family. Their situation was summed up by Scott's plaintive cry that Asquith and Lloyd George were so absorbed by their own problems that they 'held out no hand'.[3]

Labour, the younger, weaker, poorer sibling of the left, should theoretically have been the one to perish in the turmoil of 1914 to 1931. But it was the mature, confident, intellectual, wealthy, older, Liberal Party that nearly succumbed to the trial – the Liberal Party of the comfortable, the self-possessed and the complacent. The Liberal Party's lighter discipline had allowed it, in prosperous times, to encompass Idealists such as Josiah Wedgwood and Richard Acland. They and others eventually defected to Labour, but felt constrained by its harsher management regime.

Defectors went fairly equally to the right and to the left, but of those going to the Conservative Party, almost all remained happily in their new party, whereas over half of the defectors to Labour came to regret their move. The Labour Party has arguably always been the most tribal of the major British political parties and therefore has been the least comfortable at receiving incomers from a different political background. Labour also became the party most fearful of its past (although arguably the Liberals should hold this title): the mere mention of Ramsay MacDonald's name can still bring a hiss of disapproval from Labour members of the House of Lords, even in the twenty-first century.[4] Tribalism may have made the Labour Party an uncomfortable home for former Liberals, but it almost certainly helped its recovery after the serious set-backs of 1931 and 1981. In the turmoil after the formation of the National Government, the Labour Party's ruthless expulsions probably helped it survive, cohere and recover, while the laxer Liberal Party continued to crumble. The Labour Party also survived the SDP split and returned to office in the landslide victory of 1997.

Although twenty-eight sitting Labour MPs (and one Conservative) defected to join the SDP, Maclennan was the only one who stayed the course in the Commons to become a Liberal Democrat MP. He was one of only six new inward defectors between 1910 and 2010 who served as an MP for another party and then as a Liberal or Liberal Democrat MP. The SDP also provided the bridge by which the significant figures of Jenkins, Williams and Rodgers, all former Labour MPs, ended up in the Liberal Democrats. Although they became Liberal Democrat peers, they were never Liberal Democrat MPs.

Grimond, despite his highly regarded leadership of the Liberal Party and at a time when Labour was pulling itself apart, attracted no new sitting MPs as converts and only received back one of the eighteen former defectors to return to the party. However, Thorpe, Steel, Ashdown and Kennedy all attracted inward defectors during their leadership of the party.

As with the situation of the outward defectors, the inward defectors to the Liberals and Liberal Democrats mainly arrived as a result of problems within their original parties, rather than the attractions of their new political home.

The Liberal Party was either the donor or recipient of most of the MPs and former MPs who defected to or from any party. This study therefore provides an analysis of most of the defections across all parties since 1910. There have been, however, some defectors who are not covered, as they were at no time Liberal MPs. These include those who defected from the Conservatives to Labour (Mosley, Howarth,

Temple-Morris, Woodward, Jackson and Davies); those who defected from Labour to the Conservatives (A. Edwards, Bulmer-Thomas, AG Brown and Prentice); and others to or from minor parties.

The one hundred years of this study saw peaks and troughs in the annual number of defections, with the highest levels occurring at times of rapidly fluctuating party fortunes; after the end of coalitions; and in election years. While it is clearly impossible to predict future defections, there are some identifiable trends which may affect the future level and pattern of defections. There are also lessons which political parties could heed from the cases investigated here.

Several factors could encourage an increase in defections. Among these, perhaps the most significant, is the issue of coalitions. Coalition government is likely to become a more frequent feature of British politics, with the increased likelihood of hung parliaments. The mere prospect of a possible coalition may encourage parties to propose more moderate policies in their election manifestos, as they will not wish to put forward policies which will be unpalatable to coalition partners, or unfeasible in office – as the Liberal Democrats found out to their cost over university tuition fees in 2010. This factor may encourage more policy consensus between parties. Election battles may be bitter, but this tends to obscure the vast swathes of policy on which there is general agreement. Lack of fundamental policy difference between parties is likely to make the move from one party to another ideologically more palatable to potential defectors. Fervent attachment to particular policies, such as free trade, state ownership and trade union reform have become less significant in British politics. The cultural compatibility of the Conservative and Liberal Democrat negotiators in 2010 coalition bargaining was in line with the long-term findings in this study. However, all political parties are generally becoming less tribal. British politics is becoming more managerial, rather than ideological, leaving fewer issues on which politicians feel honour-bound to follow a tradition. These factors are likely to increase the propensity of MPs to defect for better prospects and to make it easier for defectors to find a comfortable new home in a different party. The same factors could also be considered to make political parties less cohesive in a crisis, as there are fewer policies which can instinctively unite a party, in the way which free trade united the Liberals in 1923. Coalition government may also be a catalyst for defections as a result of greater opportunities for cross-party relationships. During the life of the coalition, there is little incentive for defections between the partner parties. However, at the end of the coalition, as was borne out after the Lloyd George coalition, there may well be a cross-flow of personnel, motivated by career prospects, reassured by lack of serious policy difference and encouraged by personal friendships.

There are some general lessons to be heeded, both for parties and for potential defectors.

Even when faced with the same circumstances of electoral decline and party splits, some MPs defected, while others stayed loyal. Those with a military background, especially those of high rank, an Eton education, high personal wealth, those from outside the predominant religion of the party and divorcés were most likely to defect – the 'toffs' and the minorities. On average, defection *was* a career-enhancing move in terms of opportunity for office or honours; but there was usually a high price to pay in terms of ruptured friendships, media intrusion, difficulties of personal assimilation into a new party and opprobrium from former colleagues. Defections for improved career prospects frequently paid off, while defections over policy were rarely satisfactory. Defectors are unlikely to be lost due to the attractions of another party's policies, but they can be lost due to the unpalatability of their own party's policies.

Most defectors dither, debate and decide over a long period of time, during which they could be dissuaded. Most have invested too much personal capital in being elected for their party to risk defection on a spur of the moment decision. Defection is a painful process, which few would undertake lightly. Communication with the disaffected is the simplest way of keeping potential defectors within a party – leaders need to hold out that hand.

Notes

1 Oxford and Asquith, *Memories and Reflections, 1852–1927*, Vol. 2 (Cassell, 1928), p. 172.
2 Benn diary, 15 April 1924.
3 Scott diary, 26 December 1925.
4 Lord Morgan, Lloyd George Society meeting, 17 February 2008.

Bibliography

Primary sources

Private papers
Addison Papers, Bodleian Library
Beaverbrook Papers, Parliamentary Archives
Chiozza Money Papers, Cambridge University Library
Clement Davies Papers, National Library of Wales
Davidson Papers, Parliamentary Archives
Denman Papers, Bodleian Library
E.T. John Papers, National Library of Wales
Edward Spears Papers, Churchill Archives Centre
Ellis Davies Papers, National Library of Wales
Haldane Papers, National Library of Scotland
Henry Haydn Jones Papers, National Library of Wales
Jowitt Papers, Parliamentary Archives
Lees-Smith Papers, University of Hull Library
Lloyd George Papers, National Library of Wales and Parliamentary Archives
MacCallum Scott Papers, Glasgow University Library
MacDonald Papers, National Archives and John Rylands Library
McKenna Papers, Churchill Archives Centre
Mander Papers, Whitwick Manor
Mason Papers, Parliamentary Archives
Munro-Ferguson Papers, National Library of Scotland
Ponsonby Papers, Bodleian Library
Samuel Papers, Parliamentary Archives
Simon Papers, Bodleian Library
Stansgate Papers, Parliamentary Archives
Sylvester Papers, National Library of Wales
Viscount Tenby Papers, National Library of Wales
Waring of Lennel Papers, National Archive of Scotland

Party records
Conservative Central Office Papers, Bodleian Library

Interviews
Lord Allen of Abbeydale, Surrey, 5 March 2004
Lord Ashdown, by telephone, 10 September 2009
Dr Peter Catterall, Oxford, 29 February 2008 and London, 26 June 2008
Stanley Clement-Davies, London, 18 May 2002
3rd Viscount Tenby, London, 9 February 2004

Memoirs
Ashdown, Paddy, *A Fortunate Life* (Aurum, 2009)
Fisher, Herbert, *An Unfinished Autobiography* (Oxford University Press, 1940)
Haldane, Richard Burdon, *An Autobiography* (Hodder and Stoughton, 1929)
Janner, Greville, *To Life!* (Sutton, 2006)
Kenworthy, J.M., *Sailors, Statesmen – and Others* (Rich and Cowan, 1933)
Major, John, *Autobiography* (HarperCollins, 1999)
Mayhew, Christopher, *Time to Explain* (Hutchinson, 1987)
Munro, Robert, *Looking Back: Fugitive Writings and Sayings* (Nelson, 1930)
Murray, Arthur, *Master and Brother* (Murray, 1945)
Nicholson, Emma, *Secret Society* (Indigo, 1996)
Oxford and Asquith, *Memories and Reflections, 1852–1927, Vol. 2* (Cassell, 1928)
Simon, John, *Retrospect: The Memoirs of Viscount Simon* (Hutchinson, 1952)

Diaries
Ashdown, Paddy, *Diaries Volume 1, 1988–97* (Allen Lane, 2000)
Ball, Stuart (ed.), *Parliament and Politics in the Age of Churchill and Attlee: The Headlam Diaries 1935–1951* (Cambridge University Press, 1999)
Jones, Thomas, *Whitehall Diary*, Vol. 1, *1916–25* (Oxford University Press, 1969)
Nicolson, Harold, *Diaries and Letters, 1930–39*, ed. Nicolson, Nigel (Collins, 1966)
Pottle, Mark (ed.), *Champion Redoubtable: Diaries and Letters of Violet Bonham Carter, 1914–45* (Weidenfeld & Nicolson, 1998)
Pottle, Mark (ed.), *Daring to Hope: Diaries and Letters of Violet Bonham Carter, 1946–69* (Weidenfeld & Nicolson, 2000)
Smart, Nick (ed.), *The Diaries and Letters of Robert Bernays 1932–1939: An Insider's Account of the House of Commons* (Mellen, 1996)
Webb, Beatrice, *The Diary of Beatrice Webb* (Virago, 1986)

Secondary sources

Reference works
Brack, Duncan et al. (eds), *Dictionary of Liberal Biography* (Politico's, 1998)
Butler, D. and Butler, G., *British Political Facts 1900–199* (Macmillan, 1994)
Cook, C., and Ramsden, J., *By–elections in British Politics* (UCL, 1997)

Craig, F.W.S., *British Parliamentary Election Results 1885–1918* (Macmillan, 1974)
Craig, F.W.S., *British Parliamentary Election Results 1918–49* (Political Reference, 1969)
Craig, F.W.S., *British Parliamentary Election Results 1950–70* (Political Reference, 1971)
Craig, F.W.S., *Minor Parties at British Parliamentary Elections, 1885–1974* (Macmillan, 1975)
Hansard, *House of Commons Debates*
Oxford Dictionary of National Biography (Oxford University Press, 2004)
Stenton, Michael, and Lees, Stephen, *Who's Who of British Members of Parliament, Vol. II, 1886–1918* (Harvester, 1978)
Stenton, Michael, and Lees, Stephen, *Who's Who of British Members of Parliament, Vol III, 1919–45* (Harvester, 1979)
Stenton, Michael, and Lees, Stephen, *Who's Who of British Members of Parliament, Vol IV, 1945–79* (Harvester, 1981)
Who's Who (A and C Black)

Books
Acland, Richard, *Unser Kampf* (Penguin, 1940)
Anderson, Mosa, *Noel Buxton, A Life* (Allen & Unwin, 1952)
Barnes, Harry, *The Slum: its Story and Solution* (King, 1931)
Bentley, Michael, *The Liberal Mind 1914–1929* (Cambridge University Press, 1979)
Bentley, Michael, *The Climax of Liberal Politics: British Liberalism in Theory and Practice, 1868–1918* (Arnold, 1987)
Cawood, Ian, *The Liberal Unionist Party: A History* (Tauris, 2012)
Cline, Catherine Ann, *Recruits to Labour: the British Labour Party, 1914–1931* (Syracuse University Press, 1963)
Cook, Chris, *The Age of Alignment* (Macmillan, 1975)
Cook, Chris, *A Short History of the Liberal Party, 1900–97* (Macmillan, Basingstoke, 1998)
Coote, Colin, *The Other Club* (Sidgwick & Jackson, 1971)
Dangerfield, George, *The Strange Death of Liberal England* (Serif, 1935)
Douglas, Roy, *History of the Liberal Party, 1895–1970* (Sidgwick & Jackson, 1971)
Dutton, David, *A Political Biography of Sir John Simon* (Aurum, 1992)
Dutton, David, *A History of the Liberal Party* (Palgrave Macmillan, 2004)
Dutton, David, *Liberals in Schism* (Tauris, 2008)
Finlay, R.J., *Independent and Free: Scottish Politics and the Origins of the Scottish National Party, 1918–1945* (Donald, 1994)
Foot, Sir Dingle, *British Political Crises* (Kimber, 1976)
Gilbert, Martin, *Winston S. Churchill, 1922–39* (Heinemann, 1976)
Gilbert, Martin, *Churchill, Volume V Companion Part 1, Documents, Documents, The Exchequer Years 1922–29* (Heinemann, 1979)
Goodman, Jean, *The Mond Legacy: A Family Saga* (Weidenfeld & Nicolson, 1982)

Grimwood, Ian, *A Little Chit of a Fellow: A Biography of the Rt Hon. Leslie Hore-Belisha* (Book Guild, 2006)
Harris, Sally, *Out of Control: British Foreign Policy and the Union of Democratic Control, 1914–1918* (University of Hull Press, 1996)
Hyde, H. Montgomery, *Strong for Service: The Life of Lord Nathan of Churt* (Allen, 1968)
Jenkins, Roy, *Churchill* (Macmillan, 2001)
Jones, Mervyn, *A Radical Life: the Biography of Megan Lloyd George* (Hutchinson, 1991)
Lane, Michael, *Baron Marks of Woolwich* (Quiller Press, 1986)
Marquand, David, *Ramsay MacDonald* (Cape, 1977)
MacCormick, John, *The Flag in the Wind* (Birlinn, 2008)
Mayhew, Christopher, *Party Games* (Hutchinson, 1969)
McKenna, Stephen, *Reginald McKenna 1863–1943* (Eyre and Spottiswoode, 1948)
McKibbin, Ross, *The Evolution of the Labour Party 1910–1924* (Oxford University Press, 1974)
Money, Leo Chiozza, *The Triumph of Nationalization* (Cassell, 1920)
Morgan, Kenneth, and Morgan, Jane, *Portrait of a Progressive: The Political Career of Christopher, Viscount Addison* (Clarendon, 1980)
Morris, A.J.A., *C.P. Trevelyan, 1870–1958: Portrait of a Radical* (Blackstaff, 1977)
Ogg, David, *Herbert Fisher, 1865–1940: A Short Biography* (Arnold, 1947)
Outhwaite, R.L., *The Land or Revolution* (Allen & Unwin, 1917)
Owen, Frank, *Tempestuous Journey* (Hutchinson, 1954)
Rasmussen, Jorgen, *The Liberal Party: A Study of Retrenchment and Revival* (Constable, 1965)
Seldon, Anthony, *Major: A Political Life* (Phoenix, 1997)
Sommer, Dudley, *Haldane of Cloan* (Allen & Unwin, 1960)
Stocks, Mary, *Ernest Simon of Manchester* (Manchester University Press, 1963)
Swartz, Marvin, *The Union of Democratic Control in British Politics during the First World War* (Clarendon, 1971)
Trevelyan, Charles, *From Liberalism to Labour* (Allen & Unwin, 1921)
Vipont, Elfrida, *Arnold Rowntree: A Life* (Bannisdale, 1955)
Wedgwood, C.V., *The Last of the Radicals: Josiah Wedgwood MP* (Cape, 1951)
Wilson, Trevor, *The Downfall of the Liberal Party 1914–35* (Collins, 1966)
Wyburn-Powell, Alun, *Clement Davies: Liberal Leader* (Politico's, 2003)

Articles and essays
Bennett, G.H., 'The Wartime Political Truce and Hopes for Post War Coalition: The West Derbyshire By-election, 1944', *Midland History* (1992): 118–35
David, Edward, 'The Liberal Party Divided 1916–1918', *Historical Journal*, 13(2) (1970): 509–32
Dowse, Robert, 'The Entry of the Liberals into the Labour Party 1910–20', *Bulletin of Economic Research*, 13(2) (1961), November: 78–87

Dutton, David, 'One Liberal's War: Richard Durning Holt and Liberal Politics, 1914–1918', *Journal of Liberal Democrat History*, 36 (2002): 3–8

Goodlad, Graham, 'The Liberal Nationals, 1931–1940: The Problems of a Party in "Partnership Government"', *Historical Journal*, 38(1) (1995), March: 133–44

Johnson, Matthew, 'The Liberal War Committee and the Liberal Advocacy of Conscription in Britain, 1914–1916', *Historical Journal* (2008): 51, 399–420

Jones, J. Graham, 'Churchill, Clement Davies and the Ministry of Education', *Journal of Liberal Democrat History*, 27 (2000): 9

Little, Tony, 'Breaking the Mould?', *Journal of Liberal Democrat History*, 25 (1999–2000): 40–4

Pelling, H., 'Labour and the Downfall of Liberalism', in Pelling, *Popular Politics and Society in Late Victorian Britain* (London, 1968), p. 120

Reynolds, Jaime and Hunter, Ian, '"Crinks" Johnstone', *Journal of Liberal Democrat History*, 26 (2000): 14–18

Reynolds, Jaime and Hunter, Ian, 'Liberal Class Warrior', *Journal of Liberal Democrat History*, 28 (2000), 17–21

Reynolds, J. and Ingham, R., 'Archie Macdonald', *Journal of Liberal History*, 41 (2003): 11–14

Worley, Matthew, 'A Call to Action: New Party Candidates and the 1931 General Election', *Parliamentary History*, 27(2), (2008): 236–55

Unpublished theses

Baines, Malcolm, 'The Survival of the British Liberal Party 1932–1959', Oxford, D.Phil. (1990)

Catterall, Peter, 'The Free Churches and the Labour Party in England and Wales 1918–1939', London, Ph.D. (1989)

Cooper, Kathleen, 'The Political and Military Career of Major-General J.E.B. Seely, 1868–1947', Southampton, M.Phil. (2001)

Egan, Mark, 'The Grass-roots Organisation of the Liberal Party, 1945–64', Oxford, D.Phil. (2000)

Hart, M.W., 'The decline of the Liberal Party in Parliament and in the Constituencies, 1914–1931', Oxford, D.Phil. (1982)

Tanner, D.M., 'Political Realignment in England and Wales c.1906–1922', London, Ph.D. (1985)

Index

Acland, Richard 10, 22, 48–9, 78, 81, 86, 88n75, 89n76, 194
Addison, Christopher 8, 22, 50, 55–7, 89n87–93, 101
Aitken, (William Maxwell) Max (Baron Beaverbrook) 94, 108, 117, 130, 144n97, 146n146–149, 165, 178n33n35n36
Alden, Percy 8, 22, 34, 35, 52–3, 85, 180, 189, 189n4
Alexander, Maurice 9, 22, 47, 86, 103
Allen, William 8, 23, 110–13, 115, 144n87
Alton, David 10, 24, 176, 178n56
Anti-Waste League (1921–2) 55, 163
Arnold, Sydney 8, 22, 34, 35, 73–4, 77, 86
Ashdown, (Jeremy John Durham) Paddy 3, 12, 15–16, 25, 26n12, 92n180, 176, 184, 187, 189n1, 190n18n26–28 n31n33n35n38, 195
Asquith, Herbert Henry (Earl of Oxford and Asquith) 3, 5n10, 11–13, 20, 29, 31–2, 38, 40, 50, 54–5, 57–8, 67, 69–72, 89n86n99, 90n102, 91n139n140, 94, 96, 99, 101, 117, 119, 120, 122–4, 145n110n121, 155–6, 159, 192–4, 197n1
Attlee, Clement 63, 66, 79, 180

Baker, Joseph 34, 35
Baldwin, Stanley 47, 94–7, 108–9, 117, 121, 122, 125, 129, 130, 139, 141n12n17n18, 144n95n96, 145n114, 170, 178n42

Balfour, Arthur 95, 143n65
Barlow, John 34, 35
Barnes, Harry 9, 22, 63–4, 90n112n113n115n117
Beaverbrook *see* Aitken, (William Maxwell) Max (Baron Beaverbrook)
Beck, (Arthur) Cecil 8, 24, 55, 163–4
Benn, William Wedgwood (Viscount Stansgate) 9, 22, 59, 62, 68–72, 75, 76, 90n122–130, 91n131n133–135 n137–140n152, 94, 98, 116–18, 121, 141n1n5, 144n92, 145n113n119, 193, 197n2
Bennett, Albert 8, 23, 128–9, 141n2
Bennett, Donald 10, 24, 168–9
Bernays, Robert 10, 24, 58, 158–9, 177n16n17
Bevan, Aneurin (Nye) 164, 180
Beveridge, William 79, 161, 167–8, 175
Blair, Tony 184, 185
Bonar Law, Andrew 20, 23, 31, 47, 69, 93–5, 97, 125, 140, 154, 157
Bonham Carter, Violet 78, 92n163, 133, 136–7, 143n59, 147n182
Bottomley, Horatio 8, 10, 21, 24, 55, 163–4, 169, 177n28
Bradley, Tom 183
Brocklebank-Fowler, Christopher 183
Brown, Alan Grahame 196
Brown, Ernest 9, 21, 23, 71, 149, 152–4, 162, 177n9
Brown, Ron 183
Bulmer-Thomas, Ivor 90n111, 92n165, 196
Burns, John 28, 34, 35

Buxton, Noel 8, 22, 50, 52, 56, 58, 74, 86, 89n79n80
Byles, William 34, 35

Cable, Vincent 183
Callaghan, James 176
Campbell, (Walter Menzies) Ming 11, 13
Cartwright, John 181–4
Cawley, Frederick 30, 169
Cawley, Oswald 169
Chamberlain, Austen 96
Chamberlain, Neville 47, 135, 137, 139, 152, 159–60, 186
Chancellor, Henry 34, 35
Churchill, Winston 8, 21, 23, 27, 41, 49, 58, 75, 78, 98, 102, 104–9, 112–14, 116–17, 131, 133, 137–9, 141n8, 142n45, 143n53n58n59n62n63n65, 144n95, 146n151n152n157, 147n191, 152, 159, 193
Clegg, Nick 3, 13
Clough, William 34, 35
Common Wealth (1942–93) 10, 48–9, 78, 162
Communist Party of Great Britain (1920–91) 10, 46, 110, 115, 166
Conscription 28, 30–1, 33, 40, 42, 52, 73, 94, 96, 150
Constitutionalists (1924) 10, 23, 25n4, 105–14, 116, 131, 144n80, 152
Corbett, Archibald 181
Cowan, Dugald 158, 173
Cowan, (William) Henry 8, 23, 30, 61, 128–9
Crawshaw, Richard, 183
Cunningham, George 183

Dalziel, Henry 9, 24, 166–7, 169
Davies, Clement 3, 11, 12, 20, 78–9, 81–4, 92n162n166n173, 114, 120, 133, 135–6, 138, 145n104, 147n170n172n191, 156, 162, 175, 189, 189n3
Davies, David 9, 23, 118–20, 177n27
Davies, David Seaborne 167
Davies, Ellis 9, 22, 47–8, 86, 88n73n74, 161, 162, 177n27

Davies, Quentin 188, 196
Denman, Richard 8, 22, 28, 30, 34–5, 74–5, 86, 91n145–149
Dickinson, Willoughby 9, 22, 77–8, 86
Douglas-Mann, Bruce 183
Dudgeon, Cecil 9, 24, 164–5
Dunn, James 183
Dykes, Hugh 187

Eden, Anthony (Earl of Avon) 49, 136, 160
Edge, William 101, 132, 147n189
Edwards, Alfred 196
Edwards, John 8, 24, 172–3
Edwards, (John) Hugh 8, 23, 111–15, 118, 189
Elletson, Harold, 187
Ellis, Tom 183
England, Abraham 8, 23, 111–15, 118, 145n131, 189
Entwistle, Cyril 9, 23, 120–1, 124, 141n2
Evans, Arthur 8, 17, 23, 103, 105
Evans, Ernest 68, 167, 173

Fildes, Henry 157, 171–2
Fisher, Herbert Albert Laurens 101, 173–4, 178n48n49n51
Fletcher, Reginald (Baron Winster) 9, 22, 62–3, 86, 90n111
Foot, Dingle 10, 22, 80, 83–4, 86, 92n176n177
Foot, Michael 137, 155, 182
Forrest, Walter 9, 23, 128–30, 146n146–149, 148n195
Fusion (1920) 55, 93, 97, 100–2, 105–7, 120, 193

Gaitskell, Hugh 67, 83, 92n176, 180, 181
Garro-Jones, George (Baron Trefgarne) 9, 22, 61–2, 85, 180, 189, 189n4
Ginsburg, David 183
Glanville, Harold 34, 35
Grant, John 183
Granville, Edgar 10, 22, 81–2, 84, 86, 156, 162, 189, 189n3
Greenwood, Hamar 8, 23, 109, 112–14, 143n67–69

Grey, Edward 28, 54, 96, 159
Grey, George 167
Griffith, (Frank) Kingsley 168
Grigg, Edward (Baron Altrincham) 9, 23, 108, 116, 120–1, 125–7, 131, 145n135, 146n137–141, 174
Grimond, Joseph 3, 12, 62, 139, 180, 195
Gruffydd, William 167, 173
Guest, (Christian) Henry 9, 23, 27, 98, 99, 117, 140, 141n20
Guest, Frederick 9, 23, 27, 30–1, 63, 69, 71, 90n112n113n130, 91n132n143, 98–100, 102, 106, 108, 113, 116–18, 123, 131, 132, 140, 142n25–29n31, 143n55, 144n80n93n94n96n97, 146n159, 158, 171, 178n38, 193
Guest, Ivor Churchill (Baron Ashby St Ledgers, Baron Wimborne, Viscount Wimborne) 98, 117, 156
Guest, Oscar (Montague) 9, 23, 27, 98, 99, 100, 117, 131, 140, 141n20

Haldane, Richard 8, 22, 50, 53–6, 89n83–86, 96, 171
Harmsworth, Alfred Charles William (1st Viscount Northcliffe) 166
Harmsworth, Esmond (2nd Viscount Rothermere) 170, 178n42
Harmsworth, Harold Sidney (1st Viscount Rothermere) 55, 108, 130, 163, 170
Harris, Percy 59, 71, 79, 169
Harvey, (Alexander) Gordon (Cummins) 34, 35
Harvey, (Thomas Edmund) Ted 10, 24, 30, 34, 35, 174
Hemmerde, Edward 8, 22, 45–6
Henderson, Arthur 29, 32, 50, 56, 89n89, 194
Hogbin, Henry Cairn 8, 23, 110, 112, 115
Hogge, James 34, 35, 64, 69, 90n115, 155
Holdsworth, Herbert 10, 24, 160
Holt, Richard 34–5, 40, 87n45
Hope, John Deans 8, 24, 104, 171

Hopkinson, Austin 8, 24, 25n10, 169–70, 174, 178n42
Horabin, Thomas 10, 22, 78–80
Horam, John 183
Hore-Belisha, Leslie 10, 23, 25n4, 136–7, 141n2, 147n184n185, 154, 162, 164
Howarth, Alan 188, 195
Hudson Davies, Ednyfed 183
Hunter, Joseph 9, 23, 157, 172
Hutchison, Robert 9, 21, 23, 149, 152–4, 156

Illingworth, Albert 9, 23, 120–1, 126

Jackson, Robert 188, 196
Janner, Barnett 10, 22, 66
Jarrett, George 8, 23, 106–7, 113, 143n53, 144n80
Jenkins, Roy 107, 181–4, 195
John, Edward 8, 22, 33–5, 41–4, 88n50–52, 167, 192
Johnstone, Harcourt (Crinks) 168, 178n40
Jones, Leifchild Stratten (Leif) (Baron Rhayadar) 107, 113–14
Jowitt, William 9, 22, 55, 60, 75–8, 91n151n153n154n156n157, 92n182

Kennedy, Charles 3, 12, 182, 195
Kenworthy, Joseph (Baron Strabolgi) 9, 22, 27, 59–61, 71, 72, 74, 76, 89n81, 90n103–106n108, 91n144n155, 117
King, Joseph 8, 22, 28, 33–5, 38, 40

Lamb, Ernest (Baron Rochester) 8, 22, 34–5, 75, 78, 86
Lambert, Richard 8, 22, 33–5, 39–40
Lansbury, George 45, 66, 76, 91n157
Leamington Spa conference (1920) 55, 101, 118
Lee, John 187
Lees-Smith, Hastings Bertrand (Bertie) 8, 22, 33–5, 41, 88n49
Liberal Nationals (1931–48) 2, 21, 23–4, 48, 80–1, 115, 130, 134, 137–8, 143n52, 156–62, 172–3

Livingstone, Mackenzie 9, 22, 59, 68, 70–3, 86, 91n141, 117–18
Llewelyn Williams, William 34–5, 68
Lloyd George, David 3, 9, 11–12, 20–1, 24, 29, 31–2, 40, 43, 48, 50, 54, 55–63, 66–71, 73, 75, 82, 90n122, 94–103, 107, 109, 116–19, 120–7, 132, 141n21, 150–2, 154–5, 159, 166–7, 171, 174, 177n1n12, 189, 192–4
Lloyd George Fund 3, 118–19, 134, 169
Lloyd-George, Gwilym (Viscount Tenby) 9, 21, 23, 79, 82, 114, 134–7, 147n168, 154–5, 158–9
Lloyd George, Megan 9, 14, 21, 22, 68, 81–4, 154, 155, 189
Lough, Thomas 34, 35
Lyons, Edward 183

Mabon, Dickson 181, 183
Macdonald, Archibald 10, 23, 139–40, 148n193n194
MacDonald, James Ramsay 19–20, 22, 27–30, 32, 37–9, 42–3, 45, 47, 50, 52–4, 56, 58, 60, 62–3, 72–8, 80, 85, 86n5n13n15, 87n27–29n36n37n39, 89n82n92n100, 94, 109, 141n7, 154, 163, 172–3, 177n11, 194
Macdonald, Murdoch 154, 162
McKeag, William 9, 23, 157–8, 162, 189
McKenna, Reginald 8, 23, 31, 68–70, 90n123n125n129, 91n134, 94–6, 108, 141n4–6n9–12, 173, 193
Mackie, George 181
Maclay, Joseph 9, 23, 157
Maclean, Donald 15, 99, 154
Maclennan, Robert 24, 181–4, 190n11, 195
Macmillan, Harold (Earl of Stockton) 136, 164
McNally, Tom 183–4
Magee, Bryan 183
Major, John 25, 186, 187, 190n33n34 n36
Mallalieu, (Edward) Lance 10, 22, 67

Malone, Cecil L'Estrange 8, 22, 46–7, 86, 88n66
Mander, Geoffrey 10, 22, 80–1, 92n168–171, 155
Mansel, Courtenay 9, 23, 120–1, 124–5, 140, 141n2, 145n127n128, 148n196, 161
Marks, George Croydon 9, 22, 76–7, 86, 91n158
Marsden, Paul 10, 24, 25n4, 84–5, 89n78, 184–5, 188, 190n43
Martell, Edward 169
Martin, Albert 103–4
Martin, Frederick 9, 22, 61, 128
Mason, David 8, 24, 34–5, 40–1, 103, 161–2, 171, 177n23–26, 189
Maurice Debate (1918) 59, 77, 99, 193
Mayhew, Christopher 24, 180–1, 189n7–9
Meadowcroft, Michael 10, 24, 176, 178n54, 189
Meyer, Anthony 187
Mitchell, Richard 183
Molteno, Percy 34, 35
Mond, Alfred (1st Baron Melchett) 9, 23, 30, 101, 120–5, 130, 145n106n109n110n114, 146n137, 174
Mond, Henry (2nd Baron Melchett) 9, 23, 120–2
Money, Leo Chiozza 8, 22, 31, 42–4, 88n53–58, 192
Moreing, Algernon 8, 23, 105–7, 109, 112–4, 143n53n55
Morel, Edmund 29, 41
Morrell, Philip 29, 34–5, 40–1
Morris-Jones, Henry 90n119, 162
Morrison, George 9, 23, 158, 173
Morris, Rhys Hopkin 22, 67–8, 82, 117–18, 190n44
Mosley, Oswald 137, 164, 195
Munro-Ferguson, Ronald (Viscount Novar) 8, 23, 53, 94, 96, 141n16–18
Munro, Robert (Baron Alness) 8, 23, 133–5, 146n163–166
Murray, Arthur (3rd Viscount Elibank) 9, 24, 159–60, 162, 177n19, 189

INDEX

Nathan, Harry 9, 22, 65–6, 168
National Labour (1931–45) 10, 60, 73–4, 76, 86, 179
National Party (1966–7) 21, 24, 163, 169
National Party of Scotland (1928–34) 10, 21, 24, 163, 166
New Party (1931–2) 10, 21, 24, 137, 156, 163–6, 177n31
Nicholson, Emma 24, 186–8, 190n29n33
Nicholson, Otho 108
Nicolson, Harold 147n183, 164
Northcliffe see Harmsworth, Alfred Charles William

Ogden, Eric 183
O'Halloran, Michael 183
Ottawa agreement (1932) 67
Outhwaite, Robert 8, 22, 28, 33–5, 39–40, 44–5, 86, 87n41, 141n3, 171, 192
Owen, David 182–4, 190n14
Owen, Frank 9, 21, 24, 56–7, 65, 89n94, 154–5, 189, 191
Owen, Goronwy 9, 21, 24, 154, 155, 177n12, 189

Pattinson, Samuel 9, 23, 120–1, 125–6, 141n2
Philipson, Hilton 8, 23, 102–3, 105
Pitt, Bill 10, 22, 84–5, 89n78, 92n179, 190n15
Ponsonby, Arthur 8, 22, 28–30, 32–40, 52, 58, 74, 86, 86n14, 87n21n22 n31–35n37n38n39, 192
Pratt, John 9, 24, 165, 169, 178n32–36
Prentice, Reginald 196
Primrose, Neil James Archibald 90n130, 98–9, 141n21n22, 142n23
Pringle, William 34, 35, 98

Rendall, Athelstan 9, 22, 59
Roberts, Aled 10, 24, 160, 162
Roberts, Emrys 81
Roberts, Wilfrid 10, 22, 81, 83–4, 92n176, 167
Robinson, Thomas 8, 23, 25n4, 111–15, 118, 144n90, 189

Rodgers, William 181, 183–4, 190n14, 195
Roper, John 183
Rothermere see Harmsworth, Harold Sidney; Harmsworth, Esmond
Rowntree, Arnold 30, 34–5, 174, 178n52
Royle, Charles 9, 24, 171–2
Runciman, Walter (Baron Runciman) 34, 35
Runciman, Walter (Viscount Runciman of Doxford) 40, 59, 127, 156
Russell, Robert 183

Samuel, Herbert 11–12, 65, 92n164n178, 154, 157, 175, 177n11
Sandelson, Neville 183
Scott, Alexander MacCallum 8, 22, 31, 57–8, 86, 88n68, 89n96–100, 90n101, 197n3
Sedgemore, Brian 24, 184–5, 188, 190n25
Seely, Hugh (Baron Sherwood) 167
Seely, (John Edward Bernard) Jack (Baron Mottistone) 27, 57, 89n95, 108, 116, 144n91, 145n119
Sherwell, Arthur 34–5
Simon, Ernest (Baron Simon of Wythenshawe) 9, 22, 64–5, 90n118, 175
Simon, John 9, 21, 23, 31, 34–5, 42, 61, 73, 86n1, 88n50, 96, 100, 133, 149–54, 156, 159–60, 177n1n2n17, 193
Sinclair, Archibald (Viscount Thurso) 12, 79, 81, 84, 92n164n171n178, 135, 146n138, 147n170n172, 152, 154, 159, 174, 181
Social Democratic Party (SDP) (1981–8) 2–3, 24, 84–5, 176, 179–84, 188, 195
Spears, (Edward) Louis 8, 23, 75, 91n151, 108, 131–2, 146n151–157
Spen Valley by-election (1919) 100–1, 150–1, 193
Spero, George 8, 22, 58–9, 90n102
Steel, David 3, 11–12, 176, 195

Sturrock, John Leng 8, 23, 105, 109–10, 112–13, 115, 143n71n72, 144n85, 152
Sueter, Murray 163–4, 170, 178n42
Suez Crisis 67, 134

Taverne, Dick 180, 189n5
Temple-Morris, Peter 188, 190n42, 196
Thatcher, Margaret 187
Thomas, Jeffrey 183
Thomas, Mike 183
Thorne, George Rennie 9, 17, 24, 70–1, 99, 117, 155
Thornton, Maxwell 9, 23, 118–19
Thorpe, Jeremy 3, 4n2, 12, 195
Thurnham, Peter 24, 187–8
Trevelyan, Charles 8, 22, 28–30, 33–8, 40, 86, 86n10n14, 87n20–23 n25n27n29–31, 88n59, 89n80, 192

Wadsworth, George 10, 23, 138
Ward, John 8, 23, 110, 112–15, 118, 189
Waring, Walter 8, 23, 104–5, 140, 142n39n41–44n47, 171
Wedgwood, Josiah 8, 22, 31, 44–6, 86, 88n60, 194
Wellbeloved, James 183
White, James Dundas 8, 22, 45, 86
Whitehouse, John Howard 8, 22, 34–5, 40, 87n46, 171, 189
Williams, Rhys 9, 23, 79, 132–3, 146n158
Williams, Shirley 181–4, 195
Wilson, Harold 82, 180–1
Wilson, John William 34–5
Woodward, Shaun 188, 196
Woolton-Teviot Agreement (1947) 162
Wrigglesworth, Ian 182–3

Young, Edward Hilton (Baron Kennet) 9, 23, 120–6, 131, 141n2, 142n42, 145n118–122, 174, 178n51

Lightning Source UK Ltd.
Milton Keynes UK
UKOW06f0408100516

273926UK00001B/58/P